Sell Your Own Damn Movie!

Sell Your Own Damn Movie!

Lloyd Kaufman
with Sara Antill

AMSTERDAM • BOSTON • HEIDELBERG • LONDON • NEW YORK • OXFORD
PARIS • SAN DIEGO • SAN FRANCISCO • SINGAPORE • SYDNEY • TOKYO
Focal Press is an imprint of Elsevier

Focal Press is an imprint of Elsevier
225 Wyman Street, Waltham, MA 02451, USA
The Boulevard, Langford Lane, Kidlington, Oxford, OX5 1GB, UK

Notices
Knowledge and best practice in this field are constantly changing. As new research
and experience broaden our understanding, changes in research methods, professional
practices, or medical treatment may become necessary.

Practitioners and researchers must always rely on their own experience and knowledge in
evaluating and using any information, methods, compounds, or experiments described
herein. In using such information or methods they should be mindful of their own safety
and the safety of others, including parties for whom they have a professional responsibility.

To the fullest extent of the law, neither the Publisher nor the authors, contributors, or
editors, assume any liability for any injury and/or damage to persons or property as a
matter of products liability, negligence or otherwise, or from any use or operation of any
methods, products, instructions, or ideas contained in the material herein.

Library of Congress Cataloging-in-Publication Data
Kaufman, Lloyd, 1945-
   Sell your own damn movie! / Lloyd Kaufman; with Sara Antill.
      p. cm.
   ISBN 978-0-240-81520-6
      1. Motion pictures—Marketing—Amateurs' manuals. 2. Low budget films—Amateurs'
manuals. 3. Motion picture producers and directors—Interviews. I. Antill, Sara. II. Title.
   PN1995.9.M29K58 2011
   791.43'30688—dc22   2011003845

British Library Cataloguing-in-Publication Data
A catalogue record for this book is available from the British Library.

ISBN: 978-0-240-81520-6

For information on all Focal Press publications
visit our website at www.elsevierdirect.com

Printed in the United States of America

11 12 13 14 15   5 4 3 2 1

Contents

Sell Your Own Damn Movie! is dedicated to Pat Swinney Kaufman. My love for you exceeds anything in this book, on this planet, or in the heavens... And speaking of "selling," thank you for supporting 37 years of Sell-u-Lloyd!

xo Lloydie

A Special "Sell Your Own Damn Thank You" to Sara Antill

Sell Your Own Damn Movie! *co-author Sara Antill explodes with joy after receiving this Christmas gift from Lloyd.*

Acknowledgments

I'd like to take a moment to give an impassioned thank you to the following people:

Michael and Maris Herz, your dear, sweet souls have nurtured me from the very beginning of my ascent into 40 years of failed filmmaking.

Jerome Rudes, who thought what I had to say was worth committing to paper. Ha!

And…

- Elinor Actipis
- Renzo Adler
- Zack Beins
- Danielle Black
- Karen Black
- Travis Campbell
- Tze Chun
- Jason Connell
- Annie Cron
- David Cronenberg
- Michele Cronin
- Lisa Eastman
- David Ferino
- Gabe Friedman
- Maria Friedmanovich
- Nina Gielen
- Jamie Greco
- Adam Green
- Rod Gudino (*Rue Morgue*)
- James Gunn
- Matt Hoffman
- Ted Hope
- Jeremy Howell
- IFTA
- Thomas Jefferson
- Allison Jones
- Jason Kalmanowitz
- Charles Kaufman
- Charlotte Kaufman
- Lily-Hayes Kaufman
- Lisbeth Kaufman
- Pat Kaufman
- Sigrun Kaufman
- Susan Kaufman
- Mike Kelly
- Brad Kembel
- Roger Kirby
- Anne Koester
- Stan Lee
- Jonathan Lees
- Teresa Loera
- Mynette Louie
- Ron Mackay
- Matt Manjourides

- Justin Martell
- Jonas Mekas
- Jeremy Morrison
- Gary Moscowitz
- Phil Nichols
- Barack Obama
- Nina Paley
- Bristol Palin
- Sarah Palin
- Oren Peli
- Bill Plympton
- Jean Prewitt
- Jon Reiss
- John Rieber
- Stewart Rieser
- Elle Schneider
- Amanda Scott
- Richard Taylor
- Tony Timpone (*Fangoria*)
- Cory Udler
- Jenn Valdez
- Jonathan Wolf
- Strauss Zelnick

Foreword by Stan Lee

Lloyd Kaufman and I have known each other since Lloyd was at Yale in the 1960s and sought me out. He was one of the many brilliant young students for whom Marvel Comics had become a sort of shrine, but Lloyd stood out among the others. He seemed driven by some kind of strong intellectual force combined with a monomaniacal passion for pop culture. That is why in 1970 I chose him to write a screenplay with me based on "Night of the Witch," one of my stories. Lloyd had never written a movie script, but I could tell that his incredibly original ideas and incredibly "unique" personality could be wrapped up in one incredibly charged enchilada of horror! I was right. Our script was immediately optioned by Cannon, the premiere indie movie studio of its day, from whose loins sprung stars like Susan Sarandon and Peter Boyle.

A lot has changed since 1970; Lloyd and his Yale buddy Michael Herz have established Troma, the longest running independent movie studio of all time. Lloyd has put a new face on the cinematic superhero with Toxie, as well as with my personal favorite, Sgt. Kabukiman N.Y.P.D. Lloyd's body of work has now proven to be a seminal influence on worldwide film today. Just look at any film created by the likes of Quentin Tarantino, Takashi Miike, Peter Jackson, Eli Roth, Gaspar Noé, and James Gunn, to name a few, and you are likely watching a film influenced by *Class of Nuke 'Em High*, *Tromeo & Juliet*, or *Citizen Toxie*. Come to think of it, perhaps Lloyd and I should've continued working together; the only problem was that during our intense brainstorming sessions, whenever he wanted to confuse me, he'd speak in Mandarin Chinese, one of his many offbeat talents!

When Lloyd and Michael created Troma Entertainment, Inc., 35-plus years ago, nobody expected that Troma would still be around today. So many movie companies have come and gone, along with billions of dollars in production funds, yet Troma, with ultra low-budget, totally nonmainstream movies, is still here. Indeed, as Lloyd likes to say, he is the herpes of the movie industry—he won't go away!

So, how has Lloyd been able to remain an auteur filmmaker for so long? How has he been able to keep making movies that emanate out of his warped, deranged mind, or what passes for one, with no interference from outside sources? How did Lloyd manage to make movies for almost 40 years without having to compromise in any way? Who among us can say we have created completely independent films that have branched off into Broadway musicals, children's television cartoon shows, Marvel comics, action figures, and more, the way Lloyd has? (Well, I guess *I* can say that, but this is about Lloyd, not me.) You will discover the answer in this incredible, one-of-a-kind tome!

All of the above has been made possible because Lloyd Kaufman has created a brand. He has also pioneered a revolutionary new way of getting his very personal art to a wide audience while eternally worshiping at the shrine of independent cinema and entrepreneurial idealism. He was one of the first to anticipate how new technology would affect the sale of the art and the art of the sale. And though some might suggest that Troma sells tasteless, mindless sex and violence, audiences have learned to look beneath the surface and realize Lloyd's films are truly unique and personal works of art. For example, the Toxic Avenger has found his rightful place in cinematic history alongside such characters as Spidey, Jerry Lewis, and Darth Vader.[1]

Regardless of content, Lloyd has somehow found a way to successfully sell his movies these past 36 years. This is a testament to the fact that it takes a lot more than talent to sell one's own damn movie. It takes a lot more than hard work! It takes unique sales techniques—techniques developed by Lloyd—which have allowed Troma to compete successfully with the huge media conglomerates. This book will teach you Lloyd's methods and secrets so you, True Believer, can do what Lloyd and Troma do every day! So, get ready for a great ride—this book will entertain you and make you laugh, but most important, you will learn a superheroic amount about selling your own damn movie. Remember, if Lloyd can sell movies with 600-pound men expelling explosive diarrhea, Shakespearean hard-bodied lesbians, Indian zombie chickens, hideously deformed creatures of

---

[1] *The Toxic Avenger* was recently selected by the Independent Film & Television Alliance and the American Cinematheque as one of the "most significant movies of the 1980s."

superhuman size and strength crushing heads, human-cow-lady hybrids, and singing and dancing hermaphrodites, certainly *anyone* can sell a movie, especially you! By the way Lloyd, please send my love to Toxie and Kabukiman—and my check directly to me!

Excelsior!

Stan Lee and Lloyd at Studio 54 circa 1973.

Introduction: Why Jay Leno Hates You

Some of my favorite stories are about belly buttons. I don't know when I developed this strange affinity for the little hole in my stomach, but I can't deny that a little wave of pleasure passes through me each time my beautiful wife Pat sticks one of her tiny fingers in there. My eyes roll back in my head and I let out a giggle like some sort of white Bill Cosby or a Jewish Pillsbury Doughboy.

That being said, a few weeks ago, I found myself crammed between two large, fat, sweaty people on the N train between Long Island City, current home of Troma Entertainment, and Manhattan, current home of me and Jon Gosselin. It was about 6 PM and there was not a whole lot of room to wiggle on this particular train. Because I was sandwiched directly between Godzilla and Mechagodzilla, I ended up facing an advertisement for a storage facility and was unable to turn my head to look away. This particular storage facility, which my editrix has warmly encouraged me not to name, has several different posters, and they are located on several different trains. Most of these ads feature naked people in an empty apartment with the slogan "Maybe we make storage too easy..." Get it? Because when storage space is cheap, people will put all of their belongings into storage, including, apparently, their clothes. And I guess this is supposed to be seen as a positive thing. So, in this ad that I had no choice but to stare at, a naked guy and a naked gyno[1] are lying on the floor of an empty apartment. The gyno's ample bosom is hidden behind a book, and both of their special hoo-haa parts are covered by one small blanket. Kinky, right?

---

[1] "Gyno" is the politically correct word that we, at Troma Entertainment, use for the nonmale sex.

You can just imagine all the racy thoughts just limping through my head at that moment. So imagine my surprise, when, as I stare at this ad longer and longer, I realize that the gyno has no belly button. At all. Not like it was just hidden somewhere. I mean, trust me, I looked. Believe me when I say that I stared at this poster longer and harder than anyone would be expected to, and there was absolutely no fucking belly button. So, (1) either this unnamed storage facility found some belly button-less freak of a gyno to pose for this picture[2] or (2) this picture was so thoroughly airbrushed in an attempt to make these people look attractive while naked that some dipshit accidentally erased the gyno's belly button! How could no one have noticed that someone was missing one of the main 26 body parts! Then again, I can't tell you how many DVD covers I have approved that read, "Michelle Herz and Loyd Kaufmann Present..." Or maybe the lack of belly button was actually an ingenious way of getting me to stare at this advertisement and remember it in my nightmares weeks later?

STUPIDITY OR GENIUS?

That is actually the question that people have been asking about me and Troma Entertainment for years. Unfortunately, the people with money seem to fall more in the "Stupidity" category, while the people with taste but no money lean more toward "Genius." But the fact is, idiocy, lunacy, or whatever, Troma has been selling itself as something for over 35 years. By all reasoning, Troma Entertainment shouldn't even exist. It should have died out in the megaconglomerate-dominated 1990s like Kurt Cobain and beepers. You need look no further than my incredibly intelligent business and life partner, Michael Herz. He has been saying for years that Troma is a piece of shit that should just die. His beautiful wife, Maris, says that too, but I think she is talking about me specifically, more so than Troma. And Michael and Maris have every right to be pissed. *Poultrygeist: Night of the Chicken Dead*, my magnum ovum, has yet to make any money. We haven't even made back our distribution costs. We have absolutely no international sales deals, and we haven't had a movie on television in who knows how long.

---

[2] If this is the case, would someone tell this beautiful, belly button-less freak of gynohood to please call me at 718-395-9067. I have a script for her.

Mark Neveldine and Brian Taylor,[3] the guys behind the *Crank* movies, have said that, in a fair world, *Poultrygeist* would have been a worldwide hit! Unfortunately, Neveldine/Taylor fall into that category of good taste/no money.[4]

The fact is, if the Big Man wants in, you're out. Like Conan O'Brien said, you can do anything you want to in life, unless Jay Leno wants to do it too. Now just imagine that Jay Leno is a giant mega-conglomerate movie studio[5] with billions and billions and billions of dollars. And he hates you—you, the little, nipping, sweet puppy at his feet who wants nothing more than some fucking table scraps. Not only does he hate you, but he hates that fact that you even exist and will stop at nothing to crush you, just because he's Jay Leno and he can. But that's not all. Even other independents are out to get you. You think all the other little puppies are going to let you have a table scrap? No, goddamn it. They're going to fight you for it because they're starving too. Thanks to the democratization of filmmaking, everyone on earth can make a movie and does! Not only will you have to compete with *Avatar* and Almodóvar, but you'll be competing with everyone in the world; from the guys who make the formulaic crappy movies for Syfy and Lifetime networks to the guy who manages a strip club and has produced a movie for $5000! Yes, as my previous books have described, we can all Produce and/or Direct Our Own Damn Movies®, but how do we make a living from our art?

Just last week, I was at a meeting with some producers at the Independent Film & Television Alliance (IFTA). Some of the boys with $60 haircuts and "interesting" open-collar shirts were discussing their business model. They only make a movie if they know upfront that it will make a profit. One of them was actually making fun of filmmakers or producers who make movies that come

---

[3] Neveldine/Taylor also wrote the introduction for my book *Direct Your Own Damn Movie!*, which is available for purchase at www.troma.com. BUY TROMA!

[4] Actually, *Crank* and *Crank 2* were huge hits and these guys have lots of money. They just aren't giving it to me.*

    *NOTE FROM LLOYD'S CO-WRITER AND FORMER ASSISTANT, SARA: Actually, Lloyd, they paid you the SAG daily rate to appear in *Crank 2* for about three seconds. I know this because I set up the deal. I also know that the SAG daily rate was more than you paid me in two months for working on *Direct Your Own Damn Movie!*

[5] As opposed to the giant fucking douche bag that he is.*

    *EDITOR'S NOTE: Wow, Lloyd, no wonder you've never been on *The Tonight Show*.

from the heart—people who make movies that they believe in. I sat there, holding my tongue. They were laughing at people like me. Laughing! But you know what? Fuck 'em![6]

Do you know how hard it is to sell something that you don't love? Try working at Kmart or Foot Locker for a few months. Do you know why those people are so fucking unhappy all the time? It's because they hate their lives.[7] And also, because they are not passionate about what they are selling.

But enough of this ideological bullshit. You're not here for a pep talk. You're here to find out how to sell a movie. So let me get this out in the open right away: Troma sales suck. I already told you that *Poultrygeist: Night of the Chicken Dead* hasn't made any money.

So why am I writing this book if I'm such a failure? Ha! Good question. Aren't you a little smart ass. It's because I'm a fucking salesman, that's why. If I can hoodwink a smart editor like Elinor at a reputable publishing house like Elsevier into letting me write another book (for money!), you think I can't help you sell a movie? Okay, well, I'm not actually making any promises. But we'll figure this out together, hand in hand, mouth to mouth. Have a little faith. You are so good looking.

xoxo
Lloyd Kaufman
Semiprofessional Sellout

---

[6] Not IFTA. I love IFTA. I mean fuck Jay Leno.

[7] Employees of the iconic Strand Bookstore in New York City are so unhappy that I have managed to entice two of them to become my assistant by offering them *less* money than they were making there! In fact, I found my co-writer, Sara, at the Strand, trying to sell copies of *Infinite Jest* to homeless people.

Chapter | one

A History of Film Distribution, 10,000 B.C.–Present

It is impossible to understand the intricacies of how to sell a movie today without understanding how the film industry has developed and changed over the past several decades. And because the history of film distribution is so directly tied to the development of the film industry itself, I thought it might be a good idea to start at the beginning. And so here, gleaned from my studies of Chinese civilization at Yale in the 1960s, is a short history of the world, by Lloyd Kaufman.

A few thousand years ago, God created the heavens, the earth, and, most important, the Chinese. And God so loved the Chinese that he gave them the divine privilege of inventing the motion picture. That's right, friends—the most important invention of our time was actually developed by the Chinese thousands of years ago. It all began early in the fifth century B.C. when a young, hairless Chinese boy by the name of Sam Levine was born in a manger in Shanghai. There weren't many Levines in Shanghai, however, and young Sam was better known by the nickname Mo-Ti. What the hell Mo-Ti means, I have no idea. I can only assume the moronic nickname came about because he was a very thirsty child, and everyone knows that Chinese people love tea. My mother used to call me Mo-Popov, so who am I to judge?

Alas, as little Mo-Ti grew up in the slums of Shanghai, he began to notice something strange. Using careful observation, Mo-Ti noticed that when light shined through a small hole in a wall, the image of whatever was in front of that light would be projected, upside down, on the opposite wall. Now, I bet you are scratching your head out there and thinking, "Wha??" But you see, Mo-Ti was a smart little guy, and what he discovered that fateful day would change history in ways that no one could have guessed. Using what he saw, Mo-Ti began to understand properties of light and accurately described a "camera obscura," which everyone knows is a rare type of obscure Chinese camera.

Now, from this revelation, it was a simple step from still camera to motion picture camera, and Mo-Ti and his Chinese brothers took that step boldly, inventing the modern 35mm film camera in 476 B.C. With this intellectual leap, Chinese society was thrust out of the Dark Ages and into an enlightened period that we now call the Renaissance. When Chinese travelers to Europe first showed the ignorant natives their films, the Europeans were amazed. Word of the magical Chinese moving pictures spread across the land. *The Last Temptation of Toxie: The Toxic Avenger Part III* became a particular favorite of the Gauls, while the Romans preferred lighter fare such as *The Wedding Party*, staring Robert De Niro's great-great-great-great-great-great grandfather, Silas De Niro.[1] The slow-witted Europeans quickly came to worship the Chinese as gods, which kind of pissed off the real God who had created the Chinese in the first place, but at that point, there was really nothing he could do about it. With Europe, and later the rest of the world, conquered without bloodshed, humanity entered the Golden Millenia, a period of peace and brotherly love that has lasted for more than 2500 years, right up to the modern day, so named because Chinese people like the color gold. All hail Mo-Ti, our lord and savior.

But, of course, none of this really happened. It did get me a D in Chinese History and Culture 1011. I was able to graduate, however,

---

[1] Troma is proud to distribute the remakes of both of these masterpiece films. Both faithful reboots are available at www.buy.tromamovies.com. BUY TROMA!

so it can't be completely untrue. Maybe I should have spent more time studying for my Chinese classes instead of watching movies and frolicking naked with Thomas, my roommate. But then I wouldn't be the distinguished and respected film director that I am today, so there's an upside to everything.

There was, in fact, some guy named Mo-Ti who looked in a glory hole and saw an upside-down image on the other side. And anyone who can look in a glory hole and be more interested in the properties of light than the three-inch penis on the other side deserves more than a passing mention here. But unfortunately, there was never any leap from theoretical camera to motion-picture camera, and poor little Sam "Mo-Ti" Levine died, penniless, after choking on some egg foo young. And so it is written.[2]

FIGURE 1.1 *This Troma booth at Australia's Armageddon Expo was decorated by Toxie himself. All the Aussies said it was a real kick in the "Aborigi-knees"!*

[2] NOTE FROM THE NEW FOOTNOTE GUY, WHO HAPPENS TO BE CHINESE: I don't like you, Kaufman. I just want to get that out of the way. And I'm not going to put up with your funny footnote shit.*

* NOTE FROM LLOYD: Yo, Footnote Guy! My Chinese name is 多夫門人 (Kung Fu Men)! Get it? It sounds like Kaufman!

For the next 2200 years or so, nothing much happened. Some buildings were built, some people were born, some people were killed. Zoos were created for the entertainment of the rich, Haiti made a pact with the devil, and lots of Indians were murdered with smallpox blankets. I mean, this was really uninteresting stuff, and I feel like, even in this short paragraph, I have already devoted too much time to it.

And then, finally, after a long period of worthless pursuits, someone decided that the world was kind of a drag. That someone was Thomas Edison, inventor extraordinaire. And so, he started inventing a shit-ton[3] of stuff like light bulbs and phonographs and disposable underwear. The guy was a genius! You know why? It wasn't because he invented stuff like shoelaces and mochaccinos. It was because he paid other people to invent things and then he put his name on them[4] and applied for the patents. And once he had the patent, he got all the money. So, of course, Edison was mafia-like with his patents. He was the James Cameron of his day! Which actually makes his invention of the Kinetoscope all the more interesting. Let's get it out of the way up front that Edison did not actually invent the Kinetoscope, which is Greek for "magic box that you can watch porno clips in." But he put his famous name on the patent and that's all that really matters. That is, he put his name on the U.S. patent. For some bewildering reason, unbeknownst to me or *www.edisonfunfactsforkids.com* where I am getting the bulk of this information, Edison neglected to get an international patent for his one-man proto-film projector. Now, you may be thinking to yourself, "Wow, that Edison guy was a real dummy! How did he ever manage to invent Cadbury Eggs and umbrellas?" But you would be wrong. Cadbury Eggs weren't even invented in America. I would think if you, dear reader, were an expert in anything, it would be Easter chocolate. I mean, as a self-loathing Jew, even I know a little something about Easter food. Frankly, I'm a little disappointed in you.

Regardless of his reasons, the fact that Edison had no legal claim on the Kinetoscope in any place other than the United States was actually a boon[5] to the motion picture industry that was about to

---

[3] Equal to 4.4 metric tonnes and 2.7 tromatons.

[4] That's how it works with writers and co-writers too. I love Thomas Edison!

[5] NOTE FROM LLOYD: Please check if this word should be "boon" or "boom." I don't want to look like an idiot, goddammit.

be born. This freedom meant that other people, some of them even smarter and more passionate about film than Edison, were able to tinker and improve on Edison's invention. What began as one dude paying 25¢ to jerk off to Annabelle Whitford Moore's *Butterfly Dance* became hundreds of people at a time paying $12.50 to jerk off to Nicole Kidman in *Moulin Rouge*. See how great technology is?

WE'RE GOING TO THE JERSEY SHORE, BITCH!

Here's a fun fact for you: Do you happen to know where Thomas Edison, the grandfather of the film industry, chose to build his empire? New Jersey! Not New York or Los Angeles, but lovely New Jersey. His state-of-the-art film studio, the Black Maria, stood on what is today Toxie's shack. In fact, Michael Herz and I had such great respect for Thomas Edison that we decided to establish our own empire of Tromaville in New Jersey. It wasn't because we liked the smell of garbage and despair or because stuff is cheaper over there. Certainly not! It was because we wanted to honor the proud history and legacy of Thomas Edison. Being able to claim Snooki was just a bonus! Forget Los Angeles—New Jersey is where it's at, bitches.

Now that I think about it, however, Thomas Edison was kind of a dick. As the inventor of the modern power grid, he electrocuted animals to prove that AC current was more dangerous than the DC current that he was selling.[6] He also founded the company that would become General Electric, which became a megaconglomerate corporation that seeks to control all media, even the stuff that no one pays attention to, like NBC. And NBC fired Conan O'Brien, who is fantastic. So you know what? On second thought, fuck Thomas Edison too.

Once motion picture cameras and projectors were invented, it was only natural that buildings would spring up to display these amazing marvels called movies. And thus, the movie theater was born. At first, anyone could own a movie theater. All you needed was a little cash and some gumption. There weren't very many movies to play, so it may not have been the best business investment, but you could do it. When the major studios started coming up, they wanted to get in on the action, so they bought their own theaters. This vertical integration was absolutely perfect—the big studios owned the talent on the screen, the costume and set designers, the costumes and sets themselves, the

---

[6] Edison gave a deaf ear to animal rights advocates. This is because he was deaf, actually.

cameras, the editing equipment, the editors, the cafeterias, the musicians, the press relations, and, finally, the theaters. Now, at this point, keep in mind that most people could not go out and make their own damn movie. There were no small, cheap cameras like there are today, and there were no computers on which to edit. So the major studios made all the movies, and then they showed them in the theaters that they owned. It just sucked for anyone else who owned a theater or anyone who didn't want to work for the studio boss. You know who else didn't like it? The U.S. government. Apparently, it was illegal.

FIGURE 1.2 Class of Nuke 'Em High *plays at a midnight screening held at Landmark's Esquire Theatre in Denver, Colorado. Will the other films on this marquee still be playing in theaters 25 years after they were made as well?*

The United States v. Paramount Pictures, Inc, in 1948, changed everything. The Supreme Court decided that the major studios could no longer own movie theaters. They also couldn't force the owners of other theaters to buy and show a bunch of shitty movies for every decent one. This decision didn't just change which movies were shown in what theater—it actually contributed to the destruction of the studio system. When a studio could no longer count on a theater having to play its cheap movies, it had to start being a little more selective about the movies it chose to make. This led to higher production costs. Within a few years, the era of the major studio was over, and the rise of the independents had begun. And that is when I, Lloyd Kaufman, became a man.

A GLIMPSE OF REALTY

I am sitting in an Irish pub on 23rd Street. The music is loud and a large group of frat boys is causing loud havoc at a table near me. I glance up and make eye contact with one of them. He smiles at me. I smile at him and nod my head slightly. He knows I am one of them. My co-writer, Sara, scribbles furiously in a notebook, straining to capture every word of brilliance that I am spilling. I sip my vodka tonic.

"That's great," says Sara. "I can probably get part of the first chapter from your Chinese stuff."

"Great, great," I say, pleased with myself. This book is going to be a breeze. "So, what more do you need?"

"Well," Sara pauses. "I guess if you just talk a little bit about how to sell a movie?"

I put down my vodka tonic. "You can't sell a movie these days. It's all fucked."

"Well, yeah," she says. "But I mean just something about how to sell a movie today, since you've talked about the history."

"It's impossible! The whole thing is fucked. We can't even sell *Poultrygeist: Night of the Chicken Dead*, on which we spent $500,000. We haven't made a cent on it!" I'm getting really worked up now, which I think is getting the frat boy across the aisle a little excited. "How is someone supposed to sell a movie when the theaters are tied to major megaconglomerate corporations that own everything. *Poutlrygeist* played in one theater in New York for what, two weeks?"

"A week and a half, actually. *Indiana Jones* opened on Wednesday and kicked out your fowl movement."[7]

"That's right! We were the highest-grossing screen in the country, but no matter how well you do, they'll kick you out for *Step Up 2: The Streets*.[8]

---

[7] NOTE FROM SARA: I did not say "your fowl movement." Please keep your foul puns out of my mouth.

[8] Or some other, much more current reference.

"Yeah."

"Damn right, yeah. Did you want to get an appetizer?"

There is silence at our table. I take another sip of my vodka. A Chinese woman walks up to me holding a handful of DVDs.

"Movies, movies," she says, hauntingly.

I brush her away.

"DVD. Movie," she says again as she wanders away.

I take another sip.

"Maybe I should have seen what she had," I say, jokingly. Suddenly, I am hit with inspiration. I slam the glass of vodka down.

"That's what this book should be!" I exclaim, triumphantly.

"Hmm?" says Sara.

"Piracy. Anticopyright. That's the future!"

I sip my vodka, and I wink at the frat boy.

A MIDCONVERSATION EMAIL EXCHANGE WITH MY LONG-SUFFERING EDITRIX

----------------------Original Message----------------------

To: elinor@focalpress.com

From: lloyd@troma.com

Date: April 9, 2010 8:37 p.m.

Subject: Sell Your Own Damn Movie

Elinor—

I am brilliant. Distribution book will be pro-piracy. It will be a real shit disturber. Everyone will hate it!! Except the good people.

xo

Lloyd

-----------------------End Message------------------------

----------------------Original Message----------------------

To: lloyd@troma.com

From: elinor@focalpress.com

Date: April 12, 2010 9:36 a.m.

Subject: RE: Sell Your Own Damn Movie

Dear Lloyd,

I am delighted that you are moving ahead with the new book! I'm sure that you have lots of ideas that we can discuss. I'm not sure about your piracy angle, mostly because I believe piracy is illegal. We would like to sell copies of this book, unlike the last two that you wrote for us. But I continue to have faith in you. I'm sure this book will be the best yet! Please don't focus on piracy.

Regards,

Elinor
Focal Press

------------------------End Message------------------------

FUN FACTS!

(Because my co-writer usually writes children's books with titles like *Weird Animals: Platypus!* and insists that no book is complete without a fun fact page.)

- The first film clips were less than 20 seconds long. The only reason anyone was interested in making them longer was so people could watch an entire round of boxing in one continuous clip.
- In the fifth century B.C., at the same time that Mo-Ti was describing a theoretical camera, someone in Greece was describing the same thing. Why it took 2000 years to actually build the damn thing is anybody's guess.
- Platypuses are one of only two mammals that lay eggs instead of giving birth to live young!

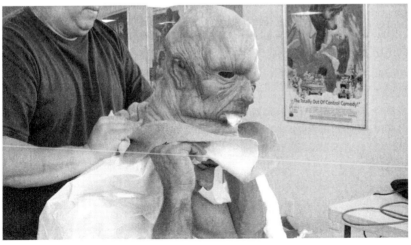

FIGURE 1.3 *When a Troma employee asks for a raise or misbehaves, he is forced to put on this suffocating rubber Toxie mask as punishment and is made to portray Toxie at various conventions and in promotional videos. This is so effective, we haven't given raises since 1989!*

KAREN BLACK SAYS, "DON'T GIVE UP!"

Oscar-nominated Karen Black has appeared in such films as Easy Rider, Five Easy Pieces, Hitchcock's *Family Plot, and Troma's* Haunting Fear. *Obviously, some of these titles are a bit more prestigious than others. Sorry, Hitchcock.*

Generally my advice is, when you're trying to sell a movie, or anything really, don't give up! I mean, maybe that's really strange advice, but that's my advice. When a person is promoting a new product, he thinks, "Oh, I'm going to irritate somebody. I'm going to make somebody mad at me. I'm going to overdo this. I'm going to annoy people." No! You're not annoying people. You're actually giving them a chance to say yes to you!

For example, about 10 or 15 years ago, somebody called me because they wanted to make Karen Black T-shirts. They had some really cute ideas. My first thought was, "Hey, this is great! I like it!" Unfortunately, I was in the middle of doing a movie at the time. The film was a very overwhelming experience for me because there was so much to memorize, and it was so hard to shoot. I couldn't phone anyone—I couldn't do anything. So finally the movie was over, and I wanted to get back in touch with these T-shirt people. But they hadn't called again, and I had lost their phone number somehow. So the result was, nothing ever happened. But if they had called repetitively, or even a few more times, I would have been very happy to give my name for their T-shirts.

What happens is, people give up because they think, "Well, I'm bothering so-and-so, and so-and-so doesn't like me." Meanwhile, so-and-so hasn't done anything, they're just busy or they don't remember you. All so-and-so remembers is that he didn't get the milk for his kid's cereal this morning and his wife is screaming at him. It has nothing to do with you.

I've always found that the more important the person, the less taken they are with their own ego. I find important people to be ego free. I find people that are worried about their own importance are the ones who might be put off by continuous communication. So to get things done, you have to communicate a lot—really do it until you get a response, and you can't give up. You can't worry about how you think the other person is feeling, because you don't know how they're feeling! You're just making it up in your head.

Make Your Own Damn Flowchart

When you've finished your movie and it's time to sell, sell, sell, there are decisions that need to be made. Will you try to sell the flick yourself, or will you use a distributor? Will you focus on big advertising or word of mouth? Will you sell the damn thing at all, or will you give it away in the name of free art? Each decision you make along the way has pros and cons.[1] I often find it helpful to channel my inner anal-retentive side and make a flowchart.

For example …

---

[1] Just like the holding cell at the 21st Street police station.

SHOULD YOU READ THIS DAMN BOOK?

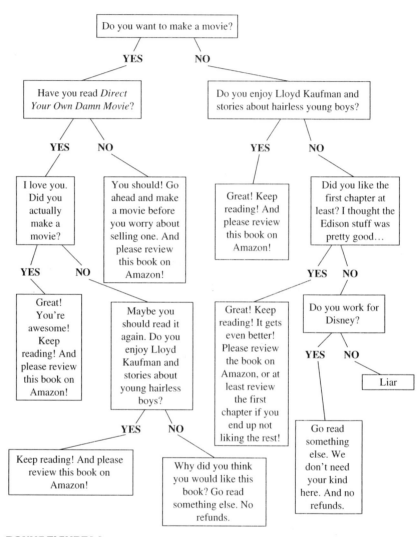

BONUS FIGURE 1.1

Theatrical Distribution: My Preferred Method of Release, Other Than Autoerotic Asphyxiation

I've spent years telling everyone who will listen (often unwillingly) that anyone can make his or her own damn movie. And that is certainly true. With small, high-definition camcorders costing just a few hundred dollars, it only takes a few birthdays worth of grandma's crisp $20 bills to become a genuine auteur. All the people who whine about how they would make the greatest movie in the entire world if only they had 50 million bucks are full of shit. If you can't make something that you are proud of for $500, another $49,999,500 isn't going to help. And Troma proves that fact every day. Even with the budget of *Avatar*, I would probably end up with *Avatarded*. And then I would have all the retarded people and all the *Avatar* fans up my ass.[1] But regardless, the fact remains that you can make a movie if you really want to. Yes, you.

---

[1] These two groups are actually composed of mostly the same people.

And if you have already made your own damn movie, then congratulations! You have now accomplished something that 98.7% of the world's population can only dream of, right after their dreams of clean water and a world without AIDS.

But let's be honest. You didn't spend the past 1 to 37 years of your life making a movie just so your mom can watch it on the flat screen in her basement (i.e., your bedroom) and tell you how great it is, even if there is no sound for those pesky seven minutes. No! You made a movie because you wanted millions of people to see it and proclaim you the next Fellini! But unless your name is Federico Fellini, Jr., that probably isn't going to happen.[2] But it's not the end of the world. Here at Troma, we make movies because we *love* making movies! No one is out there comparing me to Steven Spielberg. And we haven't made any money since 2003, but you don't hear me complaining![3]

I'm not going to sugarcoat things for you, though. Selling a movie and getting more than 50 people to see it is tough these days. Nearly impossible, in fact. What worked 30 years ago doesn't work today. So let's just wrap up this chapter and tell some stories about naked people.

----------------------Original Message----------------------

To: lloyd@troma.com
From: elinor@focalpress.com
Date: May 3, 2010 10:32 p.m.
Subject: RE: Chapter 2

Dear Lloyd,

We received your draft of Chapter 2 this morning, but there seems to be several pages missing. Please advise. This chapter can't really end on such a depressing note, can it? Also, I just wanted to remind you about our agreement on the number of pages this time around. I really don't want to press the issue, but a two-page chapter just isn't going to cut it. Please resend your completed Chapter 2. Thanks Lloyd!

Regards,
Elinor
Focal Press

----------------------End Message----------------------

---

[2] Federico Fellini, Jr. is actually my favorite dancer at the Manhole Club. Hi Federico! Can I cash in that free lap dance now?

[3] I let my employees do the complaining. They are much better at it than I am. Come tour the Troma Building in Long Island City, New York, and you can hear it for yourself!

Okay, so forget what I said about selling your movie. Of course you can sell your movie, if you click your heels together three times and try really, really hard. I mean, would Focal Press let me write a book about selling a movie if it was actually impossible? Of course not! So let's jump in the deep end with our noses held and our Speedos around our ankles and figure this out together! (The more time that passes, the more afraid of Elinor I become.)

Believe it or not, Troma movies used to be shown in actual movie theaters. I know this is unfathomable to those of you who have been waiting for six or seven years for *Poultrygeist: Night of the Chicken Dead* to cluck its way into your local cinema, but it's true.[4] Back in the 1970s, when disco was hot and Farrah Fawcett didn't have anal cancer, small independent film companies were still benefiting from the 1948 court decision that prevented the major studios from owning movie theaters. Back then, if you made a decent movie that was at least mildly entertaining, there was a pretty good chance that at least one guy would agree to show it in his theater. Even Troma's horribly indecent flicks got play.

FIGURE 2.1 *In a recent appearance tour "down under," Lloyd seems a bit distraught at how happy his wife Pat seems to be, posing next to Jamie McKinnon, a New Zealand Troma distributor in Auckland.*

---

[4] For example, at this writing, *Poultrygeist* is finally getting a modest theatrical release in Australia, four years after its U.S. theatrical run.

You see, in those days, when it came to film distribution, the United States was divided up into 18 territories. Each territory had a subdistributor, who would distribute films within that territory. So a film that you saw in Salem, Oregon, might never play in Wichita, Kansas. But this was back before President Al Gore invented the Internet, and unless little Moishe from Wichita, Kansas, had a buddy in Salem, Oregon, he would never know what he was missing. So this subdistributor would take your decent/indecent, mildly entertaining, independent film and open it in his territory—usually someplace small, like Evansville, Indiana. It wasn't a test screening with free tickets and a focus group. It was an actual opening. This could go on for weeks. And depending on how the film did, you as the producer/distribution company could then take that film to other distributors and essentially achieve national distribution, on par with anything that MGM could throw at you. You may not have the advertising budget they did, but if your film was any good, word of mouth could keep you in the theater. And because the theaters were independently owned, they kept films that made money and got rid of the ones that didn't. Novel, eh? Funny how that's not how it works today, but I'll get to that in a second.[5]

First, a subdistributor would take one 35mm print of your film and see how it played. If the film did well in one theater, the distributor would take another 35mm print, and then another. There were no DVDs to pass around, and no digital projectors, so each theater needed its own 35mm print in order to play the film. Let me tell you something about 35mm film prints. They are fucking heavier than an Oprah special. A feature-length film requires about six reels of film, which fit conveniently into two 70-lb film cans. Do you want to know something else about 35mm film prints? They are incredibly expensive to make. Each print costs around $2000, so being the cheapo that I am, of course I absolutely never make more prints than absolutely necessary. From the time we made *Squeeze Play*! up through *Toxic Avenger II*, we were making more than 100 prints of each film. That means that, at any given time, a Troma movie was playing in about 100 theaters around the country. No, seriously! I'm not kidding! Now compare that to the whopping six(!) 35mm prints that we made of *Poultrygeist: Night of*

---

[5] Or more than a second, depending on how quickly you read. You are really the one in control here.

the Chicken Dead, and you can see just how drastically things have changed in theatrical distribution.

With the rise of the multiplex theater, studios just weren't producing enough quality movies to fill up all 12 screens. And like I said, in the age of the independent theater, a movie that wasn't making money was given the boot. We gave theaters what they needed, and they *loved* us! Troma movies tended to sell a lot of popcorn,[6] which is where the theater makes most of its money anyhow. *Variety,* the Da Vinci Code of the film industry, even reported our numbers each week. Compare that to 2008 when we had to practically beg some shitty website to accurately report that *Poultrygeist: Night of the Chicken Dead* was the #1 movie in the country per screen the weekend of its New York City premiere.

Now, you may be saying to yourself, "God, this is depressing. *Poultrygeist: Night of the Chicken Dead,* Lloyd's magnum ovum,[7] was probably Troma's best film. What could have possibly changed so much in 20 years?"

One word: Reagan.

Remember that landmark court decision in 1948 that prevented film studios from owning movie theaters? I think I mentioned it a few times. Remember how the court decided that a film studio owning a theater was illegal and a little too close to a monopoly and against everything that our capitalist society stands for?[8] Well, Ronald Reagan, Mr. Studio Man himself, decided that the Supreme Court had been mistaken. His Federal Communication Commission's repeal of the consent decree once again made it perfectly legal for the major studios to own theaters and to pressure the ones they didn't own with cinematic blacklisting. It goes something like this:

Studio Head: Well, Pete, we know that *Shrek VII* isn't doing very well, but you see, we spent a lot of money on this flick, and we'd like to keep it playing.

---

[6] I'm not sure if most of it was thrown at the screen or if it was because the greasy butter-like substance makes a really good lubricant for a mid-movie hand job.

[7] NOTE FROM YOUR RECENTLY REPLACED FOOTNOTE GUY: Hey Lloyd! Remember me? Other people might not want your chicken puns in their mouths, but I don't mind!*

   * NOTE FROM THE NEW FOOTNOTE GUY: Eugene, please don't move anything on my desk. And yes, it is my desk now, okay? How did you even get in the building?**

   ** NOTE FROM YOUR RECENTLY REPLACED FOOTNOTE GUY: I'm little.

[8] God, I sound like a fucking Tea Party patriot. But in this case, it was a Republican who screwed up. Obama gets a free pass since he was still living in Kenya.

Theater Owner: Well, Mr. Studio Head, I understand. But you see, I've been playing an independent film this week that is actually making me a lot of money and selling a lot of popcorn. I'd really like to keep playing that movie for another week.

Studio Head: Sure, Pete, sure. I understand. I'm sure you've heard of a little film called *Sex and the City 2*, right?

Theater Owner: Oh sure, Mr. President. I'm really excited to have that movie here and make some money.

Studio Head: Well, you see, Pete, unless *Shrek VII* plays in your theater until I say it can stop, I don't think we'll be able to give you *Transformers 3*.

Theater Owner: But, Mr. President, I need to make some money. I need to pay my rent and feed my hermit crabs. I need *Transformers*.

Studio Head: Sure you do, Pete. Do we have an agreement then?

Theater Owner: Yes, sir.

Studio Head: And while you're at it, we'd like you to build an IMAX screen at your theater. And purchase a 3D projector. The extra fees from those ticket sales will really come in handy when it comes time to repaint my yacht this year.

Theater Owner: Yes, sir.

(Theater Owner proceeds to spend his rent money on a gun and blow his brains out.)

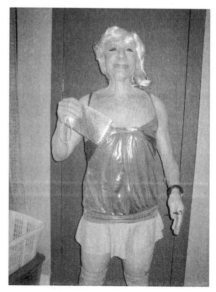

FIGURE 2.2 *A young Taylor Swift at the opening of* Poultrygeist.

I can't tell you how many times *Poultrygeist: Night of the Chicken Dead* played at an independent theater and ended up being the highest grossing movie of the weekend. But, inevitably, we would be kicked out for *Step Up 2: The Streets* or that stupid movie about beautiful people who could jump in and out of places. Oh yeah, I think it was called *Jumper*, because originality is king in Hollywood. Tell me, is a film truly a film without at least a couple of chicken puns in the title? Shakespeare himself would say nay!

This chapter clucks ass. Wasn't I going to talk about naked people? What happened to that idea?

I lean back in my chair and stare at the *Poultrygeist* props covering my desk. I blink a few times, wondering if typing this entire chapter on my BlackBerry is really a good idea. I scroll back through my email, and I find Elinor's note. Now I remember why there haven't been any hairless young boys mentioned in the chapter. Yet. I click back over to my Facebook to try and cheer up a bit. Nothing gets me going these days like a good hour of FarmVille in the afternoon. I am just about to fertilize some crops, when that tiny red banner pops up alerting me that I have an urgent Facebook message.

Troma fan Ricky Bales writes to Lloyd on Facebook. Lloyd responds to all his fan-boys because they are a valuable means of free advertising!

Ricky Bayles   5 May 2010 at 3:07

Hi Lloyd!!!

Dude, the toxic avenger rocks! It is totally awesome. i read your last book and made my own damn movie! What should I do now? How can I get it into a theater?

Shit. In a way, I feel responsible. Like I said, I've been telling people for years to make their own damn movies. It started as a way to get them to stop trying to get *me* to make their movie for them. But somewhere along the way, "Make Your Own Damn Movie" took on a life of its own, a battle cry, almost. So how can I turn my back on these poor, trusting souls who are looking to me to guide them? All right, Ricky Bayles. You want your movie to play in a movie theater? Let's tear it up!

WAYS TO GET YOUR FILM INTO A THEATER

Option A. Give your film to a major studio. Examples include Sony, Universal, and Disney. They will do all the work for you and your film will play for weeks in every movie theater across the country.

- Pros: Lots of money and prestige
- Cons: Virtually impossible

Option B. Gather about $100 million. This will go toward advertising and distribution costs. Take out print ads, television ads, and Internet ads, buy coverage in magazines, and try to buy an Academy Award. Your film will probably play in at least a few theaters in each big city, and you may make some of your money back.

- Pros: Creative control over advertising, some money and prestige
- Cons: Virtually impossible. And if you do somehow stumble on $100 million, don't spend it on a movie. Adopt a shelter dog or something. Or remember your old pal Uncle Lloydie who helped you get started!

And now that we've gotten those two fantastical options out of the way, let's try something a little more practical.

WEEKLONG RUNS

Start calling theaters and try to get them to play your film for a week, starting on a Friday night. Understand that you won't get into the AMCs and the Regals, but there are several small, independent theaters around the country that might give you a chance. Have your press kit (which I'll talk more about in Chapter 5) prepared, and it will definitely help if you have some great quotes from notable publications or websites, or if you can point to a smaller screening at a college or convention that drew lots of fans. Basically, these theaters want to make money, and if you show them that you can help them do that, they will be much more likely to take a chance on you.

Many times a theater will agree to play a film if one of the stars or the director will be there and do a Q&A. We sent the lead actress in *Squeeze Play!*, Jenny Hetrick, to Norfolk, Virginia, to promote the film. Now, most of the people who went to see the movie had never heard of Jenny Hetrick before that night, but there is something about actors and actresses appearing somewhere that draws crowds. It's like one of those experiments on *Dateline* where they put an ordinary person in nice clothes and give them a couple of bodyguards and all of a sudden people are taking pictures of them on the street. They don't know who the fuck this person is, but they know they need a picture. As a result of our promotion, *Squeeze Play!* played for seven weeks in Norfolk! When we distributed *Def by Temptation*, we sent Kadeem Hardison and director James Bond III on several personal appearances. When you're talking to a theater's booking agent, mention that the beautiful lead actress will be in town that week and would just love to stop by for an introduction or a Q&A. Also talk about how you plan to promote the film before the weekend it opens. Talk about your street team who will post flyers on every empty surface in town, or about your 5 million fans on Facebook!

If you can get your film into a theater without losing too much money, you're doing great! But if the theater seems interested, or if you have a few successful screenings under your belt, try asking for a little cash in return for the theater's honor of presenting your masterpiece. At Troma, we have a 40-year history of successful theatrical runs, so we begin by asking theaters to pay us a $500 deposit against 50% of the gross. That means we have $500 in our hands, no matter what happens at the screening. On top of that, the theater will pay us 50% of the ticket sales, minus the initial $500. So if the movie makes $147 over the weekend, we make $500. If the movie makes $2000 over the weekend, we get a cool $1000. Sometimes, when we're making the deal, we will go as low as a $300 deposit against 35% of the ticket sales. Bigger theaters may not let you have more than 10%. It's all about the best deal that you can negotiate.

Whatever happens, *get everything in writing*! It's best to have an actual contract, but even a documented email conversation is better than nothing. For the love of Dr. Phil, do not make a verbal agreement over the phone without backing it up in writing. You will get cheated. And then you will start sending nasty messages to my Facebook about how I didn't tell you to put anything in writing. So I'm telling you, and if Elinor is still reading at this point, I'm sure she will back me up:

GET EVERYTHING IN WRITING!

When we opened *Poultrygeist: Night of the Chicken Dead* in New York City, this is the model that we used. Now, because theater space in NYC is pretty competitive and the Village East Cinema is a pretty big theater, the theater owners required us to spend $30,000 to $40,000 on ads in New York before they would show the film. So we did. The premiere was phenomenal, and *Poultrygeist* was the #1 grossing film per screen in the country. The movie made about $30,000 over the weekend, of which we got about a third. So we spent $50,000 on ads and only made $10,000. Which, if you're a little fuzzy on your second-grade math, is a loss of $40,000. Losing $40,000 sucks. In years past, however, the theater would have kept playing the film for a few weeks based on such a great opening, and we would have had plenty of opportunity to make that money back, as well as make some profit. However, the Village East Cinema only allowed us to stay until Wednesday because *Indiana Jones 4: The Curse of the Skull Fucker* had to open on every single fucking screen in the theater. So we were out, just like that. The theater doesn't need you, and the owners will have no problem kicking you out, too. So remember that before your let your ego get involved and you spend $50,000 on newspaper ads, especially since no one reads a newspaper anymore.

EVENT SCREENINGS

Now, with *Poultrygeist*, we tried to have a real opening, with our totals reported by *Variety* and all of that. But you don't need to do that to get your movie into a theater! You also have the option of renting a screen yourself for a one-night event. This works best if you have a large family or a large cast full of people who will be happy to attend and bring their families and friends. For this to work you need to perfect the art of disappearing right around the time everyone is buying tickets and then reappearing with the line, "Oh! Did you get your ticket already? I was going to get it for you!"

The negative side of this option is that you have to put up the money upfront to rent the theater. So if no one shows up, you are shit out of luck. But the upside is that you make all the profits from the ticket sales! With a good turnout, there is the possibility of making a little money, but probably not much. But hey, you wanted to get your movie in a theater, right? And with a successful screening, you may be able to convince another theater to give you a weeklong run!

Ultimately, if your goal is to get your film into a theater, then go for it. Just realize ahead of time that it's probably not going to make you millions of dollars. But you didn't make the movie so you could make millions of dollars, right? I didn't think so. Try to think of any short theatrical run as an epic advertising campaign. Successful screenings can build buzz for a DVD or digital release down the road!

SELF-DISTRIBUTION, OR NECESSITY IS THE MOTHER OF *INVENTION*: AN INTERVIEW WITH MYNETTE LOUIE AND TZE CHUN

Tze Chun and Mynette Louie are the writer/director and producer, respectively, of the film Children of Invention, *an official selection at the Sundance Film Festival in 2009.*

FIGURE 2.3 *Tze Chun, writer/director of* Children of Invention.

FIGURE 2.4 *Mynette Louie, producer of* Children of Invention.

LLOYD: Did you try to make a movie that appealed to everyone at all times?

TZE: When I was writing the movie, I wanted to write an Asian American film that wasn't just for Asian Americans. When we premiered the movie, it was really nice to see that the movie played really well with all these different age groups and ethnicities. And part of the fun of going on the festival circuit is going where there's no Asian American population at all. We'll go to these places like Denver and Sarasota and places where the audiences are primarily Caucasian, and we've found that the audience reaction has been equally positive.

MYNETTE: It's interesting because there's a lot of talk right now about thinking about your audience and the target market and working backward from there and changing your script to fit that, so you can ensure yourself an audience. But with this film, it's semiautobiographical and based on Tze's childhood in Boston, so we didn't think about any of that stuff. He didn't think about any of that stuff, he just wrote the script and we found the audience afterward. And like Tze said, we were surprised. We thought it would appeal to Asian Americans and women, but we didn't expect it to appeal to middle Americans who had been burdened by pyramid schemes. It turns out there are a lot of people that had been burdened by pyramid schemes.

TZE: I guess it's something a lot of people are talking about right now, figuring out your different audiences and demographics beforehand. But if there's a story that I want to tell and spend a couple years of my life doing, I just had to trust that other people were going to identify with that as well. When I was making short films, I made a lot of short films before I made my first feature, and one of the main lessons I learned when I was making these short films was that I had gotten a production company to give us $15,000 to make a short film. And I was like, "Well, this has got to be my calling card, I'll shoot on 35mm, I'll have special effects, action sequences, comedy, drama, everything." I thought these were all the things that were going to help me in my career. At the same time, I wrote something that I felt just came from the heart. We spent $600 making it and shot it in my childhood home. We shot over two weekends with no crew, just me holding the camera and my producer holding the boom and that was pretty much it. And the movie that was supposed to be my calling card didn't get picked up anywhere, and the movie I made for $600, *Windowbreaker*, got into Sundance, and that was the one that ended up playing in 30 international film festivals and that was the film that was the basis for *Children of Invention*.

LLOYD: You had an interesting strategy with YouTube for *Windowbreaker*, did you not?

TZE: With *Windowbreaker* we played on the YouTube Screening Room, which is really great because there are so many eyes on the YouTube homepage, while the Screening Room is curated as such that there's only five new films, I think, every two weeks. So it's not like a mass of videos that people are sorting through—there's only five, and I think we got a half million hits over the first month or so. More people saw it the first day than at any film festival.

MYNETTE: It was great. Like Tze said, with the Screening Room, we weren't just in this big vat of videos. As for *Children of Invention*, we were one of five Sundance films featured this year at the Sundance 2010 Festival's part of YouTube's new rental platform. So we were one of the first five films to be featured in this rental platform where you pay $3.99 for a 48-hour rental.

LLOYD: How did you get into Sundance?

TZE: We submitted the movie, and because *Windowbreaker* had already been in, they knew us. We didn't have a producer's rep before we got into Sundance. I think that a lot of producer's reps will say that having one helps and it can't hurt, but we didn't do that.

LLOYD: What did you do at Sundance to help sell your own damn movie?

MYNETTE: We hired a publicist and got a sales agent on board. We considered doing it ourselves, but I had never been to Sundance before. We got those people on board; our publicist got us interviews and reviews. There were a couple of publicists that specialize in just doing Sundance because it's a special animal. It was expensive, though. It was several thousand dollars. What the publicist did was start about a month ahead of Sundance prepping and sending screeners out to key press and key reviewers. Our sales agent, as well, started calling people a month ahead and trying to get the screenings and trying to get them to come to Sundance. Ultimately, we were very glad we got the publicist. Like we said, Sundance is its own animal, and we did not know how to navigate around the press. And it is a press circus/zoo type situation, so their help was invaluable.

FIGURE 2.5 *A still from* Children of Invention.

LLOYD: Did you get the sales agent before applying to Sundance?

MYNETTE: No, pretty much the following hour after finding out we got into Sundance, I was emailing different sales agents and publicists and trying to get them on board and to screen the film and see if they wanted to represent it. Your sales agent is basically somebody who represents the film and tries to sell it to a distributor on your behalf. We brought a North American sales agent on board with us, and then usually you have a separate foreign sales agent that helps you with non–North American territories.

LLOYD: Do you still have the same sales agent?

MYNETTE: The deal expired the year after Sundance. The thing is, when we got into Sundance it was 2009 and just several months after the Lehman Brothers crash and the whole economy just took a nosedive. So when we got into Sundance, we knew that we weren't going to have one of these storied traditional deals of yore, like *Little Miss Sunshine*. So we were very realistic about our expectations. Our sales agent got the film in front of everybody he needed to get the film in front of. All the major distributors saw it at Sundance or got a screener, so he did his job. And we did get offers, but it wouldn't have been financially responsible for us to take any of these offers because they were, to be perfectly honest, crap. So we decided to do distribution ourselves by selling the movie on DVD on the festival circuit right after Sundance. We decided to play as many festivals as possible and sort of use that as our theatrical run and use all the press from all these little local festivals to help sell the DVD after screenings and online.

TZE: Because *Children of Invention* has an Asian American cast and has no obvious stars, we knew going into Sundance that we were going to be one of the smallest films there. And we knew going into it that we wanted to use Sundance as a jumping-off point as opposed to the end all be all. That's why we submitted to a hundred festivals and ended up playing at 45 of them. It was through those other festivals that we really were able to get this grassroots support, and even though we weren't the biggest film at Sundance, we started to win all these festival awards afterward. And we're distributing the DVD on our own so that got us some press as well. It was one of these situations where there were a couple of offers at Sundance that made no financial sense at all for our investors and we thought, well, we're just going to keep pushing forward, win more awards, sell more DVDs, and show that we're economically viable. And as we rounded out the festival circuit, we ended up rejecting all these distribution offers. As more and more of them came, they ended up getting better and better because we had done more and more of the work. But in the end, we had done so much of the work, why bother bringing on a traditional distributor for DVD?

LLOYD: How has the independent film economy changed?

MYNETTE: It's gotten a lot harder to recoup. It's harder to find your audience, because audiences are much more fragmented. There's a much bigger divide between big studio features and little films, so the middle has dropped out, I think. Because of that, we understood the deals that the distributors were offering, but we decided that we can do just as good a job as they could, or even better. And we had done so much of the work already. We didn't start getting decent deal offers until six months into our festival run, and by that time we had been traveling the festival circuit on our own, almost like a rock band, going from festival to festival on a tour and interacting directly with our fans. Which I find is really, really important. Even if you do have a distributor, I find that a lot of filmmakers actually have to keep going to these festivals because it's about developing a direct relationship with your audience, and there's no substitute for that. A distributor can't really substitute for that at all.

LLOYD: Why did you distribute to cinemas? Did you shoot on 35mm?

MYNETTE: No, Chris Teague, our DP, shot on a Panasonic HVX200 with a 35mm adapter and a [Sony] HDW-F900 as well. We ended up booking in eight theaters across the U.S., New York, Boston, L.A., and five smaller cities. We didn't four-wall anything. These art houses requested the film from us and we got pretty lucky.

TZE: We wanted to play Boston because the movie takes place in Boston. It played at the Brattle Theatre, which had been my theater growing up, and I had loved that theater. And we wanted to play New York and L.A. because the whole point of doing theatrical is that you get reviews. So we tried to keep our P&A [prints and advertising] costs as low as possible and it ended up being under $5000. So we thought that was a remarkable tradeoff in order to get great reviews in the *New York Times*, *Los Angeles Times*, *New York Post*, *New York Daily News*, *Village Voice*, etc. And because we got good reviews, then other art house cinemas started calling us. So we had planned for a three-city release and we ended up doing eight, which was really nice.

MYNETTE: Oh, and we didn't have a film print. We actually screened off of Blu-ray. I think over the last six months a lot of art house theaters across the U.S. have gotten Blu-ray projectors and that has been a huge cost savings for us.

LLOYD: Getting back to the festivals, did you pay the entry fees to get into those 45 festivals?

MYNETTE: No, after Sundance we got a lot of invitations, so those were free. And those festivals that we didn't get invited to, we asked if they could waive the fee. So out of maybe 150 festivals we applied to we paid four entry fees and the rest of them were free.

TZE: Students should apply to the big festivals first. Because if you do get into a big festival like Sundance, Tribeca, SXSW, L.A. Film Festival, etc., and you get into those festivals first, you'll get into the other smaller, regional festivals more easily. With short films and feature films you could just blanket submit, but it's better to submit to just the big festivals first, because once you get in there's a lot more leverage for you to request that the submission fees be waived at other festivals.

MYNETTE: And not just that the submission fees are waived, but that they pay you a screening fee. So we actually got a decent chunk of change asking for screening fees from festivals. A lot of regional festivals actually have a budget to pay screening fees. Some can pay between $300 and $500.

TZE: That's in addition to flying you out, usually. It doesn't mean a lot if you play 5 film festivals, but it means a lot if you play 45.

LLOYD: Can you talk a bit more about the smaller film festivals? A lot of the filmmakers we've talked to say that if you don't get into Sundance, Cannes, Venice, or Toronto, forget the other festivals because they are useless. Tell us how the other festivals are useful.

TZE: I played eight festivals with my short film before Sundance and it was really awesome because I didn't go to graduate school for film, so I didn't know a lot of other filmmakers, and when you have a short film at some of these smaller regional film festivals, your access to people is a lot greater than at Sundance. If you go to Sundance, you might not be able to have an hour-long conversation with somebody who is 5 or 10 years further down the road than you to give you advice. I think for promotion for a feature film, it's absolutely necessary to play some of these regional festivals because everyone on the festival circuit in a particular year travels together. And they might not have a chance to watch your film at Sundance, Tribeca, SXSW, but there are other producers, cinematographers, actors, collaborators, and other people in the industry. It's important to play your film so these other people can see it.

MYNETTE: And also, I think regional festivals, as opposed to Sundance or Cannes, have real audiences. Real people are going to see your movie, not just people in the biz. It was a way for us to market test, and almost every Q&A was like a focus group. We saw what people responded well to, what they asked questions about, what they were most interested in. So that was really helpful in terms of informing our marketing going forward with the film. And also, playing at a smaller festival, the press actually covers your film, whereas if you're at Sundance, the press will not necessarily cover your film if you're small because there are all these other big films there. But we actually got a lot of great reviews, and even features and interviews with local press because there's more access to the press and more access to the industry.

TZE: And every time we played one of these regional festivals and got a good review, we would see sales spike on our website for DVDs.

LLOYD: How were the time slots they gave you at Sundance?

MYNETTE: They were good. We had four screenings and one press and industry screening that they actually scheduled during Obama's inauguration, which was awful, so they gave us another screening after that. Then we started selling our DVD at our second festival right after Sundance.

LLOYD: So people have seen your movie already, but they'll buy your DVD?

TZE: Yeah, it's actually really interesting. We've found that contextual selling always works best. So after the movie has screened, 10% of the audience will buy the DVD. Since it's an Asian American film, at Asian American film festivals we found that 20% of the audience would buy the DVD. So if you're looking at a crowd of 300 to 600 people, 30 to 60 people are buying a $20 DVD. If you're going to be at that film festival anyway, it is definitely a good chunk of change. We actually continued selling the DVD through our theatrical run, so even though it doesn't show up on Rentrak, we did end up making an additional half or third on top of what we made from DVD sales.

LLOYD: And you and another movie joined together to distribute?

MYNETTE: There's a film called *White on Rice*, an Asian American comedy made by our friend Dave Boyle. He basically released the film through Variance Films, the theatrical distribution company, in a dozen cities, but he hadn't done New York yet. We had been talking about doing New York, so we were like, "Why don't we do it together? That way we can buoy our promotional efforts and support each other." So whenever they posted on Facebook, they mentioned us, and whenever we posted on Twitter, we mentioned them.

TZE: I also think that's a good strategy for smaller films because, even though we didn't four-wall a theater, there was still a minimum we had to hit in terms of our ticket sales.

MYNETTE: Yes, there was a revenue split with them that we had to make a certain minimum before the split started. The split went toward this minimum they wanted us to hit. And because our efforts were so grassroots, we didn't have a lot of money to spend on advertising. We didn't buy any paid ads at all. It was all Facebook, and Twitter, and visiting Asian American classes and Japanese language classes and telling people about the film. It's funny because you never think that this nuts-and-bolts stuff works, but it proves to be the most effective. We visited classes at Hunter College, which is right next to the theater, and tried to convince these students to come in. We held screenings at universities and nonprofit organizations that had constituencies that we thought would be most interested in the film, and that way they could tell their friends to go see the movie when it came out in theaters. We found that was more effective than a paid ad.

TZE: We didn't want to go $25,000 in debt for theatrical and then try to make it all back through DVD sales. That didn't seem logical to us.

MYNETTE: We haven't recouped our total distribution costs yet, but we made back over a third of our budget. It was a microbudget feature, but it wasn't tiny, tiny because there was SAG and WGA, we paid all our crew, we shot in three states, and we had two child leads. So it wasn't a $20,000, shoot-in-a-room-with-your-roommates film.

TZE: We think that recoupment is going to happen in about a year.

MYNETTE: In addition to our self-distribution efforts, I signed a separate video-on-demand deal and a separate DVD retail and rental deal. So we're on VOD right now—we launched in June 2010.

TZE: Our windows were theatrical, and then we did VOD, which is where you can request a movie to rent though your cable box. Probably 70% of the cable boxes in the country have *Children of Invention* as an option that you can rent for 48 hours for $5.

LLOYD: How did you do it? Did you knock on Time Warner's door?

MYNETTE: We did it through Film Movement, which is a small specialty distributor in New York and they have relationships with all the cable carriers— Time Warner, Cox, Comcast. So that's a two-month run on cable VOD. Then in August 2010, we're going to launch our DVD nationwide in retail and rental outlets like Netflix, iTunes, Amazon, Blockbuster. And we did that through a new company called IndieBLITZ. Basically they started fulfilling our DVDs for us and they have a relationship with a company called E1, which is a large DVD distributor in Canada. So they select some of the titles they fulfill the DVDs for to give to E1 to sell to their network of wholesale buyers.

TZE: We ended up bifurcating the rights, but I think as we were going in, our strategy was to find a distribution company that wouldn't take rights for 12 to 15 years, but would still have access to the big box retailers.

LLOYD: How about the sales outside North America?

MYNETTE: We have a foreign sales agent, Forward Entertainment; they were the sales agent for *Old Joy* and *Red Doors* and a lot of documentaries. And we have sales pending in about five foreign territories.

LLOYD: So if you were to give odds, is your movie going to be very profitable, exceptionally profitable, break even, what do you think?

MYNETTE: I think we'll do a little better than break even. It is a movie that's hard to sell because it's a drama, it has no stars in it, and it has Asian American leads. But I think the majority of American independent movies don't even recoup. So we consider ourselves pretty lucky to make as much money as we have already.

You know, making the movie was so easy. Between the time Tze finished the first draft of the script and the time we premiered at Sundance was 10 months. So it all seemed to happen so easily for us. The distribution was difficult because of the climate we just happened to be in. Self-distribution has always been hard and will continue to be hard. It's a lot of legwork.

I knew it would take a lot of time to distribute a film, but it has been very time-consuming. Filmmakers should be prepared if they're going to make a movie that will be difficult to sell. They should be prepared to have their other work suffer. We haven't been able to focus on our new films because of this old one. And finally, now that we're done with the distribution of this film we can finally move on. But it has been very difficult to juggle distribution with new projects.

TZE: I guess even though it was kind of a long road to get the movie out, there's not a lot we would do differently. I think that we tried to make the best choices we could, given the marketplace. But it was really educational to not just make your movie and dump it out there and let someone else handle it. You not only get to know your audience, but also how they feel about your work. And that's important, not just for the piece of work you're out there with but also for future work. What do people respond to well, what do they think the strengths and weaknesses of the film are? And having gone through self-distribution, going through a lot of these film festivals and seeing the reviews not only in festivals, but in newspapers during our theatrical run, I think it was enormously educational. It was a lot of time, but I wouldn't have wanted to give up any part of that. A face-to-face meeting with somebody after they've seen your movie in Dallas is going to be different from other cities. But also looking at a review in a major newspaper is different from reading a review from a blogger who's at the festival. That breadth of experience with the film is something I found really fulfilling.

MYNETTE: Yeah, I didn't want to end on a down note. It is really hard to self-distribute, but we did it out of necessity. Otherwise our film would have sat on the shelf or we would have sold it for, like pennies to a distributor. We made more on it doing self-distribution than we would have selling all rights to a distributor. So we're glad we did what we did, not only for the money but for the learning experience as well. I think that it's really important for producers and directors to understand what the whole distribution and marketing process is, and it's been a crash course in that. I think that our budgets for future films will be a lot better informed because of the experience we went through.

TZE: I think that distribution is in some way an extension of the creative process. You hope that you know what the strengths of your film are, and in distribution you kind of find out whether or not that's the case. I think it's important to have knowledge of distribution as a filmmaker. There's something freeing to me about it, that you have the knowledge of what's going to happen to your movie afterward. You hope that you're not going to spend a year of your life distributing your film, but you know that that's always something you can do if it's necessary.

MYNETTE: I actually enjoy distribution, and I think Tze does, too. The two of us worked together. I did the website, and Tze did the graphic design. Doing the posters, the key art, trying to find cheap ways to promote the movie using Facebook and Twitter, and all that stuff, it's all very creative. We brainstorm all kinds of things because there are a lot of free Internet tools out there where there weren't before. So there is a lot of room for creativity in getting your film out there. Being a merchant of your film is not dirty; it's part of the entire film-making process. So you make a film—great—but it has to be seen in order for your vision to be seen. Otherwise, it's just sitting on the shelf.

TZE: Unfortunately, there's no outsider that's going to be as invested in distributing your film as you are. By that, I'm including within distribution the going to festivals with it, the communicating with your audience, etc. I'm not just talking about red lining contracts and negotiating deals—I think it's something a little bit bigger than that. I think that Mynette and I have seen that there hasn't been anyone as dedicated to getting this film out there as us. When you meet with distributors you see that they're suffering too, obviously, but we've heard so many horror stories about people sending over their films for 12 to 15 years and nothing being done with them. If that's the worst-case scenario, then of course we're happy to do the work ourselves.

MYNETTE: As Tze mentioned, there's no one but the filmmaker who understands your movie as well as you do.

YOU AND YOUR FILM VERSUS THE ENTIRE HISTORY OF CINEMA, AND HOW TO WIN THE BATTLE: AN INTERVIEW WITH TED HOPE

Ted Hope graduated from NYU film school, became a production assistant, and worked his way up within the studio system to become an incredibly success-ful producer of such films as Crouching Tiger, Hidden Dragon, In the Bedroom, *and* Happiness. *In other words, he is the exact opposite of Lloyd Kaufman, and he is everything that you've dreamed about being.*

FIGURE 2.6 *Ted Hope speaking at the Sundance Film Festival.*

LLOYD: Can you talk a bit about *The Brothers McMullen? The Brothers McMullen* was a movie that certainly, on the surface, didn't have too many explosions in it, Sylvester Stallone, or any of that stuff. So how did that get distributed?

TED: I was sitting in my office, and Mary Jane Skalski, who at that time was our office manager and who has since gone on to become a great producer in her own right, had said there's this movie and this guy is really cute and I'd love it if you could look at it because I'd like to talk to this guy again. The guy came in, and I thought he was a PA, but he's the star of the movie and he's the director and he wrote it. And literally, maybe three hours later, I was talking to Tom Rothman, who we had known during our Samuel Goldwyn days when he had distributed *Wedding Banquet* and *Eat, Drink, Man, Woman* and who had taken a job at Fox and started up a new independent division for them called Fox Searchlight. And he said, "Have you seen this movie, *The Brothers McMullen*?" And I was like, "That's so funny. I actually have it in my backpack." And Tom says, "Well, you should look at it, and if you were going to be involved in it, I might be interested in paying for a first look."

At that point, the movie had been shot, but it was over two hours long. Eddie Burns and his partner at the time, Dick Fisher, had both realized it needed some work. So he sent it to us, and I looked at it. It had great actors in it, I thought, and it was really funny, but it was about 35 minutes too long. I didn't understand yet that it was a comedy. You know like, where they were just staring into whiskey bottles and pulling out their hair under silence. I looked at it and said, "I actually think there's a really great movie here." What you can see in the film was that through each of the brothers' characters, you could kind of recognize your own life no matter where you were. One person was unhappy in their relationship, one person was beginning a new relationship, one person had a loving relationship. And of course, if you've seen the movie, all that stuff changes over the course of the film. But people could identify with it. And Eddie was a fantastic storyteller.

At that time he was still a PA on *Entertainment Tonight*. And to make the movie, the guy had actually become homeless. He was living in his car to save the money from paying rent. He was working for *ET* during the day, and I would meet up with him at 10 or 11 o'clock at night, to cut the film. And then he would tell us like, "Oh my god, I can't believe it. We were on *ET* and Robert Redford was there and I thought I might be able to give him my film, but I fell asleep while we were filming him because I had been up all night cutting!" All Eddie needed was a little coaching to kind of see what that movie was. Once I spent a little time with him, he and Dick Fisher totally got what the movie should be and they cut those 35 minutes out. The film got into Sundance…

LLOYD: How did it get into Sundance?

TED: On its merits. James Schamus and I had already had films at Sundance. James had been an executive producer on *Poison*, which had won. I had produced *Trust*, which got a screenplay prize. So we had a good relationship with Sundance. And Sundance in those days was much smaller than what people think it is now. Buyers weren't going there to try to acquire a film yet. But the year before, I think actually, was when Christine Vachon had sold *Go Fish*, which I think was the first film that was sold during the film festival at the time. And it was also sold in the first half. So that was like a real game change. People started thinking that it would happen. So Tom had paid for a first look of the film and we had gone out looking for finishing funds. We had calculated that to really deliver the movie would cost about $250,000. We found people who were willing to put up the money, but they wanted half the ownership in the film. And Eddie and his dad kind of looked at it and said, "Wait a second, we could create a version of this movie that people could see at Sundance for $50,000 and own the movie outright, or we could take their money and give up half or more of the ownership. You're telling me that's a difficult question?" They chose to put up the money themselves to deliver it. As a result they owned 100% of the film, which turned out to be worth it a hundred times over.

The one step along the way that was kind of fun was when Eddie had applied to the Independent Filmmaker Project for this thing they had called Independents Night. It was at the Walter Reade Theater at Lincoln Center. It was a prestigious event and he had gotten in. But if you do that, you can't have your premiere at Sundance. So we had to try to figure out what we could do. We decided that we would be sure to have a "technical malfunction." It was a sold-out house. This was a film that everyone knew was going to Sundance. All the distributors came, and if you've seen the movie, there's a really funny joke about 10 minutes in, where Eddie is eating cornflakes, cutting a banana, and talking about how what he's doing reflects one's relationship with women. Right after the joke, which ends with, I think, the phrase "balls swinging in the wind," the tape "miraculously" broke. It's a huge joke, everybody was laughing, and the film just stopped. Nobody knew what happened. We apologized for the malfunction, and we went into Sundance on this big wind of momentum. Everybody knew it was a funny movie, that it was exciting, and they were really eager to see it. In the end, it was the right thing. It created more hype for the film.

Eddie's next film was called *She's the One*. We made this really big mistake at the time, which was casting two real unknowns in the film, in the female leads. A woman named Jennifer Aniston and another one named Cameron Diaz. Cameron had done one movie, *The Mask*, and had another one in the can, *The Dinner Party*. But to this day, who could be so lucky to have both of those actresses in a movie together? We made *She's the One* right after *The Brothers McMullen* came out. We made it for a price that was like three and a half million dollars, and we did it under a deal that New York had at the time, called East Coast Council for IA. We shared the back end with all the crewmembers. And to this day people come up to me, people who had worked on the film, and they say, "You know, this is the only film I ever worked on that I got a piece of the back end, and I still get a little check every once in a while."

LLOYD: While we're talking about that, do you find that the studios give you a fair count? Can you get fair counts? Do you have to audit the studios?

TED: I've never expected to make money on the films I've done with the studios, and I never have. I've never audited them. I get these account statements, which are ultimately hilarious because of how depressing they are. Regarding very profitable films that I have made: the studio or distributor piles on huge "interest charges," like $14 million. Sometimes the interest is more than the entire budget of my movie! So you can't see a dime!

LLOYD: Trey Parker and Matt Stone told me that the only royalty checks they've ever gotten from anyone are the Troma checks for *Cannibal! The Musical*.

TED: We've had several films, *The Brothers McMullen* and *She's the One*, both distributed by Fox Studios, pay handsomely back to everybody. But they were both films made for pennies, in comparison. And I would say that, historically speaking, the films that have had profits returned to them through the studio system run pretty close to the studio hit average of, like, one in eight. But generally speaking, the way that our investors have made money is through foreign sales and through the sale of a completed film to a U.S. studio. So it's not based on the box office performance, it's based on the earlier receipts that come in.

LLOYD: Let's talk a little bit about someone entering the industry today, because the democratization of cinema has made it possible for everyone to make his/her/its own damn movie. What do you think is the best way to have a film that's kind of personal and independent distributed today? What would you do if you were an unknown and did not have your reputation and your relationship with the stars and all that stuff? If you were Edward McMullen today and you happened to want to make your personal film... I mean Edward Burns.

TED: What I would do is first focus on the audience. Even before you make your movie, you have to think about who your audience is going to be. Not just for this individual film, but for the long term. How do you satisfy them? How do you engage them? How do you collaborate with them? How do you seed, build, corral, and travel your audience? And not just through a single film project. I think it makes a lot of sense to sit there at first and say, "Okay, I'm going to make this feature. What else can I make around this feature? Can I make five short films? Can I use those shorts to build the ramp that will allow the audience to climb aboard my movie? And when I'm done with my movie, I don't want to lose them. I've got to make sure that I stay engaged with them and give them the bridge to the next work." Those are really important questions.

People understand in a big way the question of development, of getting your script right. They understand the questions of production and how to make it. They understand even the questions of selling and bringing your film to a festival. But what they haven't paid as much attention to is the creative process of discovery and appreciation, presentation, participation, those other elements of cinema.

One of the reasons I went into making movies, and that I'm sitting here on your couch right now, is that I love talking about movies. Not just my movies but the movies I fell in love with that made me want to make cinema. When you think back, 20 years ago, 40 years ago, 60 years ago, let's be real, the movie posters were far cooler than they are today. Usually now they're just these big heads beckoning you to come see them in the 27th movie that they've done. They used to be finely drawn pictures that helped you understand what the movie would be about in a much better way than they do today. That poster, that trailer, those clips, your film blog, your website, that casual game you create, frequently will be the discovery portal to enter the narrative. They are where we start to shape the story. And the care and attention we need to pay those is huge. We have to recognize that's how we enter the story. Then we have to recognize that films don't go away, they're always there. When I make my new film, I'm not just competing against *Poultrygeist*. I'm not just competing against the new Mel Gibson movie. I'm competing against the whole history of cinema. You sit here in your home and say, "Well, next on my Netflix queue I have this Kurosawa film, this Fritz Lang film, the fourth season of *South Park*, and I have *Slither* by James Gunn." I have all these things I want to watch. I'm competing against the history of cinema. So why are you going to watch my movie tonight instead of those? I need to give you the access. I have to give you the ramp trail to get you to the wheel and make you content to keep running around. Okay, so that's not the best metaphor…

As a new filmmaker, you have to recognize, that's your job. You have to build the ramp to get us to watch the movie. You have to get us to say, "Kurosawa may be one of the greatest filmmakers ever, but tonight I'm going to watch Joe Blow's $20,000 debut film." And that can happen; you can win that nightly battle.

It always struck me as a funny thing that in America, new people are always worried about doing things the right way. The thing that's really exciting about the time we live in now is that there aren't any real experts. The expert is someone who has done it. We're at a great place where you could have a will to fail and learn from it. Get over that hang-up about getting it 100% right. Be willing to get it 80% right. Just be sure to learn as you stumble. Don't trip over the same stump twice. It's a really exciting time where the rules have been thrown out, and that's a time when the new leaders emerge and learn to take advantage of it and run with it.

Chapter three

Piracy Is Good. Long Live Pirates. Yarrr.

Several months ago, long before my editrix had perused the sales figures from my previous two books and discovered that they were selling like pancakes,[1] long before she had practically begged me to write a third installment based on my vast knowledge of how to successfully distribute films, and long, long before I had begun filling said installment with helpful advice and charming diagrams, I did something bad. In the eyes of many people, it was the worst thing I could do. Something worse than all the shitty sex jokes and sexy shit jokes. It was something that people with nothing at stake had been warning me not to do it for years.

Many months ago, as the white snow that had quickly become dirty brown slush seeped into the overflowing sewers of Long Island City (the decrepit side, not the trendy side) I, Lloyd Kaufman, gave away my baby.

---

[1] NOTE FROM LLOYD'S LATEST ASSISTANT WHO IS BEING FORCED TO PROOFREAD THIS MANUSCRIPT ON HIS OWN TIME FOR THE BENEFIT OF INDEPENDENT ART: Lloyd, I believe this should be "selling like hotcakes," not pancakes.*

*LLOYD'S RESPONSE: That's cliché, dammit! Keep it as pancakes! Nobody knows what the fuck hotcakes are. People know pancakes!

He was a cute little guy, with green, bubbly sores and one adorably droopy eye. He didn't talk much (except when I needed him to speak so we could advance the plot), but he said it all with his dead eye. We had traveled around the world together, arm in mop. I loved him. I really did. I still do. But in the end, I gave him away so that he could have a better life—a better life as a big-budget movie star. The truth is, I did it all for him. The money I received in return was just a little blessing from God. You see, God understands what I did, because she is mother, too.

FIGURE 3.1 *Chaos ensued in Australia when the young man, at left, mistaking Lloyd for Mel Brooks, bought eight Troma DVDs. He returned them shortly after this photo was taken, but he rebought them when he found out Lloyd was actually Pee Wee Herman.*

That's right, I sold the rights to *The Toxic Avenger*. So sue me. Okay, just kidding, don't really sue me. Troma's number one son (sorry James Gunn) will soon grace the big screen once again, but this time as the star of a huge, megabudget summer blockbuster. If that movie ever gets made, which it might not. But what do I care, I've already been paid.[2]

---

[2] This isn't true, but it sounds more impressive than "I've been calling for weeks and the production company phone seems to be disconnected."

But despite all the benefits that Troma's vice president and my personal life partner Michael Herz and I see coming out of this deal, there has still been backlash from the Tromaverse. Our sales director, Matt, loves to tell me bad news. In fact, I think the only things he and I ever talk about are bad news and naked people. So good old Matt just couldn't wait to run to me and tell me about all the trash talk going on on Troma's Facebook page the day the news broke.

Matt: They hate it, Lloyd.

Lloyd: Oh. Really? Well...

Matt: Yeah, they say you sold out. God, they really hate you right now.

Lloyd: Oh. Shit. (pause) Shit. (pause) Did anyone send any naked pictures to the Myspace today?

Matt: Nope.

Lloyd: Shit.

If only I could gather all these little Facebookers into my arms and explain to them how desperately Troma needed that money. If only I could tell them how we can use that money, not only to pay the bills and stay afloat, but also to make more movies! If only I could hold them all on my lap, gently stoking their sweaty backs. If only I could whisper in their collective pierced ears.

I found out later that Matt had been doing his own fair amount of Facebook trash talking. But I didn't fire him. Like Spider-man says, "Everybody gets one."

But before I continue with this Toxie turbulance, let's meet Nina Paley.

SELLING A MOVIE BY GIVING IT AWAY: AN INTERVIEW WITH NINA PALEY

Nina Paley is a cartoonist and film animator. Through the struggle to release her brilliant 2008 film, Sita Sings the Blues, she has also become an activist for free art and copyleft over copyright. Lloyd has gotten in the habit of playing her song "Copying Isn't Theft" as he drifts to sleep each night.

LLOYD: Nina, I understand you came from the comic book world. Were you able to make a living as a comic book person?

NINA: I was able to make a living as a very poor person, yes. I should add that poor people are alive, while we're on the subject of making a living. People actually manage to live without making that much money.

FIGURE 3.2 *Nina Paley, creator of the award-winning, self-distributed* Sita Sings the Blues.

LLOYD: Certainly in Africa people manage to live without money. Except for the 5 million people that died in the Congo.

NINA: Um, yeah, I don't want to get into that. But many people live with a lot less money than people think is necessary to make a living. But now as you can see I live in this beautiful palace. So it's a lot of talk now about being poor, but clearly I am fabulously wealthy now.

LLOYD: Yes, and I noticed some very lovely hors d'oeuvres and desserts—very frou-frou. Well, anyway, talk about your transition from the comic to movie world.

NINA: I started in high school illustrating my history teacher's outline for the history of the North Pole, which was quite amusing. Then in college I did a strip for the college paper and then I moved to Santa Cruz and did my first weekly strip called *Nina's Adventures in Santa Cruz,* which became just *Nina's Adventures,* and that was self-syndicated. At its peak, it was in, maybe, 25 papers—alternative weekly papers. This was like 20 years ago. All the alternative weekly papers have been going down the toilet due to media consolidation. Media consolidation! It's not just in film, it's in all media, and weekly papers have drastically changed since I did these *Adventures.* Anyway, when I was 25

I thought it was time to sell out and I really wanted to get syndicated because everyone really wanted to get syndicated, even though newspapers were well on their way to decline. Just like how filmmakers today are like, "Oh I want a distributor, I want a distributor!" Well, cartoonists all wanted a syndicate. That was our idea of success.

LLOYD: Meaning getting into lots of newspapers?

NINA: Yeah, I was self-syndicated, but that means I had to mail this stuff out and find the papers, convince them to pick me up, and remind them they needed to pay me. This was long before I got into free culture, so I felt I had to protect my intellectual property. So if some paper was printing it without my permission, I had to tell them not to, which was stupid. It was really, really stupid.

LLOYD: That sounds right to me. How was it stupid?

NINA: Because the papers that did pay me paid me maybe $10 a week. The benefit I got from this was not the money—I wasn't making a living from a self-syndicated comic strip. The idea was that *someday* I'd make a living out of it. And there was the idea that this was my intellectual property and I need to be paid for it, and they're stealing it from me if they publish it without paying me. I wasn't too much of a hard ass about it, but that was still my idea. So I'm truly a convert to free culture. All this crazy stuff I've seen artists doing, I've been doing. Of course, they wouldn't call it crazy; it's just crazy for me. So the benefit I was getting was that people were reading my stuff and I was developing fans. And there was no Internet back then, but it was still really meaningful to have fans, and part of that was that my fans were awesome. They were among the most awesome human beings. And they would send me letters because there was no email—actually physical letters. And they made my life great.

LLOYD: Have you met your fans?

NINA: I certainly have. I have friends to this day that I met because they sent me letters, including Philip "Cha-Ka" Paley.

LLOYD: Er, who?

NINA: Philip Paley. He played Cha-Ka on *Land of the Lost*. His last name is also Paley, and when he saw my comic in *The L.A. Reader* he sent me a postcard, and I wrote back, and he wrote back, and we just decided that we're third cousins. And he's just awesome. I'm still friends with him, and friends with people in L.A. and various other cities where the comic ran. I got in touch with people and other artists. One time I hurt my hand and couldn't draw the strip for several months and there was this thing called "Nina Aid." I drew the strip with my left hand.

LLOYD: So what you learned in promoting and selling *Sita Sings the Blues*, you developed in your own comic period?

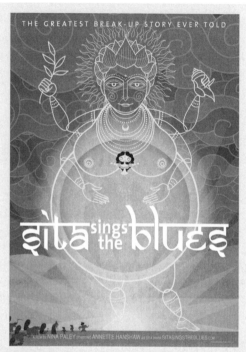

FIGURE 3.3 Sita Sings the Blues *poster.*

NINA: Well, no. I mean, I didn't truly learn this stuff until I did it. I really could not have imagined what was going to happen when I freed *Sita Sings the Blues* until I did it. And I did it because it was the right thing to do. I did it because the alternatives were absolutely broken. I could see that what was going on was not working. To be perfectly honest, since it's just between you and me…

LLOYD: Of course.

NINA: I was fairly disgusted by what I learned about the movie business in my first year. The first year, *Sita* had her festival year, which actually ended up being two years. But for the first year I couldn't legally free the film. So I was talking to distributors. And some of the small distributors I liked a lot. But the big ones—I was courting them and I wanted them to like me a lot—but let's just say I didn't like their style. I didn't like their style to the point where part of my motivation was "What could fuck up this system? Is there anything I can do?" I had many reasons to free the film, but on top of everything else, I was like, "Whoa, this could really fuck up the system." The system in place can't cope with stuff like this. If filmmakers start freeing up their films, the whole gatekeeper system that has become so corrupt, shall we say, can't survive all that. That's one of the concerns I have when artists talk trash about me freeing my film. It's like, "No, this is your way out. This is everyone's way out of the system!"

LLOYD: So you made *Sita Sings the Blues*, you didn't like what you saw in the movie distribution business, so you evolved your own system.

NINA: I didn't even evolve my own system.

LLOYD: Now, the good news is, Nina, that no one reads my books, so you can be very frank.

NINA: The film business is changing, and again, to be honest, I do like very much the distributors I have. But the distributors I have don't have a monopoly on my film. So with the distributors I have, I feel like I have a more respectful relationship with them. They can't hurt me, and they do a good job. They do a great job, I like them, and they're smart.

LLOYD: Okay, lets back up a little bit and assume that people know nothing about *Sita Sings the Blues*, other than it's a brilliant film. Had you been part of the Brotherhood of the Bell, or Tori Spelling, this movie would be all over the place and advertised with $2 million advertising campaigns. So you've got a brilliant film. Now what happens?

NINA: Well, first of all, the film was illegal because it used these songs that someone named Annette Hanshaw recorded in the 1920s. But even though her voice is in the public domain, the compositions are not in the public domain. All these compositions from the 1920s were absolutely supposed to be in the public domain by the 1980s at the very, very latest because, at the time, copyright terms were renewable for 28 years, and then for another 20 years. But Congress has been retroactively extending it over and over and over again so things never enter the public domain. We don't have a living public domain anymore. Pretty much anything that was made after 1923 is never going to enter the public domain because as soon as it's ready to, they pass another law extending it at the bidding of the big media industries.

LLOYD: Such as Disney.

NINA: Disney, Viacom, Warner/Chappell, Sony—all of those.

LLOYD: Originally it was all about public domain, wasn't it? Thomas Jefferson thought of it as public domain and then attached to it was copyright.

NINA: Right, it was this tiny little exception to public domain, and the Constitution says "for limited time."

LLOYD: Like the McRib. Fourteen years, right?

NINA: Fourteen years, and that was for authors and inventors. Authors and inventors get exclusive rights to their respective writings and inventions for 14 years. It was never for music, and it was never for pictures.

LLOYD: Well, Thomas Jefferson actually said that DVD rights would be copyrighted. He was a big fan of Blu-ray. In his day, they called it Brownray. But the point is, it's 14 years and it was supposed to give a little boost to the author.

NINA: And it was a huge compromise. Jefferson was really dubious about it. He was a real critic of it. At questioncopyright.org, we reprinted a letter that he wrote saying, "You can't own this stuff." If anything resists ownership naturally, if there's anything that shouldn't be owned, it's culture and ideas. So I think he very reluctantly went into that. But he was a complicated guy. He was against slavery, but he owned slaves.

LLOYD: Yeah, but at least he made love to them.

NINA: Yeah, at least. But certainly there were always arguments against copyrights and patents. They're both awful. Today almost nothing enters the public domain. We're talking things that should, because they're orphaned works now. And this creates a huge obstacle to anyone creating anything around culture. And of course, all creative work builds on what came before it. Something, in any movie you do, is going to be transgressing. Like if whoever made this pillow sued Lloyd's ass. It doesn't matter if I own this pillow. I own the pillow, but not the intellectual property rights behind it.

LLOYD: On the other hand, the children that wove it for you were probably slaves.

NINA: Oh, they don't matter. All that matters is the corporation that owns the idea of the pillow.

LLOYD: And certain racist unions.

NINA: So having this pillow mentioned in this book is a copyright violation. And there's a Food Emporium bag, and I just said "Food Emporium," so that's a trademark violation.

LLOYD: Don't say "superhero," either. We made that mistake once. It's owned by Warner and Marvel together, so you'd get a lawyer's letter for "superhero." It's interesting because when we were making *The Toxic Avenger* comic book, he was a superhero. But then Marvel went down the tubes and it was only Warner Bros. and they threw out Toxie. We used the word "superhero" in a Toxie press release, and we got a lawyer's letter.

NINA: Well Lloyd, remember, it's all an incentive to create and innovate. That's what these laws are for.

LLOYD: We don't want to cure cancer...

NINA: No, it's all about executives getting some money. They're not even getting money! That's what really gets me when people say, "it's all about money." It's not, it's just about control. It's not about money. Everyone would be making more money if we didn't do it this way.

LLOYD: I agree. You know, Shakespeare plagiarized *Romeo and Juliet*. If the laws of today were around in Shakespeare's time, he'd have gotten his ass sued.

NINA: Right. But, let me say that plagiarizing and copying are not the same thing. If you cite your sources, it's not plagiarism. Most copyright violations have nothing to do with plagiarism. These songs I use in *Sita Sings the Blues*, I don't say they were written and sung by me—I credited everyone that did it. But I was still violating the copyrights of Warner/Chappell Music. And to keep the record straight, I was never sued. I never got into legal trouble, except that I was trying to comply with laws because I wanted to release my film. And we live in a film world where if you want your stuff broadcast or sold or pushed into any of these channels for releasing the film, you need all this documentation to show you can legally use it. And it reminds me of back in the day, not that I can remember this time, but a time when human beings needed that, when human beings were owned by people. And if you were a southern person with dark enough skin, you couldn't travel anywhere unless you had this extensive documentation to show that you were free. And if you didn't have this documentation, everyone assumed you weren't free and you had to prove otherwise. So the same is true with film.

LLOYD: Do you consider it a mistake using this music, or did you think it was okay?

NINA: It's not that I thought it was okay. I thought it was important to use it. It was necessary. The whole power of the Ramayana as expressed in *Sita Sings the Blues*, one is that by having this 3000-year-old story with this 80-year-old music with this contemporary story really shows that the story of the Ramayana exists at different points in time, and that it transcends time and space.

LLOYD: So knowing you might give yourself a one-arm-behind-your-back fight, you went with art over anything else?

NINA: Yes, I did it for art. Art is not for pussies—that's what I say. And it's not like I had any funding or anything. It's like, "I'm going to make the film I want to make, right?" No one's paying me and I'm taking all these risks, why on earth shouldn't I make the film I want to make? So I did. I made the film I wanted to make, and that included this music. And I didn't feel like I was making any moral transgression even though back then I still bought into the intellectual property myth. But come on, no artists are going to get paid, none of the artists who worked on this are alive, they were all screwed over by corporations decades ago when they initially sold them the rights. And this music has historical significance. It has historical significance and cultural significance. It's not a product, and I'm not hurting anything. If anything, it's increasing the value of this music. So I went ahead and I did seek legal help from early on when I committed to make this feature.

I contacted the Electronic Frontier Foundation, and they put me in touch with American University, which has an intellectual property law clinic. Those students researched all those songs, because I was concerned with the recordings. I didn't know if the recordings were in the public domain at that time.

Actually, I thought that the compositions would be the easy part to clear and the recordings would be the hard part. Well, it turns out the recordings are in the public domain because the copyrights were never renewed. They're in the public domain all over the world, except, possibly, New York State. That's a whole other story. We just came out with the soundtrack and we may need to ban the soundtrack in New York State. And I say, let 'em at us. It would be great to have the first soundtrack banned in New York. It might bring attention to these ridiculous laws that we have.

LLOYD: "Banned" used to be a surefire ticket seller.

NINA: There are other things banned in the United States that aren't banned in other countries because of copyright. You really have to question when copyright laws effectively prohibit the citizens of the countries and states where the legislators are passing these laws; they basically allow everyone else in the world access to this information that these legislator constituents don't have. Now what these legislators are trying to do is to force everybody in the world to restrict everything just as much as they do. This is part of ACTA, the All Censor Together Agreement. It's this big media industry thing. They're trying to go around the WTO and the UN and create laws that are going to apply internationally behind closed doors.

With clearing *Sita Sings the Blues*, we contacted all these companies that own the publishing rights, and they just gave us the runaround. They don't want to be bothered. So here I am, and the only way you can reach them is through a paid intermediary. Everyone is like, "Well, why doesn't your music supervisor handle this?" You're supposed to have all this money and this whole position and job and you have to pay someone just to handle extortionists.

LLOYD: So what did you do?

NINA: I had to pay a lawyer to talk to these corporations because we had been trying for months and we couldn't get anywhere. I ended up paying $20,000 in legal fees and legal intermediary costs. And that's low, because toward the end, a rights clearinghouse helped out and they charged very low fee for me.

LLOYD: And how do you support yourself while doing this?

NINA: I was just going deeper and deeper into debt. I was just hemorrhaging money. And in order for it to play in festivals, when you reach them, you have to pay a festival license of $500 for each song. And you sign something promising not to make money from the film. So you pay them money for the privilege of signing a document that says you won't be making any money. How does this make sense? You're supposed to have all this money. The whole film system is set up for people that have a lot of money. People that don't have a lot of money are not welcome. Meanwhile, Pixar was releasing *Wall-E*, which had all this *Hello, Dolly!* stuff in it and that's a nonissue for them. No one talks about this because they have money. They're allowed. Pixar is supposed to be doing this because they have money. I'm not supposed to be doing this because I don't have money. Whoever has the most money to spend on lawyers wins.

So I go into debt. And I had to borrow. In the end, the rights clearinghouse negotiated what's called a "step deal," and for $50,000 upfront I could decriminalize the film. Not clear the songs, but decriminalize the film. And for every 5000 DVDs sold, I have to make additional payments.

LLOYD: What does decriminalization mean for a film? Does it clear it?

NINA: Well, I don't want to say clear, because it wasn't clearing the rights. For $220,000 I could clear the rights to those songs, but $220,000 was well over the budget of the film, so I couldn't clear the rights. And that meant if I couldn't clear the rights, the film was illegal. It was illegal beyond that first year at film festivals. It was illegal to give it away for free.

LLOYD: Even for free?

NINA: Noncommercial copyright infringement means you can be punished with up to 5 years in jail. And commercial copyright infringement is up to 10 years. But that would be giving it away for free. I did not free it until March 2009.

Decriminalization meant it's not cleared, but it's legal for people to see it. So I won't go to jail and I won't get sued. I was already wanting to free it, but this is a huge incentive to encourage the circulation of free copies. Because for every copy sold, somebody has to pay about $2 that goes to corporations and lawyers. Now, I do sell copies, I sell my DVD, other distributors sell their DVDs. This is a huge chunk of their money though, because their margins are a lot lower than mine. But basically, every DVD you buy of *Sita Sings the Blues* is supporting these god-awful extortionist giant media corporations that control our shared culture.

LLOYD: But you can give away as many DVDs as you want?

NINA: Yes, they're promotional copies. Now, they could sue me for that because there's nothing in any of these contracts that specify about promotional copies. But all distributors do that—everyone has their own promotional copies, it's very conventional. So my feeling is, they're all promotional copies. I had many incentives to do this, but I still sell DVDs and others sell DVDs and this provides some revenue for me. But I have so many other kinds of revenue now.

Even you, reading this, you can legally distribute *Sita Sings the Blues*. Just download it, copy it to DVD, sell it out of the trunk of your car in New Jersey, whatever. But for each copy that you sell, you have to pay this money to these corporations, because I'm sure you want to obey the law and respect intellectual property, which everyone knows is so important. So to do the right thing for every DVD you sell, check this compliance chart that we have, and it will tell you to send 73¢ to Sony and 92¢ to Warner/Chappell, and we have all the addresses and all that stuff. So please, please sell a copy of *Sita Sings the*

Blues. You don't have to pay me anything, but you do have to send a check to all those people on the list.

LLOYD: Now at this point, do you have a huge staff?

NINA: There's no huge staff. "We" means me and my main collaborator, a nonprofit called questioncopyright.org. They are the fiscal sponsor of the Sita Free Distribution Project, so donations sent to them are tax deductible. They have the system for sending donations easily set up online. The store where we sell merchandise is actually questioncopyright.com. We're hoping that other good projects that are released under truly free licenses want to sell merchandise. It's basically open source merchandise associated with media.

LLOYD: Let's go back to when you finally got decriminalized. What's the next step? Here's a movie that won all these awards at festivals...

NINA: It was the most highly rated film in the United States for a few weeks, according to critical consensus. And critically, it's very much acclaimed. And people seem to like it.

Once it was decriminalized, I didn't have a hand tied behind my back. I freed it and released it under a "copyleft" license. Copyleft means you can do anything you want with it. Nobody owns it, it's not intellectual property. *Sita Sings the Blues* is not intellectual property; it's culture. And culture moves through people, just like the Ramayana and the art and all these things that influenced me and came from other places. It's going other places, too. So it's just passing through me, and now my greatest pleasure in life is seeing it copied and shared and cut up and remixed and part of other things. I love that.

LLOYD: So things like Pirate Bay, you don't have a problem with?

NINA: Not only do I not have a problem with those things, I appreciate those things. Those are distributors. What Warner calls "pirates," you and I should be calling distributors. And they are much better distributors.

This copyleft license is technically called a Creative Commons ShareAlike license. Not to be confused with other Creative Commons licenses, because Creative Commons offers a lot of other licenses that are not free. But the Creative Commons ShareAlike license is essentially copyleft. Copyleft means it's total freedom. The only thing you can't do with it is copyright it. So you can share, share, share, remix, remix, remix, but everything that you mix it with also needs to be copyleft.

One reason I used this license is that if I was unable to clear those songs, the film could have leaked and people could have started sharing it illegally. And that could have been the best I could hope for. Because I met a lot of filmmakers on the festival circuit who were hoping that pirates would get a hold of their films. Even though they had deals with distributors, the distributors were asleep on the job and they had locked up the rights and they weren't distributing the films properly and these filmmakers just wanted people to see their films. So their last and only hope is that pirates would share the movie illegally. I wanted people to be able to share *Sita* legally. I wanted to make something shareable, not just for people that are willing to break the law. I wanted to show that sharing is a fun, wholesome, family activity that anyone can and should do. And in order to do that I had to pay $70,000, but it was worth it. But the more people shared the film, the more they made donations, the more they bought DVDs, and the more they bought ancillary merchandise.

LLOYD: Is the strategy, "Come and see my movie for free and donate money?"

NINA: Yes, it's all voluntary. The first thing I did was I put the film on archive.org on all resolutions. I actually sent a hard drive to archive.org because I wanted the film available at such high resolutions that I didn't have a reliable enough Internet connection to upload it. So the film on archive.org is available on up to 3 gigabytes uncompressed. The same file I used to make the 35mm negative for *Sita Sings the Blues* is available on archive.org. And I really hope that somebody else makes a negative. It costs a lot of money to make a negative from the film, but you can do it. Basically, we've just encouraged as much sharing as possible.

LLOYD: And that made you millions of dollars, end of story.

NINA: Yes, and now I live in this palace! What happened was, the more that people shared the film, the more people donated.

LLOYD: How did they know to donate?

NINA: There's a little card at the beginning of the film. It just says that it's an audience funded, audience distributed project, and for more information, go to sitasingstheblues.com. But it's up to the audience to decide whether or not they want to donate. I don't expect many people to. This is not one of those "give 'til it hurts" sort of things. They don't owe me anything. I actually believe that their attention is a tremendous gift in and of itself, and my motto this month is "Attention is scarce. Information is not. Do the math." So really, people are focusing on the wrong side of the equation. It's attention that's in scarcity and people are giving it attention for free. And I'm sure a lot of people think it's really pathetic I said that, but in 10 years everyone is going to realize this. Most movies spend more money buying people's attention then they get in revenue, which is why movies lose money. Buying attention is called advertising. *Sita Sings the Blues* has no advertising. It's all word of mouth, it's all word of keyboard—people share it. The more they share it, the more they buy DVDs, the more they buy cinema tickets when it's in cinemas, the more they buy T-shirts and merchandise. See these earrings? These are *Sita* tchotchkes.

LLOYD: So people donate, and you also have DVDs for sale. Is that off of your website?

NINA: Well, I have my own DVDs that I sell, but since the film is copyleft, anyone can distribute the DVD. Not many people are, but a few distributors are doing it and those distributors all have my endorsement. This is a complex idea for the uninitiated. It's a simple idea, but it's a very new one. I don't negotiate rights for my stuff, but I negotiate endorsements. So if someone wants to market copies of *Sita Sings the Blues*, they're putting all this money into it, they'll do better if I endorse their distribution. And I endorse their distribution if they give money to me. So we have a contract that's sort of like a rights contract, but it's not for the rights, which everyone has—it's for endorsement. It has a little "Creator Endorsed" mark they can put on it.

Film Caravan distributes the film as well. Film Caravan's distribution went to Netflix. You can get it on Netflix now. Currently I'm having a bit of a struggle because Netflix has a streaming service, a video-on-demand thing, and that's great and they want to put *Sita* on it, except that out of principle I prohibit digital restrictions management on *Sita Sings the Blues*. DRM makes things defective. It's basically a way to break technology in order to maintain the illusion of control for these media conglomerates. Stuff that has DRM on it has features and usability removed from it, so that you can't make copies from it. And I benefit when people make copies of *Sita Sings the Blues*. Most people don't make copies of your film, you're lucky when it happens, but they put this DRM crap all over your film so you can't copy it. The Netflix movies have DRM all over everything and I asked if they could make an exception for my film and not put DRM on it and they said no. I asked if they could put a bumper on it that says, "You're watching this with DRM, but you can get it without DRM from these places," and they said, "No, we can't do that." There's many a moral dilemma I face in keeping the film free, and what that means is, unless we can figure out some other solution, it probably won't go on that service. And c'est la vie, there are lots of things I turn down because of my goddamn principles, but it has all worked out for the best.

LLOYD: Good for you, that's fantastic. And ultimately, you will be remembered, and the guy that made *Harold and Kumar in Guantanamo Bay* won't be. So, how is this working? Are you able to retrieve any of this money you had to spend just to get to the point where you can make your movie available?

NINA: Yes! I just did my first annual *Sita Sings the Blues* free distribution report. I just did the numbers because it's tax time, and apparently I made $132,000 from giving my film away for free. Now, the budget of the film is $270,000 if you include the $70,000 in legal fees to decriminalize the film. So I'm still in the red. But most of this revenue came from gifts. Most of it came from donations, awards, and voluntary payments from screenings. Because a lot of places that do screenings have a budget for doing screenings. And in many cases they're arts organizations, little art cinemas, and they rely on gifts themselves. And they actually want to support filmmakers, so you don't need extortion to make this happen. I just say, "Share some money with me if you have it." And many of them are happy to, so they send donations as well.

As far as merchandise, people kept emailing me saying, "I want to buy a T-shirt, I want a DVD, I want this, I want that, I want this stuff." I'm online, I have a blog, so fans just told me what they wanted. Fans also do things like set up house-party screenings where they collect donations and send them to me. Fans are amazing! And by giving this film to the audience, the audience has thought of really cool ways to get the film out there that I wouldn't have thought of. So my model, the best way I can describe it, is make it available and create some merchandise for people to give back to you. A lot of people want to support the artist, but a straight-up gift seems weird to them. So merchandise is like a token of a gift exchange. Nobody needs a T-shirt for $25—if you're naked you can get a T-shirt for $5.

They're buying this merchandise because they want to support me and show their love of the film by wearing something that has a token of the film on it. And I should add that anyone can make *Sita* merchandise. It's open, there's no trademark on it or anything, anyone can do that. But anybody else who did that would have a competitive disadvantage because a big reason people buy merchandise is to support the artist. So that's the big difference between me and the rest of the world. We all own the film equally, but I'm the author, and that makes me different.

LLOYD: Do you think you can live off *Sita Sings the Blues* and merchandise, or ultimately must you get a day job?

NINA: I don't need a day job, but I am relying on gifts primarily. I don't know what's going to happen actually, I really don't. I rely on the goodwill of others, and friends and fans. I really trust the audience and I really think I'm going to be okay. And I really need to think like that in order to be able to make art. I can't get too caught up in "how is this going to work?" beforehand. It's a lot like making art. I don't know how my art is going to be; it's a journey of discovery. It's the same way with my life. I could not have imagined this was going to happen. I could not have imagined the generosity of the audience. I'm not banking on it, I'm not going to assume people are going to continue being generous. They're obviously capable of it though. I just want to be open to it.

By freeing the film, I made myself so open to goodness and generosity, and I didn't believe in goodness or generosity, so I've learned something. Freeing the film ended up being the best thing I've ever done. And this copyright hell helped in showing me that there is another way, and this has been great.

LLOYD: What else could you advise for someone who has a no-budget film or an underground film or even an independent film that isn't getting a huge advance guarantee?

NINA: My advice is, remember that you're doing this for art. Don't forget that. This is not about money—most films lose money. There's this really pervasive myth that films make money, but most films lose money. We only hear stories about the ones that make lots of money. People in the film business lie. It's virtually impossible to get real numbers about what movies are actually making. But only a tiny little fraction of them make money. And anyone whose film doesn't make money is going to lie about it. Because if you stand up and say, "My film lost money," then you're not going to be hired for the next stupid corporate movie. Losing money is what most films do. So just find a way to stay alive, be happy, and make art.

LLOYD: What's next for *Sita*? Where do you go from here? Is Brett Ratner going to license the remake for a billion dollars?

NINA: There's nothing to license; he can make the remake without licensing anything. Troma can do the live-action version. You don't have to pay me a cent. What's next with *Sita* is that it's on this continual rise. Unlike other films, it continues to circulate. A lot of films have this initial burst because it's propped up with advertising and once the advertising goes away, the circulation goes away and that's it. *Sita* is all word of mouth. The more people that know about it, the more new people see it and it's still just rising along. And that means anything could happen, that's up to the audience now.

LLOYD: So basically you've been letting fans direct where you go with *Sita*?

NINA: I just take opportunities. Opportunities arise and I say yes.

LLOYD: Nina Paley, this book is called *Sell Your Own Damn Movie!* How did you sell your own damn movie, *Sita Sings the Blues*?

NINA: I sold my own damn movie, *Sita Sings the Blues*, by giving it away. Lloyd, you told me to say that. Sorry, I'm not much of an actress.

So now that I've convinced you that I am a giant jackass for selling the rights to *The Toxic Avenger* instead of giving them away, let me explain why I am not a jackass for that reason.[3]

1. Nina Paley is giving away her movie to the people. I would have been giving my movie away to a giant studio. People need free art. Giant studios with lots of money do not need free art.

---

[3] Although I still retain the right to be a jackass in the future, in unrelated situations.

2. I have always said that if someone who loved *The Toxic Avenger* wanted to remake it, they could have it for free. Those with the means to whom I have extended this offer include James Gunn and Quentin Tarantino. Unfortunately, they were both busy making successful movies and lots of money.

3. We actually have given away one-time performance rights (for free) to young people in Portland and Omaha who wanted to do a stage musical version of *The Toxic Avenger*.

So, are we good now? We better be.

LLOYD'S PIRATE FANTASY (THE ONE WITHOUT JOHNNY DEPP)

I've talked a lot about history so far in this book, both real and imagined, but bear with me for one more trip back in time. We've already dealt with Thomas Edison, the James Cameron of his day. Let's go back a little further this time, all the way back to Thomas Jefferson. You know Thomas Jefferson. He was the young gun that wrote up the Constitution in his spare time,[4] when he wasn't banging his slaves or giving birth to America. But I'm not going to

FIGURE 3.4 *Bristol Palin and Toxie celebrate National Silicone Day at the Bloody X-Mas Convention in Czech Republic.*

---

[4] NOTE FROM LLOYD'S CO-WRITER, SARA: I'm sure Jefferson had a diligent co-writer who probably did 98% of the writing for him. Does that sound familiar, Lloyd?*

  *LLOYD'S RESPONSE: Absolutely not.

make jokes about Jefferson banging his slaves—that's been done. And really, who can blame the guy? I spent a year in Africa as a young man,[5] and I can tell you that there is nothing more beautiful and sensual than an African tribal gyno, shaking what her mother gave her for everyone to see.[6] So I won't judge Thomas Jefferson for taking advantage of oppressed people like any true American would have done. But enough about naked people. Let's get back to Thomas Jefferson and pirates.

Now, in case you were unclear on exactly what Nina Paley was talking about when she mentioned "public domain," allow Uncle Lloydie to enlighten you. Anything that is in the public domain is owned by the public. That means that the public, meaning you, can use it anyway that you want to. If the Sesame Street Muppets were public domain, you could make your own replicas and have them do horrible, disgusting things to each other on camera. If Lady Gaga's songs were in the public domain, you could use them as background music in your dirty Muppet video. You could then sell this video on the Internet and make money. Of course, you can do these things anyway, even though they are protected under copyright—you'll just get sued until your penis crawls back up inside your body.[7] You'll pay thousands of dollars in fines, and with the way copyright law is enforced these days, you might even end up in jail.

I met a Troma fan in Florida a few years ago who told me how he used to get eight Netflix DVDs at a time, keep them for a day or two while he downloaded them to his computer, and then return them for eight more. Once he had the digital files, he would make copies for his friends, asking about $2 for the cost of the blank DVD and the effort. One night, while extremely high, he had figured out that, based on the number of movies he had copied and the penalty for each one, if caught, he would owe the government about 2.5 million dollars in fines and face the rest of his life in prison. Now, for someone who had already sold himself to the government in the form of

---

[5] For the full story, please see my first (and far superior) book, *All I Need to Know about Filmmaking I Learned from the Toxic Avenger*. It is out of print, but available, used, like my soul.

[6] The only thing more sensual would be if it were a young tribal male with no tats—or my wife, but that's a different story. My beautiful Pattie-Pie is in a class by herself!

[7] Or if you are a gyno, and don't have a penis, you'll just lose all your money.

federal student loans for film school, the prospect of an extra 2.5 million was pretty frightening. He gave up the pirate DVD business and started selling weed instead, as there were fewer risks involved. That was how we met. Last I heard, he was in jail for selling drugs, but he'll be out sooner than if he had been caught selling $2 DVDs of *I Know Who Killed Me* to his friends.

Thomas Jefferson would have been appalled at this story. And not just because I think he would have liked trashy Lindsay Lohan movies. But because Thomas Jefferson believed that all art should belong to the public. For him, public domain was a large, thriving democracy, while copyright was a fat king thousands of miles away eating puddings and meat pies. Unfortunately, we have reversed this with current law. Now copyright is king, while public domain has been relegated to obscurity. Thomas Jefferson, who was against copyright and said himself, "Inventions then cannot, in nature, be a subject of property," finally agreed to compromise and include the issue of patents (and, by interpretation, copyright law) in the Constitution:

> The Congress shall have Power … To promote the Progress of Science and useful Arts, by securing for limited Times to Authors and Inventors the exclusive Right to their respective Writings and Discoveries;

First of all, let's understand that authors meant writers. No heavy metal singer or filmmaker was assumed to be covered under this law.[8] And by "limited times," Jefferson meant 14 years. That meant that if you invented something or wrote a book, you had 14 years to make back the money that you spent and make a profit. After that, the invention or work would become part of the public domain and other people would be able to improve on it. That's exactly what happened when Edison didn't secure an international patent for his early film projector! Everyone in Europe, including

---

[8] NOTE FROM LLOYD'S ASSISTANT: I don't think you need to say this, since filmmakers didn't exist at this point.*

*LLOYD'S RESPONSE: I'm still operating under the theory that film was invented by the Chinese thousands of years ago.**

ASSISTANT'S RESPONSE: Whatever. Lloyd sucks balls.*

***NOTE FROM FOOTNOTE GUY: Uh, should I take this out? Whatever, fuck it. I think Lloyd sucks balls, too.

those smarter and more passionate than Edison, had the opportunity to improve on his design and create the film industry that we know and love today! In fact, while Edison was shooting his films in New Jersey, some bright folks had the idea to get out of New Jersey and New York and head to California to make their movies. It wasn't because they loved the beach—it was because they wanted to be farther away from Edison so he would have a harder time enforcing his patents. And there's the irony—the entire Hollywood studio system was based on evading patent law, yet now they are the strictest enforcers! They are the ones suing sweaty prepubescent fanboys (and their parents) for downloading copies of *The Hurt Locker*!

FIGURE 3.5 *Lloyd promoting Troma movies with the winners of the popular reality show* America's Next Top Model.

Once patent and copyright law had been written into the Constitution, it was decided that everything created before the law would be considered public domain. That's why the writings of Plato and Homer are free for anyone to use. But considering that the ancient Greeks created democracy and civilization, you would think they would have created copyright law if they had wanted to. The fact that they didn't makes me think they would have supported truly independent art. In fact, I may start calling myself a modern-day Socrates![9]

---

[9] Like Socrates, I want to drink poison and die. But unlike Socrates, I am a chicken. Or at least a (Night of the) Chicken (Dead). (Shameless plug.)

So with Jefferson's 14-year copyright, everything seemed fine. So you had to wait 14 years to create your dirty puppet Lady Gaga masterpiece. So what! But then a man named Walt Disney created a little shit named Mickey Mouse, and everything changed.

HOW MICKEY MOUSE BEAT THE SHIT OUT OF THOMAS JEFFERSON

In 1928, Mickey Mouse appeared in the first sound-synchronized cartoon, *Steamboat Willie*, which was a parody (in Disnenglish, a copyright infringement) of a Buster Keaton film, *Steamboat Bill, Jr.* Mickey Mouse became an instant star and Walt Disney's meal ticket. By 1956, when *Steamboat Willie* was all set to enter the public domain, Disney had become a powerhouse corporation, and it interceded on little Mickey's behalf:

> **Disney Executive:** You see, Senator, if *Steamboat Willie* were to belong to the public, they would pretty much own Mickey Mouse, too. And we can't let that happen.
> **Senator:** No, no. We must protect Mickey.
> **Disney Executive:** What we need, Senator, is an extension of the copyright law. That way, we can keep Mickey safe.
> **Senator:** Yes, yes. We must protect Mickey.
> **Disney Executive:** Yes, Senator, we must protect Mickey.

The Disney executive puts away his hypnotist materials, leaves a pile of cash on the table, and leaves. The hypnotized senator wakes up with the overwhelming urge to protect Mickey Mouse. Days later, copyright law is extended. Buster Keaton, however, continues to receive food stamps. This scene is repeated in 1984 and 2003. *Steamboat Willie* will remain the intellectual property of Disney until 2023, almost 100 years after it was created and many, many years after the last person who worked on it became snail food. And at some point before 2023, I'm guessing the copyright laws will be extended once again. An interesting little twist to this whole story, which was sent to me by steamboat4eva@hotmail.com, is that someone at Disney discovered in the 1990s that *Steamboat Willie* may actually be in the public domain already. This was due to a mistake in the wording of the original copyright. A law student at Arizona State University investigated this claim and agreed. Then another law student at Georgetown wrote another paper confirming the claim. At this point, Disney threatened to sue the student, and the claim hasn't been uttered since.

WHEN TURNER CALLS, YOU CHANGE YOUR POSTER

When corporations own art, it is the people who lose. And by people, I mean especially me. And Troma. In 1985, my brother Charles (who also directed the original *Mother's Day*) wrote and directed a delightful comedy about a family who leaves New York City for a wilderness trip, called *When Nature Calls*. The poster featured a large bear wearing a shirt, embracing a woman. It was cute, clean, and completely harmless, except that the bear vaguely resembled Clark Gable.[10] Now, the film had nothing to do with *Gone with the Wind*, and I have no idea now why we chose to have the bear resemble Clark Gable, but at the time, we thought it was great. Great, that was, until we received a cease-and-desist letter from Turner Broadcasting. Apparently, the bear in our poster looked a little too much like Clark Gable for their taste, and they were afraid that someone would confuse the *When Nature Calls… You Gotta Go* poster (featuring a bear) with a *Gone with the Wind* poster (featuring humans). This moron might even go see our film when what he really wanted to see *Gone with the Wind*, and Turner would lose money. Now, this was complete and utter bullshit, and I'm sure Turner knew that too. I imagine that the lawyers drafting that letter had a really good laugh about the whole thing. But we knew that it would cost a fortune to hire our own lawyers and fight one of the biggest megaconglomerates in the country. So we pussied out and changed the poster art by flipping the image around. Now it just looked like a backward Clark Gable bear.

On the flipside, we at Troma sent our own cease-and-desist letter one time. It was the early 1990s, and the *Toxic Crusaders* cartoon was airing on television. Troma was receiving some mainstream attention for the first time in a while, and there was even talk of turning the *Toxic Crusaders* into a feature-film à la *Teenage Mutant*

---

[10] NOTE FROM BORED FOOTNOTE GUY: I should probably add something here about who Clark Gable was, but frankly, my dear, I don't give a damn.

Ninja Turtles.[11] So you can imagine our shock when we saw that the incredibly popular *Tiny Toon Adventures*, produced by no less than Steven Spielberg, had created its own version of the *Toxic Crusaders* and the *Toxic Avenger*, called the *Toxic Revenger*. Clever, huh? Now, in the same way that no one was ever going to confuse our *When Nature Calls* poster featuring a bear for *Gone With the Wind*, there was a *very* good chance that someone (especially a kid) would confuse a cartoon called the *Toxic Revenger* for a cartoon called the *Toxic Crusaders*. And there was also a very strong chance that this confusion would extend to merchandise purchases. Television stations were even calling our TV syndicator, thinking that we had made some sort of side deal with *Tiny Toon Adventures* behind their back! We sent Turner a letter asking them to stop. They finally agreed to stop making new *Toxic Revenger* features for *Tiny Toons*, but not to stop re-airing episodes that included the segment.

Even though in court we surely would have won, it was a battle too expensive to fight. We had actually been in the right in both cases, but each time, our lawyers told us that it would cost roughly $400,000 to take the issue to court. In today's dollars, that's about $2 billion!

Dear Lloyd,

I finally wrote the script that I've been talking about for 12 years!! Remember I told you about it at your daughter's debutante ball? Well, when I saw you outside your daughter's debutante ball after I waited for two hours in the rain. So anyway, I want to start sending it out so that I can make 10 million dollars!! But I have a question—should I copyright my script before I start sending it out? I don't want anyone to steal my idea! I just know that this musical/horror/comedy/time travel/space alien adventure story will be a hit!

Sincerely, Todd

P.S. I love Toxie!! Why the hell did you sell the rights to Akiva Goldsman?[12] You are a greedy fuck, but I still love you!

---

[11] The fact that it never happened is just another example of how Troma was screwed by a big studio. I'm sure I've told the story in one or more of my other books, so please, please go read those. And then review them on Amazon!

[12] Akiva Goldsman won an Oscar for the screenplay of *A Beautiful Mind*. He also wrote the screenplay for one of the best movies ever, *Batman & Robin*!

Dear Todd,

If I had a nickel for every time someone called me a greedy fuck, I would have seven nickels. If you want to copyright your script and register it with the WGA, go right ahead. I think it costs a few bucks, but that little copyright symbol-thing will probably make you feel like a big man, so go for it! I think you can even just put the © in there and it's legal. However, keep in mind that the reason something is copyrighted is to prevent someone else from using the same idea. If the idea is shit, no one is going to want it! And the truth is, Todd, most no-budget movies are horrible. That doesn't mean you/we should stop making them! But most of them are so awful that no one in their right mind is going to steal the idea! So if you want to support the WGA, send them your money. But if you don't copyright your script, I have a feeling that you will be completely safe.

xoxo Lloyd

P.S. I love you too!!

AMSTER-DAMN COPYRIGHT LAW!

In March I was invited to a Troma retrospective in Amsterdam. This was a real, high-class event,[13] held at the Netherlands' equivalent of the Metropolitan Museum of Art. Now, I'll be Amster-damned if I am ever honored at a retrospective at the U.S. equivalent of the Metropolitan Museum of Art, the actual Metropolitan Museum of Art, but in Europe, they aren't afraid to celebrate true independent art![14] The odd thing about all of this is that Troma has not had any distribution in the Netherlands, or any part of Europe, for about 10 years. The only way that they know anything about us is through piracy. Also, Troma doesn't have any 35mm prints of *Surf Nazis Must Die* or *The Toxic Avenger Part II*, but somehow, the Dutch did. How? Piracy! And apparently we are so popular, that this retrospective and the master class I presented were completely sold-out events. They even stuffed the room with a few extra seats that they could gather and raffled them off. And why? Because of piracy! I was so overwhelmed that I cried like a baby. Usually I have a cup of coffee before I present a master class,

---

[13] Although, to be fair, most events are pretty high in Amsterdam.

[14] NOTE FROM LLOYD'S WIFE, PAT: Actually, that's not true, Lloyd. You had a retrospective at the AFI/Kennedy Center in Washington, D.C., circa 1990.

but this time, I was completely stoned. I thought that I was brilliant, but who knows. I could have been talking about baby pigs and shoelaces for an hour—I really have no idea.

This Dutch retrospective (which I kindly convinced my lovely wife that she did not want to go to so that I could get catatonically high for 72 straight hours) hasn't been the only time that piracy has helped Troma in Europe. In Russia, piracy has made us famous. Sometime in the late 1990s, around the time of *Terror Firmer*, I was asked to come to Russia and appear in a music video for a leading Russian band, Korable. They wanted "the blind guy from *Terror Firmer*," so off to Russia I went. I even pretended to be blind on the airplane so that I could really get into character.[15] I was surprised enough that the Russians even knew what *Terror Firmer* was, since we had never had any distribution in Russia whatsoever. But I was even more surprised when I got there. The band had rented a bar and announced a Troma party. The place was filled with Toxie and Kabukiman posters and the smell of vodka. It was like a dream come true! All night, drunk ruskies kept coming up to me and begging me to autograph their mimeographed videocassette covers of *Toxic Avenger* and *Class of Nuke 'Em High*. How did they get them, you ask? Piracy! And it was great! I guess someone figured out, after the Berlin wall came down, that they could make money selling Troma tapes, as long as we didn't have any movies that made fun of Putin. Which is why you will never see a copy of Troma's jazz age musical extravaganza, *Putin on the Ritz*, floating around Russia. Also, Russians hate Ritz crackers—they are too buttery and indulgent. If you've ever met a Russian, they will always choose a saltine over a Ritz—preferably a stale one.

But back to distribution.

As a result of piracy and Troma becoming sort of known, we attracted a legitimate Russian distributor and actually made a few rubles there!

We've actually had distribution offers from Europe, but these deals were so shitty that we turned them down. I would rather have people see our movies through piracy than not see them at all. And that is what would happen if we signed some crap distribution deal.

---

[15] And into the hearts of the lovely Russian gyno flight attendants.

----------------------Original Message----------------------

To: elinor@focalpress.com
From: lloyd@troma.com
Date: May 9, 2010 8:37 p.m.
Subject: New title for book

Elinor,

We must change the title of the book! Selling a movie is an outdated idea! We can call the book *Give Your Own Damn Movie Away!* This is inspired!!

Also, book should be very short so that people can carry it in their pockets and refer to it always. This is the future!!

xoxo
Justin Bieber

----------------------End Message----------------------

----------------------Original Message----------------------

To: lloyd@troma.com
From: elinor@focalpress.com
Date: May 9, 2010 8:39 p.m.
Subject: RE: New title for book

Dear Lloyd,

I am thrilled by your enthusiasm! However, as I said before, piracy is still illegal, and I hope that you don't choose to focus on that.

Regarding the book being very "short," please refer to our contract. I would appreciate it if you didn't think I was stupid.

Regards,
Elinor
Focal Press

----------------------End Message----------------------

----------------------Original Message----------------------

To: elinor@focalpress.com
From: lloyd@troma.com
Date: May 9, 2010 8:42 p.m.
Subject: RE: New title for book

A quote from *There Will Be Blood*! That is my favorite comedy!!

xoxo
Daniel Day Lewis's milkshake

----------------------End Message----------------------

I'm not advocating breaking the law. I can't, because then if you do break the law, you can come back and say, "Kaufman told me to," and that would be a gigantic goiter in the ass for me. So I'm not telling you to become a pirate and break the law. What I am saying is, be a shit disturber. Be like Nina Paley and do your best to fuck up a corrupt system and the tyranny of an elite club of huge devil-worshipping media conglomerates. Be like a Troma intern and just fuck everything up. What we need is to once again make public domain the Earth, and demote copyright to a dwarf planet. Some people say that if a work is in the public domain then people can ruin it with shitty copycat efforts, but this isn't the case. Just look at Shakespeare. Furthermore, if the plays of Shakespeare had been copyrighted, who knows if we would have ever heard of them! But because we were free to print them and distribute them and perform them any way we wanted, they spread like a case of herpes on a Troma film set. And no amount of shitty reimaginings from Baz Lurhmann are going to diminish the original beauty of *Romeo and Juliet*. And I feel that the good interpretations, like our very own *Tromeo and Juliet*, only expose a greater number of people to the original! And let's remember that Shakespeare himself would have been a copyright infringer when he copied an Italian play of his day and turned it into *Romeo and Juliet*. Today he would be sued up his rosey-red iambic pentametrical ass!

Another good example is the work of H.P. Lovecraft, which slipped into public domain by accident. Director/producer Stuart Gordon has made several films based on Lovecraft stories, and I have been perusing Lovecraft myself in search of a story for the *Toxic Avenger Part V: The Toxic Twins*. If Lovecraft's work was copyright protected, it may have been forgotten years ago.

And as my final argument for the dominance of public domain.

It's what Thomas Jefferson wanted. That's reason enough for any Republican, conservative or Tea Party member to support it. The founding fathers are like gods to those people. It's creepy.

HOW TO BE A LITTLE CRAZY, YET VERY SUCCESSFUL IN THE WORLD OF AVANT-GARDE FILM: AN INTERVIEW WITH JONAS MEKAS

Jonas Mekas is often called the godfather of American avant-garde cinema, even though he was born a Lithuanian. If Sarah Palin were president, he wouldn't have even been allowed in the country! Thus, we would not have the Film-Makers' Cooperative, the Film Museum, or the Anthology Film Archives, all of which Mekas founded. We also wouldn't have his brilliant film The Brig, *which is one of Lloyd's favorite movies!*

LLOYD: Do you consider yourself to be a good salesman?

JONAS: When we made films in the 1960s, we wanted our films to be seen. It wasn't a question of selling; we just wanted people to see them. It was a question of dissemination, of distribution. We knew we couldn't sell them—nobody wanted our films, there's no money in them. So 20 of us got together and created our own distribution center, Film-Makers' Cooperative, in January 1962. Now the Film-Makers' Cooperative has 700 filmmakers. Because we could not get into official commercial distribution channels, we said goodbye and created our own. Why waste energy trying to perpetuate our movies? We'll go our own way! We went to all the universities and colleges and alternative places where people could see films and we bypassed Hollywood.

LLOYD: How were you able to make your own films, and also have money to eat?

JONAS: By watching movies and publishing in *Film Culture Magazine*. By not relying on my poetry and cinema. I did all kinds of things. I worked in factories. We did all sorts of things that paid, such as teaching, like Stan Brakhage.[16] When he was making films, he had to teach at university in Chicago and Colorado. I succeeded by working and believing in what I am doing, and I still believe in what I am doing, and I am now crazy. You have to be a little crazy.

LLOYD: You are a world-famous person. How did you live when you were with Amos Vogel[17] and those guys?

JONAS: When I came to New York from a displaced persons camp in late 1949, for like 5 years I worked in various factories in Brooklyn. Then for next

---

[16] NOTE FROM LLOYD: Stan Brakhage was mentor to Trey Parker, and as such he is featured in Troma's *Cannibal! The Musical!* BUY TROMA!

[17] Amos Vogel is the author of 1974's *Film as a Subversive Art* and the founder of Cinema 16, where he showed the early works of Roman Polanski, Stan Brakhage, and Kenneth Anger.

10 years I worked in a photo studio on 22nd Street. I did the international edition of *Life* magazine as a cameraman. That covers my first 15 years. Then I started *Film Culture Magazine*. I was still working as a cameraman for several years part-time. Then I began in 1958 writing for the *Village Voice*. I was still in the graphics studio, but I was already writing for the *Village Voice* and getting $5 a week. I did that for 20 years. I survived on that $5, which went to $15, $18, until in 1978 I got $200. I lived in cheap places and ate cheap food, like today. My breakfast costs 50¢.

LLOYD: And you were making your own damn movies all that time. Was there an attempt to get people to see those movies?

JONAS: I began screening films myself in 1953 on Orchard Street, downtown. It covered the expenses of the rental and I made a little extra.

LLOYD: And someone paid for *Film Culture Magazine*?

JONAS: I paid. I was even taken to court for late payments to printers. The first issue came out December 1954. I had made an arrangement with the Franciscan Monks who owned a printing shop. The monks printed the first issue, then there were issues with the printer that I went to court over. Then, in issue #7, came Jerome Hill, a filmmaker who made a film on Albert Schweitzer and got an Academy Award for best documentary.[18] He got interested in supporting *Film Culture*. It was thanks to him that I managed to continue. With every issue I was losing hundreds, sometimes thousands of dollars. He always picked up the deficit. So thanks to Jerome Hill, who later sponsored creation of Anthology Film Archives. It was with his money. In the early years, whenever the Film-Makers' Cooperative failed, he covered the bills. Later, he asked me to give him the names of 12 needy filmmakers. And then every month he sent those needy filmmakers $40. He did that until he died. That was a lot in 1965— you could pay your rent and still eat. Jerome Hill was a little bit of a poet, so he sided more with noncommercial sensibilities. And he saw my craziness, my passion, my obsession, and he believed in that. It just happened that the chemistry was right, and he stuck and helped until he died. There is nobody like him now.

Last year Film-Makers' Cooperative was losing its space. There was a piece in the *The New York Times* on the problems we had. This guy by the name of Charles S. Cohen saw the article and called me and said, "I want to help." He had several buildings in New York, he's connected with art, he has written a book on cinema, and he produced a film. So he gave Film-Makers' Cooperative new space on Park Avenue South for $1 a year for next 5 years, then he will extend it. There are people who still understand the needs of independent filmmakers. He is as close as you can get to Jerome Hill and he asks for nothing in return.

---

[18] This film is one of Troma's Roan Group releases, available at www.troma.com. BUY TROMA!!

LLOYD: I don't doubt that. I'd like to ask you about the world of grants.

JONAS: The world of grants has ruined avant-garde film, and has ruined good cinema. Until 1970, there were no grants to cinema, only one or two given by Rockefeller or Ford to filmmakers. After that there were state councils created, or the National Endowment for the Arts, and now we've got 2, 3, 4, 500 grants given every year. And who gets them? People who make socially conscious, useful films on how to vote, or how to do this, how to be a good citizen. If you said, "I'm an avant-garde filmmaker, I want to make a personal film, how can I give you a synopsis?" you didn't get grants. All of the bad filmmakers made bad films, and there were thousands of them, because of all the grants.

LLOYD: So they have to know what the grant giver wants to hear.

JONAS: Since we live in a grant world, one has to keep proposing and writing. But there are some filmmakers not interested in getting a grant at all.

LLOYD: Now, you are from Lithuania.

JONAS: Yes, I was just a farmer boy. I saw my first film when I was 13 or 14. There were no cinemas in the village, so the movies I saw were the Soviet propaganda movies, and then the Germans came in and I saw the German anti-Semitic propaganda movies. That was the beginning of my cinema.

LLOYD: It's not that different from today with kids seeing the toothpaste commercials on TV. You were in the labor camps? Were you able to sell yourself? Were you valuable over there?

JONAS: I was very valuable in the German factories making weapons to fight the United States and Britain.

LLOYD: How did you avoid being made into a lampshade?

JONAS: You had to be silent, don't talk. Those who talked did not stay long in factories. They disappeared. You come into work one day and five or six people are missing.

LLOYD: So it wasn't like you had a talent you could sell.

JONAS: No, I had a talent for being silent and doing what they told me to do. That was wartime Nazi Germany.

LLOYD: What about for young people in the age of technology?

JONAS: I say don't go to film schools. Buy a camera and start filming. When you discover what you want to do, and you need to know more about lighting, then you go and study lighting. Don't study general cinema. You may never need certain things. If you discover you have to know more about lenses for what you want to do, then take courses on lenses. Again, I am against this very general study, unless your parents say "Son, or Daughter, I will support you for three years if you really go to study something useful." It's very often parents support their kids to finish some kind of school. So they may as well. Cinema is very easy. You don't have to study something very serious, so they study movies and the parents are paying. Equipment is available sometimes at film schools. There are some positive aspects to it. But film schools have not produced filmmakers. People say Scorsese went to New York University, but Scorsese was making films before he went to university.

LLOYD: Getting back to sales...

JONAS: Nobody is buying my movies. Someone had a great plan on how to sell through the Internet. So I opened *www.jonasmekas.com* from Stendhall Gallery, which I am no longer with. Supposedly I put my films on the Internet, and everybody will buy. It doesn't work at all. Everybody was downloading for free, everybody wanted for free. So the Internet is not really for selling films, or at least I don't know how. Everybody is very clever about downloading; you cannot keep anything secret on the Internet. The Internet is not going to save us. The Internet will help us have our works be seen by many people, which is good for the ego, but I don't see yet how the Internet can save us.

LLOYD: Do you have a feeling about piracy?

JONAS: In the 1970s I said, "Pirate my films, please. I don't care. I don't have money to make copies of my films, but if you do, go ahead." You can't stop it. Why should I stop people from making copies of my films? Go ahead, do it. From them, many classic films survived because people made copies and never told anyone. Once, we wanted to have a retrospective on Epstein. So we bought 15 films from Cinémathèque Française and showed them in 1971 at the Anthology Film Archives, then we returned them. Then a year later we decided that we should have a copy of one we really liked. So we sent a message to France asking to have a copy of one. We got a message that said, "You Stupids! We sent you all these films and you did not make copies of them!?" I will never forget that.

LLOYD: Let us sum up what a young person should know.

JONAS: Do it without ever expecting to sell it, without ever expecting anyone else except yourself and your friends to see it. It may happen that your friends will see it and like it, and through them, someone else will see it and like it. I believe in Darwin's theory of art. Someone sees a bad film and doesn't recommend it because it's boring. And then someone sees something like Kenneth Anger's *Scorpio Rising* and says you should see it. You can't stop that; it grows and grows and grows by itself. Darwin's law of survival of art or any product is good. You don't have to call it art, I don't like to use that word.

I have been to film screenings at university and they ask, "Why did you keep that scene in?" And I say, "Because I like it, it's there. I could cut it out. Who else thinks I should cut a scene out they don't like?" And then they say cut out a different scene. So I could ask a hundred people and end up from a two-hour film to a two-minute film by listening to others. It's your film.

Don't expect to survive on your film. It may happen that you survive by appealing to certain areas of people. Maybe you'll figure out how to sell it and how to make money, which I haven't. So it's possible, but don't rely on it.

LLOYD: We had a good interview here. Anything else you'd like to say?

JONAS: You have to be a little crazy to survive, to continue.

LLOYD: Van Gogh and Picasso were both geniuses. Picasso ended rich, Van Gogh didn't. Picasso was a salesperson.

JONAS: He was a great artist. He just lived in a different time. Between the nineteenth and twentieth century there was a big difference in publicity. In the nineteenth century you could be great and nobody would know. But in the twentieth century, everything was already faster.

LLOYD: Picasso promoted himself and put on clown makeup.

JONAS: Dali did all that, but Picasso was more subdued. They said that about Warhol, "Oh, he was looking for publicity." But he did not seek anyone; they came to him. It was the same with Picasso. Dali was the exception. People came to him, but he also promoted himself. He was an actor and clown. I knew him quite well. But Warhol, they flocked to him, he didn't seek them. It's not about seeking publicity; it's much easier if something reaches a point where you don't have to do publicity. That's what happened to Picasso and Warhol. So hopefully we'll reach the point where they flock to us.

LLOYD: The only things flocking to me now are chickens.

SELLING YOUR OWN DAMN ANIMATION, IF YOUR NAME ISN'T WALT DISNEY OR JOE PIXAR

By Bill Plympton

Bill Plympton's cartoons have been featured in The New York Times, Rolling Stone, *the* Village Voice, Penthouse, *and Lloyd's favorite magazine,* Vanity Fair. *His 1987 film,* Your Face, *was nominated for an Academy Award for Best Animated Short Film.*

If some people don't know me, it's understandable. My name is Bill Plympton, and I create animated shorts and animated feature films. And because they're animated, it's very difficult to get any press, respect, or even distribution for my films. I also have two other strikes against me—these are not family-oriented films, and they're very low budget. So there you go! That's my dilemma. How do I get distribution for an animated film that no one wants to touch?

For over 20 years, Lloyd Kaufman's Troma films have been my inspiration for survival in the film business. His brand of sex, violence, humor, and low-budget filmmaking has guided me through my successful career as an animator.

I think a lot of the prejudice against my films is because there is sex and violence in them, and the audience in America believes that animation is sacred territory. How dare I put raunchy material in a purified, Disney-created art form? That's blasphemy! I'm tainting the holy art form of cartoons.

Yet Quentin Tarantino puts tons of sex and violence in his films and they're very close to being cartoons. So, why can't I? Why can't the American public make that great creative leap from kid cartoons to adult animation?

Sure, when I was a kid I loved the Disney cartoons, but now I'm an adult, and I don't want to see animation about kids playing with toys and animals singing. I want to make my animation about love, passion, jealousy, revenge, sex, and adultery—the really cool topics!

When *Idiots and Angels* opened at the Tribeca Film Festival, we got wonderful reviews and enthusiastic sold-out audiences. We were sure that a distribution deal and riches were coming our way. But we must have shown the film to 50 distributors, and none of them picked it up. It was very frustrating. The film went on to win numerous prizes all over the world and sold to over 10 territories, so it's done quite well internationally. In fact, it was a big theatrical success in France.

I believed in the film enough to try for an Oscar nomination, and thus, according to the Academy rules, I had to enter the film this year or forget it.

So, without a distribution deal in place, I decided to handle the release myself. Now this isn't the end of the world. In fact there are some positive aspects of self-release. But let me first list the negative points:

1. I had to lay out a lot of money for prints and trailers.
2. I had to hire press agents.
3. I produced posters and postcards myself.
4. I called all my press friends, begging to get any kind of interview or articles.
5. I organized street teams of students to canvas the city.
6. I booked myself at every art school I could think of that would give me a master class, to make the schools aware of the screening.

However on the positive side, here are the benefits of self-distribution:

1. The rights to the film remain in my hands, thus I can control when it's released, how it's released, and where it shows. And if I want to rerelease it, it's my decision. Often times, as you know, distribution companies will decide to put the film on the shelf and refuse to release the film, and you're stuck with a film that will never see the light of day, and there is no recourse.
2. All the money, if there is money, comes directly to me. So many times I've had a distribution company handle my film and all the royalties get gobbled

up in crazy expenses—transportation, prints, luxury hotels, miscellaneous expenditures… or I may not get a statement at all. One exception was when Lionsgate Films released *I Married a Strange Person* and I actually got a royalty check from them! Whoopee! So miracles do happen.

3. I get to control the images and style of the release. I can talk directly to my audience.

It's interesting that when I released my first animated feature film in 1992, with October Films, *The Tune* was the first low-budget, self-animated film to hit the theater. Now it seems like everyone I know is working on an animated feature. I started a whole movement of cartoonists who think they can make their own films—*Sita Sings the Blues, Queer Duck, My Dog Tulip, Waltz with Bashir, Persepolis*, and many others. And I think it's very cool. I love the competition because I believe that these filmmakers will prove that there is a market for non-Pixar, non-Dreamworks homemade indie films.

Lloyd Kaufman is the king of indie filmmaking like I am the king of indie animation. God bless Lloyd Kaufman.

Chapter four

Look at Me! How to Make People Want to See Your Movie, Part I

LLOYD'S DIARY, 6/15/10

My Facebook is down, so I'm having a tough time writing today. On one hand, it's one less distraction. On the other hand, I'm going nuts wondering if anyone has commented on the picture of me and Miley Cyrus where you can see her hoo-ha. So now, instead of getting a quick fix from Facebook, I am stuck distracting myself in other ways, such a looking up what Perez Hilton's real name is[1] and whether or not I should buy a Christoph Niemann print for my downstairs bathroom.[2] Please load, Facebook. I need you.

ONE HOUR LATER...

Still no Facebook. I honestly don't know how much longer I can last before I start chewing off my own leg. My beleaguered, yet

---

[1] It's Mario, in case you were curious.

[2] My favorite is the one where the toothbrush is hugging the toothpaste.

beautiful young male assistant just came in and reminded me that I am meeting with my co-writer, Sara, tomorrow afternoon and that I needed to get off the interweb and do some writing. You see, Sara is such an amazing and reliable co-writer that I know she'll have lots of writing done, and I don't want to look bad.[3] God, my assistant is beautiful. Facebook, why hast thou forsaken me?

Fuck it, I'll write the chapter. Is that what you were looking for, God? Did you really need to take away my social networking? I could have scribbled something down on the train on my way to the meeting. You didn't have to go this far.

So it occurred to me earlier this morning, when I got an email from Elinor mentioning it, that there is very little in the book thus far about selling a movie. So let's talk a little bit about what exactly sells a movie. You think you have passion? You think you have a great story? You think you are meant to do great things in film? Bullshit! All those things may be true, but they aren't going to sell your movie.

THE 1.7 SECONDS RULE, BY DR. LLOYD KAUFMAN[4]

When it comes right down to it, people are going to give your precious film about 1.7 seconds of their attention,[5] based solely on the time it takes their eyes to transmit the information to their brain and the time it takes their brain to process the fact that they have come across a film that is not *Sex and the City 2*. Physical and biological processes aside, it's up to you to hold their attention for any longer than that. And how do you do that? Let me offer you Dr. Kaufman's Definitive Remedy for Getting People to Possibly Pay Attention to Your Movie.

---

[3] NOTE FROM SARA: Okay, so I added this sentence in the copyediting phase once Lloyd was back in Yemen and out of touch with the editor. But I'm trying to build a career, here. And this chapter is about selling yourself.

[4] NOTE FROM THE EDITOR: Lloyd Kaufman is not actually a doctor. However, he does enjoy playing doctor.

[5] Unless your film is actually called *Precious: Based on the Novel "Push" by Sapphire*. For some reason, this film, which has one of the worst titles in the history of film, got quite a bit of attention.

FIGURE 4.1 *The gassed-up Troma Toxicab about to embark on its maiden voyage with filmmaker Dennis Woodruff, also gassed-up!*

DR. KAUFMAN'S DEFINITIVE REMEDY FOR GETTING PEOPLE TO POSSIBLY PAY ATTENTION TO YOUR MOVIE, PART A

The Title

Nothing represents your film better (or worse) than the title that you choose. Back in the old days, it was important to choose a short title that could fit nicely on a theater marquee.[6] These days, a short, attention-getting title is just as important! Every time a fat, sweaty kid is flipping though On Demand or Hulu, he's going to watch a title that reaches out and grabs his interest. If you're not sure what I mean, take the following quiz:

QUESTION 1
When my girlfriend is out of town, I would rather watch

- **(A)** my cat lick himself
- **(B)** *Elizabethtown*
- **(C)** *Slime City Massacre*

---

[6] And speaking homonymically, regarding the marquee, it is a little known fact that the Marquis de Sade had "Poultrygeist: Night of the Chicken Dead" tattooed on his right ass cheek.

When I can't sleep at night and the Ambien just isn't working, I'd like to flip on the television and watch

(A) lions lick themselves
(B) *An Education*
(C) *Bloodbath in the House of Knives*

QUESTION 3
I'd never tell anyone, but my favorite movie is really

(A) *Big Gus, What's the Fuss?*
(B) *Sgt. Kabukiman, NYPD*
(C) *The Toxic Avenger*

- If you answered mostly A's, you're kind of a dick, and I'm not really sure why you are reading this book.
- If you answered mostly B's, you are either extremely pretentious, extremely whipped, or just kind of boring. I'll let you decide which.
- If you answered mostly C's, you are one cool guy or gyno. I think you're really catching what I'm throwing here. Let's do lunch. I'd like to move this relationship to the next level.

Your title is arguably the most important feature that will convince people to watch your movie. The less-than-groin-gripping film *A Nymphoid Barbarian in Dinosaur Hell* was #1 on Comcast/GE/NBC/Fox/Universal's Hulu.com during the weekend of March 2, 2010, due primarily, I'm sure, to its title—certainly not the nymphoidinal storyline. Nine months later, *A Nymphoid Barbarian in Dinosaur Hell* is still one of Hulu's top-viewed movies—it's all about the title! It is vital to keep your title interesting, original, and, if you're like me, to add several exclamation points on the end!

Troma's early films:

Stuck on You!
Squeeze Play!
Waitress!
The First Turn-On!

When we were preparing to distribute a film called *Surf Nazis* in 1987, we were concerned that people might think that the titular

Surf Nazis were the good guys of the movie, which they are definitely not. To avoid confusion, I suggested changing the title to *Surf Nazis Must Live*, because everyone likes optimism, but unfortunately Michael Herz said no. We finally agreed on *Surf Nazis Must Die*, which, in its day, was still a very risky choice for a title. There was a very good chance that we could have been even more blacklisted than ever. Even today, you don't see too many theatrical films throwing Nazis into their titles, and this was almost 25 years ago! The young man who did our theatrical bookings at Troma even threatened to quit if we distributed the film! However, I don't respond well to threats, and a year of working at Troma had so depleted this guy's bank account that he couldn't afford to be unemployed. So we agreed to disagree. Later that year we premiered *Surf Nazis Must Die* at the Cannes Film Festival. Luckily for us, Cannes is in France, and if anyone loves Nazis, it's the French. Putting the word "Nazi" in the title turned out to be cinematic genius! Roger Ebert may have walked out of the screening after 30 minutes, but at least he showed up in the first place. Rex Reed did a piece on us and the title, and it was great publicity. Unlike the French, Jews hate Nazis. They also run most of the film industry, so putting "Nazi" and "die" together was a great move! We lucked out there, too!

FIGURE 4.2 *Confusion ensued for a near-sighted Lloyd after misreading the marquee that listed* Little Ashes, *when he went into the Plaza looking for "little asses."*

And speaking of Jews, before Troma acquired the independent film *Bloodsucking Freaks*, it was actually called *Sardu*. The name was then changed to *The Incredible Torture Show*, which was a better fucking name than *Sardu*, but still not quite right. We at Troma changed the name to *Bloodsucking Freaks*, and a modern classic was born! Restoring the original generous doses of graphic misogynistic violence certainly didn't hurt either!

Is it sinking in how important a title is? Pick one that works well for the tone of your film. If you are aiming for serious, don't choose a silly title. If you are going for slapstick horror, don't choose something pretentious that makes you sound like a pretentious fuck. And if you have two great puns in mind, like "poultrygeist" and "night of the chicken dead," use them both! And then throw a shit fit whenever anyone refers to the movie by just one of the titles.[7]

One Last Tip: Pay Attention to the Phonebook

Laugh if you want, but when you are picking a title for your movie, try to choose one that starts with the letter "A" or another letter close to the beginning of the alphabet. When people are flipping through pages and pages of movie titles, looking for something to watch, chances are that they are going to lose interest and just pick something right around the time they get to *Babe 2: Pig in the City*. In this modern age of instant gratification,[8] the average attention span is shorter than Zelda Rubinstein in flats.[9] By choosing a title that starts with A or B, you'll be sure that someone at least *sees* your title before he passes it up and decides to watch something else. At Troma, we have completely ignored this tip, and most of our movies start with "T" or other various letters at the end of the alphabet. Consequently, we don't make any money.

Troma titles:

The Toxic Avenger
Troma's War
Tromeo and Juliet
Terror Firmer
Tales from the Crapper

---

[7] And if you choose an incredible title like "Poultrygeist," you may also benefit from some illiterate theatergoers who think they are buying tickets to the 1982 classic, *Poltergeist*.

[8] Also known as premature ejaculation.

[9] Zelda Rubenstein stood about three minutes tall, and four minutes in high heels.

I recently announced to the Troma staff that we will be changing the title of *The Toxic Avenger 5: Toxic Twins* to *AAA Locksmith*. They appreciated the effort, I think, but they were less than enthusiastic.

DR. KAUFMAN'S DEFINITIVE REMEDY FOR GETTING PEOPLE TO POSSIBLY PAY ATTENTION TO YOUR MOVIE, PART B

The Tagline

Remember *A Nymphoid Barbarian in Dinosaur Hell*? Now, the title alone pretty much did the job that it was asked to. It's sexy, yet forbidden, and it has dinosaurs. Sounds great, right? But just to up the ante a little, we added the tagline, "Where the prehistoric meets the prepubescent." Oh yeah, now your stinky juices are really flowing, aren't they?

Unfortunately, the movie is incredibly tame and offers very little sex, zero prepubescents, and hardly any dinosaurs. And for 20 years, no one really cared. Then, as you already know,[10] about a year ago we added the film to our Hulu account for download. Suddenly, in March, some dickhead named Chadwick Matlin[11] wrote a four-page article on *Slate* condemning the film, which he describes in the opening paragraph as "a film that features a girl besieged by hordes of rapists, dinosaurs, and one giant phallic monster called the 'Chromasaurus.'"[12] Now if that were what the movie actually was, I would still stand behind it. However, the movie is not nearly that exciting. And Chadwick[13] seems oddly fixated on the prepubescent "girl," who, if you watch the film, you will see is obviously a grown woman with grown-woman breasts and crow's feet. So what is Chadwick so pissed about? It's not that a prepubescent girl (which she clearly isn't) is being ravaged on film—he mentions how it was fine for Dakota Fanning (who is, in fact, prepubescent) to be raped on film in *Hounddog*, because that was "high art." What he seems most upset about is that the movie comes from Troma. I wrote a response

---

[10] NOTE FROM THE NEW (IRRITATED) FOOTNOTE GUY: Of course they already know this, you just said it a couple of pages ago. Maybe if you're lucky, Kaufman, your readers will be smoking a little more pot than usual today. I know I am.

[11] Real name. No joke, the fuckhead's name is Chadwick.

[12] Which is actually the famous Troma (crappy-sound-distorted) Tromasaurus!

[13] Yep, real name. His mother must have been as big of a dick as he is.

to Chadwick's article on my own blog, which got 10 times the response of the original article, but maybe I should have just let it go.

When creating a tagline, follow the same advice as for picking out a title (except that part about starting with "A"—that doesn't matter for a tagline). Be creative! Be poetic or witty! Remember that if your movie is online, it will be among thousands of other movies. It must stand out.

And whether Chadwick likes it or not, *A Nymphoid Barbarian in Dinosaur Hell* is consistently one of the most viewed movies on Hulu. See what a great tagline can do for you? I doubt as many people would check it out if the tagline read, "Middle-aged woman talks to clay-mation dinosaurs!" Of course, some people might still watch it. But I don't want to know those people. In fact, most of the people who watch it are so upset by the lack of prepubescent girls and hoards of rapists that they leave angry comments below the video clips demanding more smut!

Some of Lloyd's favorite Troma taglines:

"Humans... The other white meat. Unless you're black, then it's dark meat... Or if you're Asian, then it's yellow meat... Or if you are Native American, it's red meat." (*Poultrygeist: Night of the Chicken Dead*)

"The first superhero from New Jersey!" (*The Toxic Avenger*)

"Body piercing, kinky sex, dismemberment... all the things that make Shakespeare great!" (*Tromeo and Juliet*)

"The South shall rise again... and again... and again!" (*Curse of the Cannibal Confederates*)[14]

DR. KAUFMAN'S DEFINITIVE REMEDY FOR GETTING PEOPLE TO POSSIBLY PAY ATTENTION TO YOUR MOVIE, PART C

The Key Art

Whether it shows up on a poster, a computer screen, or a DVD case, your key art is going to rival the title in importance when it comes to getting people to watch or buy your film. A good title may be more effective in drawing people in, but bad art is more effective

---

[14] My lovely southern belle debutante wife Pat came up with this one.

FIGURES 4.3 AND 4.4 *Troma DVD art, before and after.*

in pushing them away. In a browser's mind, crappy art = crappy movie. And they are usually right.

"No crappy drawings, no ugly people" (Lloyd Kaufman)

This should be the golden rule when it comes to key art. It should be as familiar a mantra as "We're here, we're queer," or "Don't tread on me," or "Winston tastes good like a cigarette should," depending on your political affiliations and smoking habits.[15] Lots of young filmmakers spend time and money on their film but think it's okay to have their art school-dropout buddy scribble them up some quickie box art. *It's not okay!* Nothing screams, "I'm a shitty movie! Don't watch me!" like bad box art. This is one of the few places where it is okay to spend money. If you don't have the money and you're not friends with Christoph Niemann, my bathroom artist, then don't use a drawing!

---

[15] If you lean more toward the "Don't tread on me" camp, I apologize for the previous chapters, as well as the next six. Just kidding, you wouldn't be reading a book by a New York liberal elite, would you?*

  * NOTE FROM THE CHINESE FOOTNOTE GUY: I have it on pretty good authority that Lloyd Kaufman is a closeted Republican. Don't let him fool you. I found a picture of Glenn Beck mixed in with these manuscript pages that was covered with a suspicious, sticky substance.

When we don't have money to spend on decent art at Troma, we use photographs. It's still necessary for the photo to be good, but a decent photo is a lot cheaper than a decent commissioned drawing. Especially with all the free photo editing software available on the Internet, there is no excuse for bad photos.

In fact, nowhere is it even written that you have to use the actors in the film as the photo subjects. So the only person that you could convince to wallow in mud and act like a half pig/half human monster was your 300-lb neighbor? No problem. Pay a model $50 to pose for your photos. Throw some artificial mud on her gorgeous bikini-clad body and start snapping pics.[16] Once someone gets to the end of the film and realizes that the hot gyno on the cover wasn't in it, he'll hopefully be so in love with your cinematic style that he won't even care!

Most of all, make your key art eye-catching. Bad art will almost guarantee that your movie will be ignored. But good art can sell 1000 DVDs at a convention. Check out Appendix B at the back of this book for some examples of Troma art across the decades.

One Last, Last Tip: Confuse Grandma!

If you happen to make a movie where a human head is crushed or other horribly offensive and disgusting things happen, try to design your DVD cover so that it can easily be confused with a children's cartoon. Then Grandma will buy said offensive film for her grandchild, and you will gain a whole new audience of perverted five-year-olds. This actually happened when *Toxic Crusaders* videos were being sold next to *Toxic Avenger* videos, and we got plenty of angry letters. It didn't help that Blockbuster put a "Family Suggestion" sticker on the covers of the unrated *Toxic Avenger* videos, even though the covers themselves clearly stated, "Adults Only, Disturbing Scenes of Violence." But how many of those emotionally scarred five-year-olds are reading this book right now![17]

You only get a few chances to sell your film to the viewer—don't waste any of them.

---

[16] And send some to me.

[17] Recently, we actually met scads of demented, disturbed fans in Australia and New Zealand who were warped at the age of five or six by "tromasposure." What's most shocking is the percentage who were introduced to Troma by their parents!

BROKEBACK FILMMAKERS, OR HOW A COUPLE OF COLORADO FILMMAKERS HAD A RAUNCHY TITLE AND OFFENDED AN INTERNET CONGLOMERATE

BY RICHARD TAYLOR AND ZACK BEINS

The Internet is an amazing place! You can do so much more on it than look at your local weather report. You can also sell your own damn movie(!) using a website such as PayPal!

We at Bizjack/Flemco Productions made our own damn movie called *The Misled Romance of Cannibal Girl and Incest Boy* and did just that! We were selling movies like hot cakes and earning some extra (hot cake) dough to make up for the cost of the film, when all of a sudden, we were shut down for selling pornographic material. What the fuck?

Our film, *The Misled Romance of Cannibal Girl and Incest Boy*, is a psychedelic/horror/romance/comedy shot on Super 8. It's about a girl (who is a cannibal) falling in love with a boy (born out of incestuous relations) and trying not to eat him. Sure, it features hot goth/punk girl boobies, gore galore, castration behind an abortion clinic, and a cameo by Uncle Lloydie himself. But it sure as hell ain't no porno! Turns out our "pals" at PayPal didn't even watch the movie. Rather, they shut us down because of the word "incest" that appears in our title. I guess they weren't too sure exactly what we were selling. For two

FIGURE 4.5 *As publicity for Troma, Lloyd works in other independent and student films. After Lloyd was cast in the film* Stripperland, *the director, Sean Skelding, decided Lloyd would serve him better dead than actually having him attempt to act.*

months we had to fight with them over the phone and through email, trying to resolve the problem and to get our film back online for sale. Finally we got a hold of the head honcho who could get this restriction off our account. We explained the whole situation, but she was less than understanding.

"You're sick and disgusting and the movie is not my cup of tea," she said to us.

"That's fine," we calmly told her. "It's not for everybody, but it is not, in any way, pornography. It's as legit as any film being sold on PayPal or playing in the theaters. A woman can sell her used panties on the Internet but we can't sell our own damn movie?"

Eventually, after convincing her that the film did not feature any acts of incest but that our character was simply a *product* of incest, she agreed to let us sell our film once again on PayPal.

What we learned and would like to share is, I guess, watch out what you name your film. We are all trying to be shocking and original, but sometimes it seems impossible to sell your film if someone gets pissed at the word "incest." If you name your film something like *Cock Hammer*, *Gayniggers from Outer Space*, or even *A Nymphoid Barbarian in Dinosaur Hell*, expect people to react, and not always in a good way. And don't forget to check out our film *The Misled Romance of Cannibal Girl and Incest Boy* for yourself in all of its *incest* and cannibal goodness on *The Best of TromaDance Vol. 5* from troma.com!

How's that for selling our own damn movie, Lloyd?

Putting the "Miss" in Mismarketing: Five Good Movies That Poor Marketing Almost Ruined

OBSERVE AND REPORT (2009)

Observe and Report is a brilliant black comedy starring Seth Rogen as a bipolar mall cop who goes off his meds while trying to stop a deranged flasher and win the girl of his dreams. Sounds hilarious, right? Coming on the heels of a string of Judd Apatow–produced hit comedies including *Knocked Up*, *Superbad*, and *Pineapple Express*, the marketing ignored the film's darker tones and instead presented it as more of the same, only this time in a mall. And it could have worked. However, *Observe and Report* had the misfortune of being released a mere two months after *another* very successful, yet atrociously unwatchable mall cop comedy starring the King of Queens, with the witty title *Paul Blart: Mall Cop*. Facing an audience that was already getting tired of the same old Apatow-styled movies (as seen by the middling receipts for *Zack and Miri Make a Porno*, released earlier the same year) and confused by film reviews that used words like "bleak" and "nihilistic," *Observe and Report* didn't find its audience on opening weekend and died a swift death at the hands of more family-friendly fare like *Hannah Montana* and *Monsters vs. Aliens*.

OFFICE SPACE (1999)

As I mentioned earlier in the book, one of the most important pieces of marketing you can create for your movie is the poster. An effective poster should communicate the most interesting and marketable ideas a film has to offer. What a poster should not do is make your movie look like a boring piece of shit. Unfortunately, that's the direction that the designers of the *Office Space* poster decided to go in. In other words, *Office Space* has a fucking awful poster. A visage of what looks like a yellow Michelin Man (who, on closer examination, is made out of Post-its) stands against a sparse background with the too-concise tagline, "Work sucks." And combined, this communicates three ideas to me: "confusing," "work," and "sucks."

Office Space is a great movie—an incredible satire of modern-day office life that's gone on to become one of the biggest cult films of all-time! Too bad the marketing team had no idea what they were selling and instead presented it as a quirky romantic comedy starring the girl from *Friends* and directed by the creator of *Beavis and Butthead*. It might be hard to make a film about middle-class white people with severe ennui seem interesting, but these guys barely even seemed to try. They couldn't even get the lowest common denominators into seats, and the film was crushed on its opening weekend by memorable classics such as *My Favorite Martian* and *Message in a Bottle*.

FIGHT CLUB (1999)

First rule of *Fight Club*: You do not talk about *Fight Club*! That rule apparently carried over into the marketing of *Fight Club*, as the trailer played down the nihilistic philosophy and dark satire of the film and instead presented it as a quirky action comedy about a dissatisfied office worker whose life is changed forever by a macho dreamboat who just wants to fight and a gothic beauty who just wants to fuck. The poster is even worse and counterproductive to the trailer. On it, a sudsy pink bar of soap inscribed with the *Fight*

Club logo hovers over pictures of the lead actors that look like they were taken in the local YMCA shower room. This left me waiting for a hot, steamy shower scene that never happened. What is this movie? Is it *Lethal Weapon* or *Brokeback Mountain*? Few cared to find out, and *Fight Club* flopped with a disappointing domestic gross of $37 million.

The geniuses behind the marketing of *Fight Club* also made a fatal error by leading women everywhere to believe that the movie was not for them. Rubbish! Plenty of women, forced to watch *Fight Club* on DVD years later, ended up loving it! This emphasis on bare-knuckles, barbarian-esque fight scenes over the story may have worked for *The Expendables* years later, but with a film that already looks boring enough to men, you might not want to alienate the other half of the population right off the bat. Save that for after they've bought their tickets!

BONUS FIGURE 4.1 *It's hard to believe, but a line actually forms as people wait to buy signed Troma posters. Oddly, Lloyd's signature actually makes the poster worth less on eBay.*

GEORGE A. ROMERO'S *SEASON OF THE WITCH* (1973)

While relatively obscure compared to other films on this list, *Season of the Witch* is a great example because it was mismarketed not once, but twice! Better known for horror classics like

Night of the Living Dead and *The Crazies*, George Romero stepped outside of the genre to make this portrait of an unhappy housewife who begins to suffer from delusions while embarking on an extramarital affair. Originally titled *Jack's Wife*, the distributor behind the film's original release decided on the much sexier title *Hungry Wives*. Amazingly, this strategy did not work, and *Hungry Wives* fell into obscurity until another distributor decided to take advantage of Romero's horror fan base and rerelease it as the supernatural thriller now known as *Season of the Witch*.

With the tagline "Every Night is Halloween," this third marketing strategy emphasized a minor subplot of the film that dealt with witchcraft. And although the film features no sequences of malicious black magic, new promotional materials were released featuring the lead character on a broomstick. As an added bonus, the film shared a title with a song written and made famous by Donovan in 1966. The song was licensed and thrown into the film. However, the song was not literally about witches, but rather the infamous celebrity pot busts in London during the previous decade.

Is this film supposed to be *Rosemary's Baby*? Is it supposed to be *The Graduate*? No one knew then and now no one cares!

BONUS FIGURE 4.2 *Typical fan art that gets spread virally, much like AIDS.*

ADVENTURELAND (2009)

I hope that director Greg Mottola was appalled at how Miramax handled his next film after *Superbad*. A more refined approached to young love than his previous cinematic endeavor, *Adventureland* is a heart-warming, believable film about a summer romance between young people. Instead of marketing the film as such, Miramax took advantage of the fact that the film was, in fact, directed by the director of *Superbad* and that it featured *Saturday Night Live*'s Kristen Wiig and Bill Hader. All of the promotional materials for the film portrayed it as *Superbad II*, when the actual product was much more sophisticated and appealed to a much wider audience than teens interested in films about high school parties, alcohol, drugs, and teenage sex. I thought I was going to see a ridiculous comedy, not leave the theater reminiscing about my summer of 1968 fling with Thomas, a fellow member of the Yale Film Society.

THESE DECISIONS PROBABLY MADE A LOT OF SENSE AT THE TIME: A REBUTTAL

By Ted Hope (producer, *Adventureland*)

I think we're in a transitional place in our culture in terms of film marketing. Frequently, I've heard this said to me by the experts over the last 15 or 20 years: You want to market your film to the widest audience, and publicize your film to specific audiences, and your core audience will always find your film if you do that. With that in mind, *Adventureland* was Miramax's biggest hit of last year. They knew they had the "star of the moment" in Kristen Stewart. They didn't know if they could get that audience out to see this film, though, as it was an R-rated movie. But she was, at that moment, the most recognizable element that was there.

We all made the decision together—Greg, the director, myself, the other producers—that it made sense to sell this as a youth comedy. The film was made by a bunch of over-40 filmmakers, the director specifically, though he had just come off of making *Superbad*, a film that was very much geared to this younger audience. So the question would be, how do we get the most people to see this film? Do you sell it for nostalgia, for adults in their mid-40s and their teenage kids? Or do you try to sell it more to the college audience crowd with all the things that were there? It did have some broad humor in it. Yes, it had deep emotions and a level of reflection in it. It was a hard choice. I certainly heard from a lot of people that they were sold one bill of goods and received another. And that complaint is something we have to deal with, because as an industry that's been the practice for a long time, and the audience isn't stupid. They know that it keeps being done time and time again. And they get angry and they get frustrated. The question is, can you sell the exact same thing and get as large of a result? It's a really pertinent question. How do we do that? I don't really have the answer.

Ultimately, *Adventureland* gets a lot of love. Would I have preferred that the film was sold as a great work of art, an incredibly literate script, with deeply human performances, and a level of artistry, mastery in both the direction and production? Yeah. That would have helped buff my ego a little bit, and I'm sure everyone else's. And I think we would've made about 7 million dollars at the North American box office instead of 16 million, which is what we made. It cost a lot to get to 16; it wouldn't have cost as much to get to 7. I'm not sure which ultimately proves to be profitable. But I think the film in its true nature is what will survive over time and not the marketing campaign and its attempt to reach the biggest broadest audience. A lot of times I haven't had distributors who were willing to spend and try to reach the widest possible audience for the film. And I was really frustrated, so I don't mind them erring on that side.

Chapter five

I Said Look at Me! How to Make People Want to See Your Movie, Part II, or Probably the Most Important Chapter in the Book (after the One about Thomas Jefferson and Pirates)

When you've spent weeks, or even months, choosing a captivating title, crafting elegant puns for your tagline, and lovingly Photoshopping photographs for your engaging key art, it can be tempting to take a little break.

"Wha?" you might say. "But that means the movie is done, Lloyd! Why would I stop now?"

Good question, guys. But the fact is, many of the people who want to make a movie—even the ones who really, really care—essentially just want to make a movie. They want to know that they "did it," and when they're at a party, someone can introduce them as "the guy who made a movie." It makes them feel good, and when the next question at the party is, "Oh, a movie, eh? Why haven't I heard of it?" they can spout some canned-ham answer about how the industry is unkind to independent filmmakers and megaconglomerate corporations are taking over the world.[1]

Of course, that's all true. But it's no fucking excuse, you lazy shit. The industry has never been truly kind to independent filmmakers. We might have had it a little easier in the 1970s as far as distribution, but making a movie in the first place was a heck of a lot harder back then. Independents have always had to suffer for their art!

Once you've made your movie, you may think your job is done. If you never really *try* to get it out there, then you can't really fail, right? You can just spout egotistical bullshit and play the part of the tortured artist at parties, while the movie that you bled for sits on a shelf above your iMac. Carl Jung would be so ashamed.

Making someone who doesn't know you from Justin Bieber want to see your movie is tough. It takes a lot of effort and creativity, hopefully two concepts that you're cool with, since you actually finished making your own damn movie. In the words of Sigmund Freud, "You can do it!"

THE POWER OF THE MOUTH

Nothing will help your movie, or kill it, like word of mouth. Just look at the *Friday the 13th* remake or *Sex and the City 2: Queens of the Desert*. These movies were so unbelievably horrible and off-putting that no amount of massive-budget marketing campaign could win people over. *Friday the 13th* had a decent opening weekend, but once all the people who had seen it went home and told their friends that sitting through it was actually worse than being killed by Jason Voorhees himself, I don't think a single person bought a ticket the next weekend. The producers of *Sex and the City 2* spent

---

[1] I just used this excuse at a party a few days ago.

millions and millions of dollars trying to convince women that they should put on their old prom dresses, get wasted, and go see the movie with all of their "girlfriends." This marketing strategy was not only offensive, but it was also completely ineffectual after critics and preview audiences had pretty much said the movie was unbearable to watch, with or without a bunch of drunk girlfriends.

FIGURE 5.1 *Trouble occurred at Tromapalooza Denver, 2010, when Lloyd thought he was hosting a band called Open Mic.*

The good news is that both of these movies, and most other films that the studios release each year, actually have one disadvantage that you do not. That is, that people expect them to be good. After all, they are written/directed/produced by and featuring the best professionals in the industry—they should be great, right? So when they're not, and they're usually not, people are understandably pissed. Because it concerned lesbians, and I am one of the very few Jewish men who get off on hard-bodied lesbians, I snuck off to a screening of *The Kids Are All Right* a few weeks after it was released. This movie had been the darling of Sundance and was supposedly the new revolution in modern family comedy/drama. Guess what. It was shit! Not only that, but it was a laughable insult to lesbians everywhere! And for the next several weeks, I told everyone so because I was understandably disappointed.[2]

[2]NOTE FROM THE INCREASINGLY BORED AND IRRITABLE FOOTNOTE GUY: Kaufman is a jerk. *The Kids Are All Right* was a huge hit. It even got Oscar nominations!

But unlike all of these pretentious shit Hollywood movies, no one really expects your homemade movie to be any good. Even your parents, friends, and dentists who invested money probably did so because they wanted to make you happy, not because they really thought that you were going to win an Oscar. So if your movie *does* suck, it's just another sucky homemade movie. However, if your movie is anything even *close* to good, people are going to go nuts!

"Have you seen this amazing movie? My son made it, but it's actually really good!" your mother will say to the members of her Oprah Book Club.

"Have you seen this fantastic movie? A friend-of-mine's son made it, but it's great!" your mother's friend will say to her hairdresser.

"Girl, have you seen this shit? It is fierce!" your mother's friend's hilariously gay hairdresser will say to his domestic partner.

"Bitch, you gotta see this movie. I don't know who made it, but I love it. It's on my new favorite things list, just like Oprah," your mother's friend's gay hairdresser's domestic partner will say to his cousin, Quentin Tarantino.

And so on, and so forth. And it used to take weeks, months, or even years for word of mouth to spread around the country. Today, with a few clicks of a mouse, a link to your trailer can travel around the world in minutes!

FIGURE 5.2 Cannibal Holocaust *director Ruggero Deodato and a young Julia Roberts use a horror festival in Spain to promote Roberts's latest underground hit,* The Horror of the Humongous Choppers.

Back when I was a young lad at Trinity School, I entered a speech contest. Instead of preparing something dignified, I decided to do something goofy, so I sang a song about Kentucky.[3] I guess I must have been as charming then as I am now, because somehow this blatant disregard for decorum got me into the finals of the contest. Word spread around the school that little Stanley Lloyd Kaufman was going to do something crazy in the finals! The next week, when the finals actually came, of course, I panicked and folded. I vaguely remember standing on stage stuttering something about horses and pretending to pull a covered wagon. I was a complete mess, and my dream journey had come to an end, much like the career of Mel Gibson. But my point is that, because of word of mouth, the turnout for the Trinity School speech contest finals was huge! The auditorium ran out of chairs, and they had kids waiting outside just to get a glimpse of me making a fool of myself! The next year, I did a speech about cable cars, and I acted out horses pulling wagons, complete with galloping sounds and a few "naaaaaayyyy"s. I was not asked to participate the year after that.

GRASSROOTS MARKETING, ALSO KNOWN AS GUERILLA MARKETING (WHICH MAY OR MAY NOT HAVE ANYTHING TO DO WITH THE MARKETING OF *KING KONG*)

When I'm looking for a new, innovative idea, I always look to porn. The porno industry has led the way for years, in everything from home video and cable to the Internet.[4] Back in 1970, when we were looking for ways to advertise *The Battle of Love's Return* for little money, I noticed that the guys in Times Square handing out strip club fliers had a pretty good technique. They would wave the fliers in your face as you walked by and yell, "Check it out! Check it out! Check it out!" They'd say it three times like that, and invariably, the hapless passerby would take the flier and, for all I know, end up at the strip club later that night, checking it out. I decided to borrow this technique when it came time to get the word out

---

[3] Stephen Foster's 1804 tune, "My Old Kentucky Home," which has recently been rerecorded by Jay-Z as "Eat My Hairy Ass."

[4] Unfortunately, the porno industry has also convinced women that any man who can't sustain an orgasm for 90 minutes is gay. Therefore, I am gay.

about our movie. I called everyone who had worked on *The Battle of Love's Return* and was still talking to me,[5] and we started blanketing New York City with little yellow fliers. Of course, the few people who went to see the film as a result of our "check it out" fliers were understandably furious when they were presented with my boring movie instead of naked, dancing sluts.

For our second attempt at cheap marketing, we made a cardboard stencil of the film's title and went to work spray-painting the sidewalks. Unfortunately, the cop who saw us doing this was under the impression that it was illegal, and he grabbed our stencil, broke it over his knee, and threw it in a garbage can. Luckily, he didn't know who he was dealing with. I dove right into that garbage can and got our stencil back the minute he walked away. The cop need not have worried, though. Even before he broke the stencil, our spray-painted stenciled titles were unreadable. But if there had been a movie called *BADD DLEI%*#* in theaters at the time, it would have benefited greatly from our stenciling attempt.

FIGURE 5.3 *Grassroots promoting at Fantazi Festival in the Czech Republic. It is important to travel to foreign countries where people know less about you and, therefore, don't know that you suck.*

---

[5] Which was actually just three guys—Gerard Glenn, Frank Vitale, and some guy named Oliver Stone. At least I think his name was Oliver. I don't really remember... he never went anywhere...

Learning from the spray-paint fiasco, we moved on to posters. And like smart guys, we figured we would glue them in a place where a lot of people would see them. For some reason, we chose the storefront window of a Chinese restaurant. Now, let me impart some practical knowledge on you in this chapter—if you are going to put up a poster on a Chinese restaurant owner's window and royally piss him off, make sure that the poster does not say who you are and where you will be at a certain time on a certain day. Because, if you do, that irate Chinese restaurant owner will know exactly where to find you. Since our posters were advertising our film's premiere at the prestigious Thalia Theater, this particular irate Chinese restaurant owner knew exactly where to find us. He came to the theater on the night of the premiere, yelling in Cantonese[6] and looking like he'd been waiting his whole life to beat up a skinny Jewish kid in a bowtie. Poor Mrs. Lewis, the owner of the theater, was horrified. We agreed to take down the posters and clean the windows that next day, but the whole thing was embarrassing. But you know what? After the irate Chinese restaurant owner beat the shit out of me, he sat down and watched the film, and gave us our first great review, which was printed entirely in Cantonese in the 报纸 *Daily*. We were the hit of Chinatown![7]

Back then, we didn't need the Internet to get the word out, and we still don't! In fact, we use it far less than we should. Don't think

EXTRA TIP

Walking down the street in New York City, I often see a whole row of posters, all identical, covering a block. When you are postering your town, it may seem like common sense to put up one poster in one location and another poster somewhere else, so more people will see them. But consider how a person may walk by a single, small poster without really noticing it, whereas three or four posters in a row might actually get their attention. Spend a few extra dollars and get as many posters as you can afford if you are really going to use postering as a marketing tool. And then blitz that shit like a German fighter pilot.

---

[6] Cantonese makes people sound like they are angry even when they are reading *Goodnight Moon*. But this guy was really, really angry.

[7] Unfortunately, Chinatown is at the south end of Manhattan, while the Thalia Theater was way up north, so the Chinese rave review was actually useless.

that the Internet is your only option when it comes to generating word of mouth. Sure, the Internet is great, and it can make it easier for word to travel over distances, but don't ignore your own hometown! These are the people that are most likely to support you, so get them on your side first! And don't forget the Chinese![8]

THE CAUTIONARY TALE OF *SUGAR COOKIES*

In the 1970s, Troma distributed a film called *Sugar Cookies*. As an X-rated[9] film, it seemed a sure thing to make some money. We booked it at the Lyell Theatre in Rochester, New York. This was around the time when multiplexes were first being built, and the major studios just didn't have enough movies to fill all eight screens, so smaller producers like us benefited enormously. I, along with Gerard, the guy who had stenciled *The Battle of Love's Return* on the streets of Manhattan with me, and my (soon to be not my) friend Oliver Stone, headed up to Rochester spread the word about *Sugar Cookies*. We decided to leave leaflets on the cars parked at the mall where the Lyell Theatre was located. The leaflets mentioned that the movie was X-rated, but they were pretty tame, and the idea sounded innocent enough at the time. Little did we know that an angry mob of motorists would see fit to return their fliers to the theater, complete with anti-Jewish scrawlings! My guess is they were a health-conscious bunch and were upset that their families had been exposed to the words "sugar" and "cookies." In any case, it didn't matter. The national distributor that we had hired made up some cheap, ugly advertising materials and pushed the movie as a generic sex film, which it was not. It was a boring, lesbian take on *Vertigo*. Of course, it bombed. Maybe if it had been sold as what it was and not had a horrible trailer, it might have done better. As it is, it stands as the only X-rated film to ever lose money.

TIT FOR TAT

People love swag. They love getting stuff, and they love getting stuff for free. I recently met a young filmmaker who printed up 2000 stickers with his film's title, and then offered to send a sticker to everyone who sent him their email. So for the cost of 2000 stickers,

---

[8] No, really! I'm starving!

[9] Today this film would be rated a mild R, or maybe PG!

which was maybe a couple hundred dollars, he not only amassed a 2000+ strong email list with which to send film updates, but he also had 2000 folks advertising his film every time they opened a binder, drove a car, or whatever else people do with stickers. If you can't afford 2000 stickers, start with 500, or 200! "Free stuff for an email address" is a creative way to combine new technology with old-school techniques like postering and leafleting.

MONEY FOR TAT

Many young directors love to design T-shirts, hat, jackets, condoms, and the rest with their film's title and logo, and distribute these to crewmembers. And if you have millions of dollars to throw around, by all means, spend it on novelty condoms.[10] I always say, "Safety to Humans," after all. But with a limited budget, there are probably better ways to spend your money than free swag for yourself and the crew.

Cheap T-shirts are one thing—they can serve to constantly remind your sound guy that he needs to show up next weekend while also reminding your makeup guy that he should talk up the film to friends whenever he can. But many directors get $1000 in their hand and all of a sudden want to be James Dean. Before buying 30 leather jackets embroidered with your movie's title and "A Film by Lloyd Kaufman,"[11] remember what makes swag so great in the first place. The purpose of swag is to alert people to the existence of your movie. So why spend a third of your budget on the people that already know about your movie because they have been working on it for three years? Nothing is gained by letting your boom guy know that a movie is being made through hats and jackets. If he isn't aware that a movie is being made, he is clearly not a very good boom operator.[12]

The exception, of course, is if you have people buy things from you instead of giving them away. If you haven't lost any money, then who cares if your DP wears his shirt once and then uses it to wipe his cat's litter box. Stores do this all the time—they sell you an environmentally sound tote bag for $3 so that you can carry home

---

[10] We have done this.

[11] You would put your name here, obviously. Unless you like my name better.

[12] But it sounds like he's kind of dumb and willing to work cheap, so please send him to Troma! We need him for *Toxie 5*! And tell him to bring a script with him, too!

your books/groceries/cockrings, and in the process they (1) make money by selling you a tote bag, (2) save money by not giving you a plastic bag, and, most important, (3) turn you into a walking billboard for their store because you're walking around with a logoed tote bag! And each time you go to the store and forget to bring the environmentally sound tote bag and you are forced to buy another one, like I was last week at the D'Agostino around the corner from my house, they make even more money! Follow their lead! There is nothing wrong with selling merchandise and putting the money back into your film. Pretty soon, your friends, parents, and strangers alike can all be outfitted in your *Zombie Lesbian Sex Slaves in Outer Space* gear!

FIGURE 5.4 *After reading Lloyd Kaufman's* Direct Your Own Damn Movie! *and* Produce Your Own Damn Movie!, *Phil Nichols uses guerilla marketing in his signature Dick Cheney costume at AFM to promote his own damn movie!*

MEDIA MARKETING, OR PAINTING THE TOWN GREEN

If you're lucky, sooner or later all of your guerilla marketing at the grassroots level will attract the attention of some media. But even with a lot of hard work, it's very likely that the mainstream media won't be coming to you. So what should you do? Sit on the couch and eat Nutella? Yes! And also, go to the media yourself.

All-Nude Revue!!

Every director wants her film reviewed. Many have no idea how to go about this.[13] Thousands of movies are made each year, and the

---

[13] Myself included.

fact is, Roger Ebert[14] can't review all of them. If you have a film with no stars, it's probably wise to not waste your time trying to convince A.O. Scott[15] to give you your first review. Wait until your film is a major "indie" success, and then go knocking on his door.

In 1971, I was not able to afford to rent a screening room for a critics' screening of *The Battle of Love's Return*. My only option was to hold a screening in my bedroom at my mother's house on 62nd Street. Naturally, *New York Magazine* film critic Judith Crist, like most females, refused to come into my bedroom. However, the *New York Times* critic actually showed up to see the film in my bedroom and we had hot sex. This would never happen today! Well, not in my bedroom anyway, because my wife is usually there. Judith Crist eventually saw *The Battle of Love's Return* in the cheapest, crappiest screening room that I could find. Even though she refused to come to my bedroom, after seeing my film, she became very loving. She even gave the film a good review and compared me to Woody Allen![16]

Press Kits

When approaching a film critic, either through email, regular mail, or in their driveway, your introduction will be your press kit. A press kit can be either paper-in-a-folder or electronic, and both contain roughly the same materials. Troma's favorite press kit-of-choice is a crappy 33¢ folder from Duane Reade. The following list is a good start for your press kit. Feel free to be creative, but don't go so nuts that no one can figure out what the movie's title is.

PRESS KIT GO-LIST (TAKEN FROM A HASTILY PREPARED *POULTRYGEIST* PRESS KIT)
- Cover should feature key/poster art and website URL
- One page with title/one- to two-sentence description, director's name/notable stars
- film stills
- any positive reviews that you have already received (can be full review or page of snippets)

---

[14] Roger Ebert is the highly regarded film critic for *Gun World* magazine.

[15] A.O. Scott pens film reviews for the Queens Community College student-run paper.

[16] The actual quote was, "Twenty-two-year-old Kaufman displays a keen eye for the absurd, reminiscent of Woody Allen. With luck, Kaufman's career will mirror that of Allen, and he, too, will one day marry his own daughter."

- Cast list
- Screener DVD/link to film on the Internet[17]
- Your contact information
- Short bios of director/cast
- Anything else that will make your press kit distinctive

Now put it all in a two-pocket folder and send it to as many media reporters and reviewers as you can find! Do some research and see if there are any genre magazines that would suit your film. This is easy for a horror film, slightly more complicated (but not impossible) for a balloon-fetish musical. Contact the reviewer and address a letter to her by name. If you ever plan to address a letter, "Dear Reviewer," or "Dear Madam Film Critic," just stop reading now. Put the book down, find the nearest train tracks, and lie down on them.

Wide-Load Trailers

A poster is a great way to sell your film with one, strong image, but with a trailer, you have anywhere from 30 seconds to 4 minutes to convince people that they need to see your film. Not that they *want* to see your film, but that they *need* to see it. There are three types of trailers—ones that show you everything, ones that show you absolutely nothing, and ones that show you enough to get you interested but not enough to satisfy you. There is no right way to make a trailer, except to make it interesting. Different movies benefit from different styles.

TRAILERS THAT SHOW EVERYTHING

In 1999, on the verge of the new millennium, Castle Rock released a film called *The Story of Us,* staring the gritty Michelle Pfeiffer and the beautiful Bruce Willis. The trailer for this film looked hilarious! There were lots of montages and funny lines and plenty of those cute little exasperated looks that husbands and wives give each other when they're on the brink of divorce. I couldn't wait to see it! But when I actually saw the movie, that little montage in the trailer was in the movie! There was literally a montage of funny lines and cute exasperating looks *in the fucking movie.* I'd been had! I could have

---

[17] If your film has already been bootlegged by pirates, just put up a link to their site! Let the pirates do your work for you!

just watched that montage for free in a TV commercial, but instead I had paid $8 to see it again in the theater! And it was far less cute and funny for $8. In 1996's *Ransom*, the entire first half of the movie is spent questioning whether Mel Gibson will pay the ransom demanded by his son's kidnappers. Unfortunately, the entire first half of the movie is pointless because the trailer had already given away that, no, Mel Gibson will indeed *not* pay the ransom, and will instead go rogue on some kidnapper ass. And that is why I've hated Mel Gibson for the past 15 years, unlike all the other posers who only started hating him when he made *Passion of the Christ*.[18]

On the flip side, I had absolutely no interest in seeing *Piranha 3D* until I saw the trailer during my seventh viewing of *Inception*. Who is going to pay $13 to see what is essentially a Syfy[19] channel movie shot in cheap 3D? Me! It looked awesome! There were all sorts of piranha attacks and scantily clad young boys frolicking in lakes. If *Piranha 3D* had given me some ambiguous trailer about something mysterious in the water, I wouldn't have given a fuck. But by showing me all the cool stuff they got, I'm oddly intrigued to see it for real! Sure, I'll probably be disappointed, but by then, they'll have my $18.

TRAILERS THAT DON'T SHOW ANYTHING

Occasionally a trailer will show you very little because the actual movie has not been completed yet. This happens a lot with horror films that have a simple story or a recurring character, but have not yet been shot. What better way to get you excited about *Nightmare on Elm Street 15* or *Saw 10* than to give you a haunting glimpse of Freddy Krueger hiding behind a hot water heater or some young, beautiful person whimpering in a dark basement. You don't need to see any kills, because you know what to expect. You just need to be titillated a little. This also happens occasionally with CGI films, like *Toy Story 3*.[20] You can create a little trailer starring Buzz and Woody to get people excited while you spend two years creating the actual movie.

I would say that, unless your film is all about suspense, try to err on the side of showing too much rather than showing too little. In many instances, showing too little is just lazy on the part of the

---

[18] Which, clearly, is enough of a reason in itself.

[19] Formerly the far more pronounceable "Sci-Fi" Channel.

[20] This, by the way, is a great movie!

filmmaker. The right editor can create a compelling trailer out of an incredibly boring movie.

TRAILERS THAT SHOW ENOUGH TO GET YOU INTERESTED, BUT NOT ENOUGH TO SATISFY YOU

Since most of the people who will see your trailer have no idea who you are or what your film is supposed to be, that image of Freddy Krueger in the shadows isn't usually going to work. If you have some funny lines, put them in! If you spend a lot of money on a great special effect, put it in! If you have the rights to use a great song that fits, use it in the trailer, even if it isn't in the movie! If you use a voice-over, tell the audience that they are going to see something they have never seen before! Use images that they will never forget! A good trailer is priceless. The trailer for *Human Centipede* has millions of views on YouTube. Compare that to the trailer for *Poultrygeist*, which has about 62 views.

For Troma's current production, *Father's Day*, we made a trailer and posted it on YouTube before the script had even been written! There was a very good media response, so we proceeded with principal photography. In this digital-DIY age, promotion should start from the moment your film gets the green light.

SOCIAL NETWORKING (WORK THAT 'NET, GIRL)

For the first 20 years of Troma's history, we depended on word of mouth. We couldn't afford to run advertisements for the *Toxic Avenger Part II* during *Cheers*. Putting up posters and handing out leaflets were the best ways to get noticed, and we only hoped that the buzz would lead to a review in *The New York Times*. But in the early 1990s, Al Gore birthed the Internet, and everything changed. In its earliest days, most major studios were either unaware of the interweb or they just didn't give a fuck. We at Troma, however, jumped in balls-first.[21] We were the first studio to have a website, and since we love to honor our past, we haven't changed the design since 1994!

The reliable techniques like postering and leafleting and dressing up like a chicken that I've been using since 1968 are still important, but it would be moronic to ignore the interweb as a means of getting the word out about your movie!

---

[21] The women of Troma jump in vagina-first, except for my former cross-dressing assistant Jamie Greco, who actually has balls, and can, therefore, jump in balls-first.

Facebook Addicts Anonymous

I'm not going to lie. I still love my Myspace page. However, the last six assistants I've hired have all done their best to convince me that, since Rupert Murdoch purchased it, Myspace is dead, and Facebook is where it's at. So now I have a Facebook as well. But the sterile Facebook environment, though efficient, just doesn't do it for me the way dirty Myspace used to. I miss being able to rank my friends based on sexual favors and ankle beauty. I miss being able to express myself through the Green Day song on my page. And above all, I miss the fake Justin Bieber page that I made and then used to friend beautiful hairless and shirtless males.

I also have a Twitter page, much like Charlie Sheen. And unlike some other famous, brilliant, and important directors, I actually do my own tweeting. You can tell by all the spelling and grammatical errors that come from an old man typing on a tiny BlackBerry keypad. What kind of major director has the time to tweet all day? I do![22]

Facebook, Myspace, and Twitter are great tools to reach a lot of people at the same time.[23] Sure, they may all be obsolete in two years, but then I'll just delete this part of the chapter and sell the book as a "New and Updated Revised Edition!" For now, Facebook, Twitter, and, to a lesser extent, Myspace are some of the best vehicles to sell yourself. While your film is still in production, create a Facebook page and Twitter account for it! As director/producer, you may not have time for frequent updates, between the casting, special-effects supervision, and cameo song-and-dance numbers, but that's what your unwashed/unpaid crew is for! Choose someone with a moderate-to-good grasp of the English language and have him or her craft at least one funny update each day. Or maybe hold a contest each week to see who can come up with the funniest update, and give the winner a slice of pizza. Then use the best five as your updates for the week![24] The point is to make the updates interesting. Many people will ignore requests from film and band pages because they've been burned by boring/needy/

---

[22] So do directors Eli Roth, Adam Green, and James Gunn!

[23] So are Ron Jeremy's penis and incredible, stretchy arms!

[24] Wow, that's a really great idea. Matt, remind me to use this at Troma on Monday!*

*NOTE FROM LLOYD'S CURRENT ASSISTANT: Um, Lloyd, Matt quit last year. I'm Allison.**

**NOTE FROM LLOYD: Just remind me!!

pretentious postings in the past. So when someone does add your film page or follow your Twitter, don't blow it! Don't overload them with updates, but don't just add people and then forget about the page. And keep in mind that no one wants to hear what a great director you are. That needs to be something that they discover on their own, like a hidden jewel.

Example of a poor tweet:

> This crew sux!! Why can't people be where they r supposed 2b??
> I can't make do my job when u don't do urs!!

Example of a somewhat-entertaining tweet:

> Today I yelled "cut," too soon and my crew attacked me like juggalos on Tila Tequila. The only difference is, I'm way hotter than Tila Tequila, but far less talented.

I recently played a small role in James Gunn's *Super*. James, producer Ted Hope, and star Rainn Wilson were tweeting daily from the set. Before the movie moved to the editing stage, millions of consumers around the world knew about *Super*!

Your updates shouldn't be a chore to read but should be entertaining in their own right. For better examples than what I spent two hours crafting above, check out James Gunn's (@jamesgunn) Facebook and Twitter pages. He's hilarious, and I love him! For poor examples, check out my tweetfeed, @harriettubman!

Once your film is complete and you've built up a rabid fan base with your amusing tweets, it's a cinch to use the page to alert people to screenings. And when your film is selling for $10 on Amazon, everyone will know![25]

TRIFECTA! CONVENTIONS: A WORLD OF THEIR OWN!

Isn't it ironic that with all the modern technology that Troma has embraced, we still have our greatest success with person-to-person contact. And nowhere is this better exemplified than at a convention. That's because, as an independent studio that has produced and distributed many horror/sex-filled/humorously perverse films over the past 35 years, the people who attend horror/sci-fi/porno conventions

---

[25] Once they've bought your movie, guilt them into reviewing it on Amazon. Also, please review this book on Amazon!!

are *our* demographic! Very few other places can you interact with so many people who have a reason to be interested in you.[26] I would say with certainty a dozen, if not dozens and dozens of new fans have discovered Troma though conventions over the past 35 years.

In fact, conventions are a perfect, organic combination of all three types of marketing mentioned earlier. Troma uses social networking to get volunteers to work our booths and of course to attract the beautiful Tromettes and Tromen who show up to dazzle the attendees. We also use social networking to alert fans to where I'll be and if there are any Troma-riffic events taking place. Fans then spread our tweets themselves.[27] Then we use the volunteers to literally litter the convention with fliers and posters, and attract some grassroots attention. And once the attention comes, we use our charismatic president and creator of *The Toxic Avenger*, yours truly, to give interviews to media outlets, and I always make sure to have a press kit or a Troma promotional information DVD (such as *Fistful of Troma*,[28] which contains trailers, etc.) in my hand.

Comic-Con, which we attend every year, has 150,000 attendees, and I would say maybe 5000 are there to see us. The other 145,000 may not have had a clue what Troma was before, but if they passed the H-wing men's bathroom or followed the smell of overpriced nachos and swampass, they've seen us now! Each year, in addition to all the exposure, we've sold enough DVDs to cover our expenses. It probably costs $2000 to take out an ad on Ain't It Cool News. Instead, spend that money on a booth at Comic-Con, and you'll also be listed in the catalog, programs, and so on. We've also been interviewed by G4, Fox, NPR, and countless small Internet radio guys at Comic-Con.

And though Comic-Con is great, there are hundred of other, smaller conventions around the country and around the world. For a brief introduction, compiled by Troma's own convention expert, Ron Mackay, check out Appendix C.

I'll be in Big River, Arkansas, and Deer Tick, Nebraska next month. See you there!

---

[26] The only other place I can think of is JDate. And if you're reading this Moishe, I still want to meet!

[27] In fact, I am proofreading this chapter in Melbourne, Australia, where I am a guest at the Armageddon Convention. There have been lines around the block of people who are buying DVDs and who want my autograph, thanks in large part to Facebook and Twitter!

[28] NOTE FROM THE FOOTNOTE GUY: Oh boy, does Kaufman have a fistful!

FIGURE 5.5A *Lloyd, pictured here with Jean-Claude Van Damme, uses conventions to network with fans, media, and celebs.*

FIGURE 5.5B *An ecstatic Mia Matsumiya and James Gunn pose with Mel Gibson* (left) *at the Tromabooth for Comic-Con 2010.*

The following is a partial schedule of my activities over the course of 2010, all of which, ideally, contributed to a few more Troma DVDs being sold. There were many events, however, that I simply couldn't remember and therefore could not include here. Also, now that I'm looking over it, some of these appointments don't seem to have anything to fucking do with selling. That's the danger in turning the responsibility for your life's schedule over to an underpaid Troma employee, though.

January 2010

Monday 1/4
- Return from the Middle East (hopefully)

Tuesday 1/5
- Depart for Shreveport, LA
- Flight Information:
  - Northwest Airlines # 5689
  - Newark Liberty Intl (EWR) to Memphis International (MEM)
  - Departure (EWR): January 5, 4:25 PM EST (afternoon)
  - Arrival (MEM): January 5, 6:29 PM CST (evening)
  - Class: Economy Seat: 17C
  - Northwest Airlines # 3697

FIGURE 5.6 Sell Your Own Damn Movie! *exclusive tip #6503: If you have to wake up at 6 AM to promote your film on a morning program, you can do what Lloyd does and just sleep in your clothes!*

- Memphis International (MEM) to Shreveport Regional (SHV)
  - Departure (MEM): January 5, 7:35 PM CST (evening)
  - Arrival (SHV): January 5, 8:48 PM CST (evening)

Wednesday 1/6

- Acting in *Super* w/ James Gunn (9 AM to 5 PM)
- Playing "911 Man"
- James' Assistant's cell: xxx-xxx-xxxx

Thursday 1/7

- Return from Shreveport
- Flight Information:
  - Northwest Airlines # 4116
  - Shreveport Regional (SHV) to Memphis International (MEM)
  - Departure (SHV): January 7, 4:20 PM CST (afternoon)
  - Arrival (MEM): January 7, 5:27 PM CST (evening)
  - Class: Economy Seat: 6B
  - Northwest Airlines # 5722
  - Memphis International (MEM) to Newark Liberty Intl (EWR)
  - Departure (MEM): January 7, 6:50 PM CST (evening)
  - Arrival (EWR): January 7, 10:39 PM EST (evening)

Friday 1/8

- Meeting with Sean Pomper at Troma Building @ 2 PM

Sunday 1/10

- Fly to Los Angeles
- Flight Information:
  - American Airlines # 3
  - New York John F. Kennedy Intl (JFK) to Los Angeles International (LAX)
  - Departure (JFK): January 10, 12:00 PM EST (noon)
  - Arrival (LAX): January 10, 3:22 PM PST (afternoon)
  - Class: Economy Seat: 31G

Tuesday 1/12

- IFTA meeting @ 9 AM
- Return from L.A.
- Flight Information:
  - American Airlines # 180
  - Los Angeles International (LAX) to New York John F. Kennedy Intl (JFK)
  - Departure (LAX): January 12, 4:30 PM PST (afternoon)
  - Arrival (JFK): January 13, 12:45 AM EST (morning)
  - Class: Economy Seat: 37G

Wednesday 1/13
- Lunch with Porter Bibb at Brassiere Restaurant @ 2 PM to discuss Ted Turner

Thursday 1/14
- Interview with Lola Rock'n'Rolla to discuss Ted Bundy

Monday 1/18
- Meeting with Joe Randazzo

Friday 1/22
- Leave for Denver, CO
- Midnight screening of *Poultrygeist* at Landmark Theatres (men's room sweep)

Saturday 1/23
- Book signing and media interviews all afternoon
- Interview w/ Barry Wurst
- Denver Tromapalooza @ 7 PM!
- Midnight screening of *Poultrygeist* at Landmark Theatres (merchandise for sale, men's room sweep with George Michael)

February 2010

Tuesday 2/2
- Arrive in Los Angeles @ 9 AM
- IFTA Finance and Executive Committee meeting (budget review)
- Meeting w/ Sony to discuss online content partnership
- Meeting w/ FEARnet

Friday 2/19–Sunday 2/21
- ConNooga 2010 (Chattanooga convention)
- Flight Information:
  - Depart: 9:00 AM New York, NY (LGA) Delta Flight 1775
  - Arrive: 11:48 AM Atlanta, GA (ATL)
  - Change plane in Atlanta
  - Depart: 12:55 PM Atlanta, GA (ATL) Delta Flight 5417
  - Arrive: 1:44 PM Chattanooga, TN (CHA)

Monday 2/22
- DVD/Book Signing at Forbidden Planet, NYC

Tuesday 2/23
- DVD/Book Signing at Forbidden Planet, NYC

Thursday 2/25
- Arrive in Los Angeles
- IFTA Board of Directors meeting @ 9 AM

Friday 2/26
- Yale Jewish Alumni Weekend, film Purim movie pro bono (try to make movie pro Bono, even though Bono is not Jewish)
- Contact: Rabbi Jim Ponet

March 2010
Tuesday 3/2–Thursday 3/4
- Detroit Film Festival, Troma Retrospective

Saturday 3/6
- Manicure appointment w/ Soo Lum Kwan @ 1 PM

Friday 3/12–Sunday 3/14
- MegaCon 2010!
- Orange County Convention Center Hall D
  - 9899 International Drive, Orlando, FL 32819
- *Class of Nuke 'Em High* screening
- Points Theater Horror Festival, Jacksonville, FL

Friday 3/18–Monday 3/21
- Dutch Film Museum in Amsterdam
- Troma Retrospective
- Investigate methods to conceal pot breath

Thursday 3/25
- IFTA Executive Committee meeting in Los Angeles

Friday 3/26–Sunday 3/28
- Attend Horror Hound convention in Indianapolis as guest

April 2010
Friday 4/2–Sunday 4/4
- WonderCon in San Francisco

Tuesday 4/6–Saturday 4/10
- In Winnipeg to act in *Mother's Day* remake

Sunday 4/18
- TromaDance 2010 in New Jersey!

Monday 4/19–Tuesday 4/20
- In Detroit to act in *Sucker*

Wednesday 4/21
- Arrive in Los Angeles
- Book signing at Vroman's Book Store
  - 695 E. Colorado Blvd. Pasadena, CA 91101

Thursday 4/22
- IFTA Board of Directors meeting @ 9 AM
- Troma 35th Anniversary Event @ 6:30 PM

- New Beverly Cinema, screenings of *Toxic Avenger* and *Poultrygeist*

Saturday 4/24–Sunday 4/25
- Arrive in Alberta, Canada
- Calgary Comic & Entertainment Expo

Tuesday 4/27
- Social Week Cinema Panel @ 6:15 PM

Wednesday 4/28
- Lunch with Shawn Durkin, winner of Troma survey

Thursday 4/29
- Arrive in Indiana for River Bend Film Festival
- Introduce *Toxic Avenger* screening @ 9 PM

Friday 4/30
- Interview w/ local FOX morning show @ 7 AM
- 20-minute intro to festival opening night @ 7 PM
- Introduce *Poultrygeist* @ 9 PM

May 2010

Saturday 5/1
- Make Your Own Damn Movie seminar @ 4 PM
- Meet & Greet @ 5 PM
- Depart Indiana

Monday 5/3
- Interview w/ Strauss Zelnick for *Sell Your Own Damn Movie!* @ 3 PM

Tuesday 5/4
- Meeting w/ Tony DiSanto (MTV) @ 2:30 PM

Wednesday 5/5
- Cinco de Mayo party at the Manhole Club, 11 PM (bring Jello!)

Friday 5/7
- Arrive in Detroit
- Shoot w/ Scott McKinlay for *Creep Van*

Sunday 5/9
- Mother's Day
- Guilt people into buying Troma's *Mother's Day* for their mothers

Saturday 5/22
- Arrive in Michigan for Lakeside Film Festival
- Q&A and master class

Monday 5/31
- Shoot w/ Steven Clark for *The Octogon Man*, Collegeville, PA

June 2010

Friday 6/4
- Long Island Film Festival shoot at Troma Building @ 11 AM

Monday 6/7
- Leave for Los Angeles
- Flight Information:
  - Delta Air Lines # 2863
  - New York John F. Kennedy Intl (JFK) to Los Angeles International (LAX)
  - Departure: (JFK): June 7, 11:00 AM EDT (morning)
  - Arrival: (LAX): June 7, 2:14 PM PDT (afternoon)
  - Class: Economy Seat: 37C

Tuesday 6/8
- Lunch with Stan Lee @ 12:30 PM
- Meeting at POW Entertainment office @ 3 PM

Thursday 6/10
- IFTA Executive Committee meeting @ 9 AM
- Leave for NYC

Tuesday 6/15
- Meeting w/ Alan Lorenzo @ 10 AM
- Meeting w/ Stephen Margolis @ 1 PM

Wednesday 6/16
- Creative meeting with Sara Antill to discuss *Sell Your Own Damn Movie!* @ 6 PM

Friday 6/18
- Florida SuperCon in Miami!

Wednesday 6/23
- Filming scene for *Donovan and the Vast Ancient Conspiracy*

Thursday 6/24
- IFTA Board of Directors meeting @ 4 PM
- Shooting segment for Joe Dante's *Trailers From Hell* @ 8 PM
- Interview for Stream.tv

Friday 6/25
- Film cameo in *Stripperland*, Portland, OR

July 2010

Sunday 7/4
- Pregame w/ Joey Chestnut before hot dog eating contest, 7 AM
- Figure out a way to get Kobayashi arrested
- Bet $500 on Joey Chestnut to win!

Thursday 7/8
- Arrive in Los Angeles
- IFTA Executive Committee meeting @ 9 AM
- Radio appearance on "Grand Theft Audio" @ 6:15 PM

Sunday 7/11
- Shoot w/ Aaron Vnuk for *Demon of Lataran*, Connecticut (script attached in email)

Wednesday 7/14
- Interview w/ Calum Waddell for 42nd St. documentary

Thursday 7/15
- Arrive in Germany for *Attack of the Tromaggot* screenings (bring Toxie mask and DVDs)

Thursday 7/22–Sunday 7/25
- Arrive in San Diego for Comic-Con!
- Judge in Comic-Con Film Festival; they will provide hotel and transportation

Saturday 7/31
- Film shoot in Connecticut, contact Sam Bahre

August 2010

Saturday 8/21
- Monster Mania convention, Cherry Hill, NJ

Friday 8/27–Sunday 8/29
- Arrive in Toronto for Rue Morgue Festival of Fear
- Find David Cronenberg for an interview/autograph!

September 2010

Wednesday 9/1
- Doctor's appointment @ 11 AM (ask about Botox options)

Friday 9/3–Monday 9/6
- Arrive in Atlanta for DragonCon!

Friday 9/10–Sunday 9/12
- Arrive in Los Angeles for Horror Film Boot Camp

Friday 9/17
- Arrive in Tampa, FL, for Black Box Film Festival
- Master class @ 10 AM
- Film screening (TBD) followed by Q&A @ 7 PM

Saturday 9/18
- Master class @ 10 AM
- Film screening (TBD) followed by Q&A @ 7 PM

Thursday 9/23
- Arrive in Los Angeles
- IFTA Member meeting @ 12 PM

Friday 9/24
- Fly from Los Angeles to Indiana

- B Movie Celebration, contact Bill Devers
- Master class @ 5 PM

Wednesday 9/29
- Master class, LaGuardia Community College @ 6 PM
- *Toxic Avenger* screening @ 8 PM
- Ask about veterinary technician classes

October 2010

Friday 10/1
- Cinema Wasteland, Cleveland, OH

Sunday 10/3–Saturday 10/9
- LK in Venice

Sunday 10/10
- 10/10/10 Party @ 10 PM on 10th Avenue Manhole Club
- *Just the Ten of Us* marathon in José's hotel room

Friday 10/15–Monday 10/25
- Armageddon Expo, Australia and New Zealand
- Film shot-by-shot remake of *Lord of the Rings*, but with koalas. This will be YouTube gold!

Thursday 10/28
- Arrive in Seattle, WA, for ZomBCon
- Travel and hotel provided

Sunday 10/31
- Buy a Snookie poof wig
- Lead the Village Halloween parade

November 2010

- Wednesday 11/10
- Arrive in Los Angeles
- IFTA Member meeting, 12 PM

Monday 11/15
- Interview w/ Bradley Creanzo, possible Troma intern @ 1 PM

Tuesday 11/16
- Meeting w/ Sara Antill @ 6 PM, *Sell Your Own Damn Movie!*

Thursday 11/18
- Arrive in Colorado
- Lunch w/ Richard (Starz Media) @ 12:30 PM in Castle Pines
- Dinner/screening/Q&A at UCCS @ 6 PM
- *Class of Nuke 'Em High* @ 12 AM

Friday 11/19
- Lunch/master class @ 12 PM, UCCS
- Interview on Clear Channel's "Uncle Nasty" Show @ 4 PM

Saturday 11/20

- Colorado Tromapalooza, contact Brett Marottoli

Thursday 11/25

- Thanksgiving Day!
- Demand that Troma employees come into work early so as to avoid parade traffic

December 2010

Thursday 12/2

- Arrive in Los Angeles
- IFTA Board meeting @ 10 AM

Tuesday 12/7–Saturday 12/11

- Arrive in Spain for Weekend of Horror Party Festival
- Participate in Troma sections
- Hotel and travel provided

Monday 12/13

- Film shoot w/ Pete Guzzo

Thursday 12/16

- Arrive in Winnipeg, Manitoba
- *Father's Day* shoot

Sunday 12/26

- Boxing Day (see if LaGuardia Community College offers boxing classes)

JAMES GUNN TALKS SOCIAL NETWORKING WITH LLOYD ON THE SET OF *SUPER*

James Gunn is the incredibly successful writer of the Scooby Doo *movies and the 2004* Dawn of the Dead *remake, as well as the fantastically creative writer/director of* Slither. *However, he got his start as the incredibly fantastic, yet shit-upon, assistant to Lloyd Kaufman and co-writer of* Tromeo and Juliet *in 1995. Among all of his recent accomplishments, such as writing and directing the sure-to-be-a-hit-by-the-time-this-book-comes-out film* Super, *he, unfortunately, is probably best known among Troma audiences as one of the few men who has ejaculated on Lloyd's desk, other than Lloyd himself.*

LLOYD: So how has what you, as a filmmaker, can do to sell your own damn movie changed since you and I did Troma's *Tromeo and Juliet* together in 1997.

JAMES: I think things are much more accessible today. When I lived in New York in 1995 and was making *Tromeo and Juliet* with you, I was very interested in alternative cinema. I would travel around the city going to all theses weird video stores, getting movies that were very difficult to get a hold of. Old films, HK action films, foreign films, and I really reveled in the discovery of those things. Today people don't need to do that. Because you just basically put the search into your computer and you buy it from Amazon or eBay or a private site. So it's much easier to give people access to your films than it used to be. The problem is today, as back then, most people still want what everyone wants, which is the mainstream Hollywood films. So while films like Troma movies are more accessible online, they're less accessible because it's harder to get them into theaters. Theaters only play 5 or 6 films at a time today, and even in 1995 theaters played a lot more films than they do today. So that's not so great.

LLOYD: So what do you, James Gunn? During the time of *Tromeo and Juliet* or *The Specials* the director could have a PR agent maybe, but you couldn't really do much like what you do now to support your films.

JAMES: I think I do a lot to support my films in terms of social networking online. I have a network of, um, "fans," for lack of a better word. On Twitter I have 24,000 followers right now. On Myspace I have another 30,000 people, and on Facebook I have another 10,000 to 15,000 people.

LLOYD: Is Myspace still useful to you? Because each new assistant I get tells me that Myspace is dead, but I think it's just because they don't want to check it for me.

JAMES: Myspace can still be useful, but Myspace is dropping rapidly and I imagine that within a certain amount of time it will be irrelevant. It has been overtaken by Facebook and Twitter. About a month ago Facebook was the #1 website on the Internet, ahead of Google, which is the first time that has happened in years. So Facebook and Twitter are very popular and very successful at doing what they want to do, and Myspace is dropping rapidly. Every week it goes down. But still, I think it's the 22nd biggest website as of today, and people forget that you can still get a lot of action there.

LLOYD: I certainly get a lot of action there.

JAMES: Yeah, that's not the type of action that I really mean. Ultimately, I get most of my traffic on my website, and a lot of traffic is driven to my website from Myspace, Twitter, and from Facebook.

LLOYD: Can you give us some advice how to be a successful Facebooker or Twitterer? You know, I mention you in my book as an exemplary twatter.

JAMES: Do you mean tweeter?

LLOYD: Sure, yes, that too! But about the advice…

JAMES: Well, I think you need to have a feel for it. I think you need to enjoy social networking. You need to enjoy interacting with people. People really like when filmmakers want to talk with them and answer their questions personally. Formspring is actually another site that's very useful. People can go and ask questions, and you can answer whatever questions you want to answer. Just go to Formspring and set up an account and then people ask you questions anonymously or not anonymously and then you answer them. People ask me everything from when was the last time I had sex with my girlfriend, to what type of cameras do I like to use on a movie, to how big is my penis. That one I've gotten asked a lot more than the camera one, actually. To be quite frank, it's a little bit above average.

LLOYD: Doesn't it take a lot of time to have so many of these networking websites? Wouldn't it be better to put all your energy into just one of these?

JAMES: No, because the truth is that my Twitter and my Facebook are essentially the same thing. Basically I have my website and then I post links to my website on Twitter and Facebook. On the website I talk about making my movie *Super* and what happened that day on set and what are the struggles I'm going through in editing and all that sort of thing. And I'll post weird videos people send me off YouTube and you'll have strange stuff like that. My brother will post his 100 favorite hip-hop songs. There's just a lot of different info. And I get up to 15,000 to 20,000 hits a day. It does pretty well.

LLOYD: How does *Super* benefit from this? I mean, how do you promote *Super* without being too heavy handed?

JAMES: I enjoy social networking so, for instance, on Twitter I make a lot of jokes. So when people sign up for my Twitter account they get a lot of jokes and they get a lot of links to weird things, and that is why they follow me. Then as an added benefit for me, when I am pimping something out, whether it be the release of the new *Tromeo and Juliet* Blu-ray which I'm about to pimp out, or when *Super* is in theaters and I'm like, "Hey guys, please spread the word and go see *Super*," people give me that because I'm not on there *just* doing that. If I was only doing that, I'd probably have a lot less followers. But I think it's better because I provide other types of content on Twitter rather than just selling myself.

I mean, Facebook is alarming—it is hugely successful. I have more than 25,000 followers on Twitter, so if I post a link, that's more than 25,000 people who see that link, which is pretty interesting. I went to the baseball game the other day at Giants stadium and the place was packed and there were less than 24,000 people there and I thought, "Holy shit, every time I post that I'm taking a shit, there are this many people reading about it." But then someone like Rainn Wilson, the star of *Super*, has 2 million followers on Twitter! For us, on *Super* alone, we have Rainn Wilson, and Nathan Fillion who has half a million followers. So right away our movie opens up and we have two guys that have a combined Twitter following of about 4 million people, plus another million from the other people involved, so we have a few million people to whom we can tweet, "Hey, get the word out and help us promote *Super*!" And that is why I really think that Twitter is by far the most useful of all the sites because the way things spread is like wildfire. Now if nobody has any interest in your movie it doesn't help that much, but if people do have interest then right away that's a lot of people that have knowledge of your movie.

There was a big drop from *Iron Man* to *Iron Man 2,* and I think one of the reasons is just Twitter. I mean the word just went out instantly that *Iron Man 2* wasn't as good as *Iron Man*. And nobody went to see it. I mean, not *nobody* went to see it, but I mean it dropped, when a lot of times movies like that make more money than the first one. But that's the power of "word of mouth." I personally think it's a good thing. I hope word of mouth starts making a difference again in films like it used to, as opposed to having all these movies that come and make 50% of the opening weekend box office just because of the idea. People go and they're swindled and they don't like it.

LLOYD: So let's say you're not James Gunn with 5 or 6 million people out there that are possible supporters. You're the no-budget guy who made *Bloodbath in the House of Knives*. What do you do with a social network?

JAMES: Well, I think that a lot of the same things apply. I think if you did *Bloodbath in the House of Knives*, you'd want to make sure that you're on Twitter, make sure that you're on Facebook, make sure that you are able to post stuff about your movies. That way if people are interested, they'll know about it, but also perhaps think about providing other content. Find cool links out there. People love weird shit! Re-tweet people! If you re-tweet people, they are more likely to follow you and read what you have to say. You can follow or re-tweet people like me. The other thing is, if you follow people back, that gives you a lot more followers. I don't follow back that many people. I think currently I follow about 100 people, and that's a lot more than I used to follow. I've been on Twitter for over 2 years, and I think that when I first started I followed 30 people for over a year. But I decided to be a little bit looser and follow a few more people. But if you follow people then a lot of people will follow you back. So a lot of people that you see that have 125,000 followers on Twitter are people who aren't necessarily well-known, but they're pretty good Twitterers and they're also possibly following 125,000 people as well as being followed by that many people. But you have to provide them with some reason for them to hang out. You've got to entertain them.

LLOYD: How about the campaign, the advertising, posters, trailers, things like that. What do you advise on that? One thing I learned two or three times when we were starting out was that distributors are idiots.

JAMES: Yeah, well, I can say that from *Slither* because *Slither* was a difficult sell as a movie. It was a horror comedy, and there was a lot of talk about how the movie should be sold. Quite honestly, I just kind of stepped back from it. I had an idea of how it should be sold, but who knows if that would have worked any better than the way Universal wanted to sell it. But I did have an idea about it and I wish that I would have maybe been a little more controlling and stronger about the way we were selling the film.

There's a lot of conversation about how to go about selling *Super*. One way to go is the big festival circuit. We don't have a U.S. distributor yet.[29] So we need a distributor, and what's the best way to do that? Is it better to go to the Toronto Film Festival in September and those other, bigger, classier festivals? Because there is an element to the movie that is like an art film and that might help us. The other way is that we can show the movie at Sundance in January. If we go to Sundance, it can be a great thing and we can show it to distributors and say, "Hey, this thing is going to Sundance." And we can do either the midnight screenings there or be in competition or whatever we want to do. So if we go to Sundance, it's something we have in our pocket when we're showing it to distributors. But we're not actually selling it at the festival. Does that make sense?

LLOYD: Absolutely not.

JAMES: So, we either sell the movie at a festival, or we sell the movie on its own because it has the prestige of going to a festival.

LLOYD: Ah, yes. I see. And the cast will be a major part of selling the film.

JAMES: Yes, we have the advantage of having very famous people in a very low-budget movie. I didn't think anyone else was going to put up with this stuff, but immediately Ellen Page read the script and wanted to do it because

---

[29]IFC became the U.S. distributor of *Super*.

she was attracted to the character, and I couldn't believe it. Then Liv Tyler read it, and she was, like, the biggest star we could hope for, and she wanted to do it. Then Kevin Bacon read it and he wanted to do it. It was astounding to me! I was really surprised. And then filling in the smaller roles, Michael Rooker, who had been in *Slither*, flew in on his own dime to come and act in the movie. Gregg Henry and Nathan Fillion who were also in *Slither* came out in support of me, and that makes a big, big difference. And, of course, Lloyd Kaufman came out in support of me. That's what's going to put us over the top.

LLOYD: Exactly, those 4000 Twitterers.

JAMES: Exactly!

LLOYD: Any other thoughts about selling?

JAMES: I'm a big believer in really truly committing yourself to a process. And if you're writing a screenplay or making a movie, I say just finish what you start. Just finish it. People get caught up in their own judgments about things, and they get caught up in obstacles along the way, but if you commit yourself to finishing something and finishing becomes the most important part, then that's really the first, and most important, step to success. Maybe the first thing you finish isn't going be that incredibly successful, maybe the second thing isn't, maybe the third thing isn't. But eventually you're going to get to something amazingly successful and incredible. So finish what you do. And I think in the same way, when you finish your movie, you have to commit yourself as if it's a job to sell that movie and get it out there. You may not be successful, but you have to know that you fully committed yourself to doing it and that you went about doing it as well as you possibly could.

You just have to go out there and put your ass on the line and make mistakes. I think people need to be willing to make mistakes and, to be really successful, they need to be willing to look foolish. Lloyd is a great example of that.

LLOYD: Thank you, James. I think we have enough.

JON REISS ON THE NEW CREW POSITION OF "PMD"

Rather than compete with the big, penis-waving 3D multibajillion dollar Smurf *movies from James Cameron, filmmaker Jon Reiss has found a way to be true his own art and also stay on the ball to make a living out of it. Reiss's film* Bomb It *was an official selection at the Tribeca Film Festival, and his book,* Think Outside the Box Office, *consistently sells way better on Amazon than Lloyd's books.*

FIGURE 5.7 *Jonathan Reiss, the award-winning director of extremely profitable and self-distributed* Bomb It.

LLOYD: Greetings from Tromaville! We're here at the Word Trade Center and there's a big stink in the air. Apparently something happened here in 2001 and these poor people want to build a mosque two blocks away and there's a huge stink about it. Apparently they don't have a right to religious freedom anymore. People won't let the Islam religion exist, which is an interesting statement since Thomas Jefferson seemed to think it was a good idea. Speaking of freedom, we are lacking in many freedoms of information in our country and that is why it is very hard for us to sell our own damn movie. The pathways to information are controlled by devil-worshiping international media conglomerates. Luckily, Jon Reiss is showing the way. He had a masterpiece called *Bomb It* and he has really forged a new path. Now Jon, in your writings, such as your wonderful article in *Movie Maker*, you talk about the PMD. Tell us what you mean by that. It sounds like a new sort of profession.

JON: The PMD is the producer of marketing and distribution. It's a recognition that there used to be people that would take films and connect them to people. Those people were called distributors. There aren't so many anymore, and now there are many more films that are created by filmmakers than could be handled by any kind of distribution apparatus. So it's a recognition that filmmakers need to now be responsible for distributing their films and connecting their films to an audience. It's a further recognition that this process needs to be integrated into the filmmaking process as well. And this person who is the PMD should start at the very beginning of production to help build that audience, because it takes a long time to build an audience and connect with an audience. So it's essentially a new crew position—someone who is responsible for that other half of filmmaking. One half of filmmaking is making the film; the other half is connecting that film to an audience. The producer of marketing and distribution is the person who is in charge of that half of the filmmaking process. I'm actually starting up a PMD academy this fall. There are already people in the world calling themselves PMDs, and in Australia they're going to start training people to be PMDs. In one city they're going to hire one PMD to supervise all the independent films being made there. There's one guy in Holland who's actually already working as a PMD on a film and calling himself that.

The reason I gave the position a title is whenever you have work on a set or on a film, that work is not going to get done unless you assign a person to do it. The best way to assign a person to do that work is by giving it a title. Because there's a title for the position, people will train for it and when you are starting a film you can put out a call for it just like you would for an editor or DP or any other crew position. The idea is that in two to five years you'd get as many résumés for PMD as you would for a DP.

LLOYD: Let me ask you about *Bomb It*. How did you get it into the Tribeca Film Festival? What did you have to do? Because it seems like Tribeca is pretty elitist. My wife would not appreciate me saying that, but would you agree?

JON: It does take a little bit of strategy and planning getting films into premier film festivals. Essentially with *Bomb It* we were initially following the old path of what I call the "festival acquisition system," which is where you make a film, you take it to a major sales festival, and you get a lot of excitement on the film because you hire a publicist. You actually spend money marketing your film at the festival with the hope that a distributor's going buy it and give you a chunk of change and take it off your hands and release your movie and you can go and live happily ever after and make your next film. That system doesn't exist for 95% to 99.9% of filmmakers anymore. So filmmakers have to try to figure out for themselves how to release their film. Having your film in even a major film festival, even the top film festivals, is not a guarantee for distribution. I would say the last 2 years at Sundance and even Toronto there were maybe 4 films that were sold, out of 150, for any kind of deal that makes financial sense. Then I think maybe 10 more films at Sundance this year made a chunk of money, but [did not get] all of their money back. And when you think of 5000 to 7000 feature films being made in North America alone, and maybe 10 to 20 get bought by distributors, that's a heck of a lot of films not getting traditional distribution.

A few years ago, there weren't so many films being made. There also used to be a lot more distributors and they were spending a lot more money. So if you were at Sundance or Cannes or Toronto, or even Tribeca, you had a pretty decent chance of recouping at least most of your money from a sale. And then at film festivals like Tribeca and the L.A. Film Festival, if you made a really good film and really worked hard at it, you had a good chance of making a sale. But that changed in 2007. There was a big global shift. A lot of distributors went out of business and others said, "Why are we paying money for all these films that don't make us so much money?"

LLOYD: What do you think is the biggest mistake that an independent first-time filmmaker can make once he/she/it has completed his/her/its project?

JON: I think the biggest mistake is to wait until you've finished the project to start marketing and developing an audience. I would say to anyone starting a film or conceptualizing a film that you need to start developing your audience from the inception of the project. And frankly, you should be developing a long-term audience. I would look at Cory McAbee[30] as an example. He is someone who has moved to the new model where you create a brand for yourself as a filmmaker and you connect your films as a filmmaker and you create a lifelong audience for yourself as a filmmaker. So if you're starting off with your first film, start doing that from the first film at the very beginning so you're not at the end of the film and saying, "Oh no, how do I distribute this film?" Then you have to spend that much more time engaging your audience.

With *Bomb It*, we didn't think that we were going to have to rely on ourselves to distribute the film. We were deluded into thinking, like most filmmakers, that someone else was going to come along and distribute the film. But still, we were developing audiences. I guess instinctively we knew that if you go through this process, a distributor is that much more likely to pick you up since you've already built an audience. It was 2004, so our audience lived in Myspace at the time. We had 4000 friends on Myspace by the time Tribeca hit. We also developed a very interactive blog where we engaged our audience. By

[30] Cory McAbee wrote and directed short films including *The Ketchup and Mustard Man* and *The Man on the Moon.* As a means of self-distribution, McAbee developed a live musical performance that incorporated his short films. The show was called "The Billy Nayer Chronicles." It became one of Sundance Film Festival's first multimedia events.

the time we hit Tribeca, we had 10,000 unique visitors a month with 30,000 visits—that's about half a million hits. When we were in release, we kept building, and we doubled that.

The key was that we started at the very beginning. We started developing our audience while we were shooting. The first thing you have to do is figure out who your audience is, and you have to be very specific about that. We knew our audience was graffiti artists and street artists and fans of graffiti artists and street artists. We started reaching out to them on Myspace. We had all the people we had interviewed and met connect with us on our Myspace. We connected all their email addresses. We did something on our website where we mailed people stickers for their email address. Because no one is just going to give you their email address just because you say, "Give me your email address." You have to give them something in exchange. So we spent $500 on postage sending stickers to everyone who requested a sticker and we got 2000 people on our email list before we even finished the film. Those are the main things we did during development. Then we blogged, not only about the film but about graffiti and street art in general so that we became a hub for information on graffiti and street art. It wasn't just about the film.

I think it's really important for filmmakers to think about branding themselves, if it's appropriate. And I always qualify it when I say that because I think that not every method is for every filmmaker. But if it makes sense to you, I think it's smart to think of yourself as a brand and where you fit in the media landscape. Lloyd certainly has a very strong brand, and he's done that naturally, much like Cory McAbee. When I interviewed Cory about this he said, "Well, I didn't set out to be a brand. It just seemed to make sense to unify my projects."

FIGURE 5.8 Bomb It *production still.*

As far as branding myself, I actually have two brands. One is Subversive Filmmaker Guy. Most of the time I brand myself as the alternative distribution and marketing guy for independent filmmakers. I do that through my website, my blog, my Twitter, and Facebook, et cetera, and I speak with a unified voice. The key thing is, and we're getting very nitty-gritty, that you want your personal sites to be in your own voice, while your project sites can be the voices/styles of multiple people. But with your own site and your own branding, you need to keep it authentic. Provide some unifying voice in connection with your fan base. And use a good email list.

The other thing is to realize that people don't just want to hear about your film. They want to hear about more things than about your film and filmmaking and they want to know about you as a person. In terms of branding, most filmmakers that you admire, like Lloyd, or Quentin Tarantino, or Robert Rodriguez, or Woody Allen, or David Cronenberg, or Martin Scorsese—if you think about them, they're all brands. And Lloyd has such a direct relationship with his fan base. Most filmmakers don't have a direct relationship with their fan base.

LLOYD: I am a fan of having direct relations with my fan base. Especially my young, hairless, male fan base. Can you talk a little about your feeling about live audiences, as in theatrical distribution?

JON: I'm a big fan of live audiences and theatrical distribution, so in my book I conceptualize film rights into three categories. There are all these film rights that have been developed by the studios to service how they distribute films, but don't work or make sense from a filmmaker's perspective. So they have theatrical, semitheatrical, nontheatrical, DVD, cable, VOD, conventional digital, merchandise, et cetera, and all these different categories are treated differently.

For me, there are three main categories. I call the first Live Event Theatrical, which emphasizes the live audience engagement aspects of theatrical screenings. They don't only have to be in conventional theaters, though. You can do them in a cemetery, you can do them in a parking lot, you can do them in a church, you can even do them in someone's house. Just so long as they involve other people and you show the film in the manner the filmmaker intended, beginning to end in the dark.

The second major category is merchandise, of which DVDs are one aspect, but I encourage filmmakers to think of many different kinds of merchandise. You can go to the *Bomb It* store (*www.bombit-themovie.com*) to see examples of different kinds of filmmaker merchandise you can create for your audiences.

The third category is digital, which to me includes television, VOD, and all conventional digital. The reason I put those together is that they're now all competing in the same landscape. They're competing for the same rights, and you have to be very careful with your contracts and how you assign those rights. Each of those entities will want all those rights, and you have to be very cautious and aware of that—they essentially treat themselves as competitors and ultimately they all treat themselves as operating in the same rights category. At one time, these were all separate, but they're all now blending.

Digital rights are so complicated and the contracts are so complicated—I call them a minefield, and I recommend you get a "bombsquad," which is someone who is really versed in digital rights, to help your negotiate the terrain. My film *Bomb It* has been used as a case study because the rights are so complicated. We divided them up in such fine ways we created a rights grid for them. I have a DVD distributor and a VOD distributor. I have a television sales agent that handles domestic and foreign who does not have my VOD rights or my digital rights. I have a separate digital aggregator. I have several different people handling various aspects of my digital rights. I have *Bomb It* streaming online and with Babelgum, an online web channel, and those are different rights. They have some of my rights, New Video has some of my rights—different companies have different aspects of my digital rights.

The other thing is that you can do a lot of your digital rights yourself now. You just have to be very careful as far as whose toes you might be stepping on in how you allocate these digital rights. For instance, when I was doing my Babelgum deal, I almost lost my Canadian television deal because my Canadian TV distributor had sold my streaming rights to the Canadian broadcaster, but he didn't have the rights to do that, while my streaming rights were exclusive to Babelgum because they paid me a fee for that. That's just a clear example of where this can get very slippery very fast. Then again, I've been lucky. We've had a lot of television sales for the film, and those are also dwindling. But because they're dwindling, there are actually more tiny deals around with very small amounts of money. There are TV stations still buying product, but for very small sums of money. But when you add all those up it becomes a decent chunk of change.

LLOYD: So for DVD, do you have a company that does that?

JON: I advocate working with a DVD distributor if you can get a deal that makes sense and if they have a history of treating filmmakers right. It's great to work with them and they can get your film into more stores than you as an individual filmmaker can. I also feel you should reserve the right to sell your own film from your own website and most good DVD distributors will allow you to do this. That way you can connect with your audience and sell through a distributor.

For other filmmakers, you may want to sell your film only from your website. You may have fewer sales because of that, but for every sale, you have a direct connection with that fan. It just depends on what your goals are, and one of the first things you should do is determine what your goals are. My primary goal was to recoup my money for my investor. Having a DVD distributor allows me to sell more DVDs and I make more money for my investor. If my goal was only to have that relationship with my ongoing fan base, I would probably make a little less money, but I would be building a greater audience for the future.

LLOYD: If you could go back in time, is there something you would have changed or some other path you would have taken with *Bomb It*?

JON: If I had known what I know now, New York would have been my theatrical release. I would have released my film at Tribeca, and I would have sold DVDs there. I would have planned to have the film in theaters right after Tribeca. I would have arranged to have my film with a DVD distributor and online at that time. Or I would have just released it and sold it myself, then gotten a DVD distributor, which I feel is possible.

In full retrospect I would have had a PMD on board. They would have been doing all this work in advance, they would have already been connecting with theaters. At that time, in 2007, it would have been moderately possible. With the way things are now I believe it would be more possible. But in order for you to do what I'm saying and release your film at a festival, you have to be very savvy and very, very prepared. I had already released two feature films, so I felt like I could have done that myself. For another filmmaker with no experience, it might have been a little tougher. At Tribeca, we had 4000 people come out, and we turned away 200 people per screening. We had a huge amount of audience and a huge amount of buzz there, so it would have been smart for us to capitalize on that.

LLOYD: What were your expenses at Tribeca, and have you been able to make a profit?

JON: To open a film in New York with a publicist traditionally is expensive—about $10,000. Then we did street teaming, and we basically treated it like a theatrical release. We spent money for me and the producers to travel from L.A., street teaming, parties, promotions, et cetera. We spent what any other small independent would spend opening a film theatrically in New York. In retrospect, I would not have spent that much money opening my film at Tribeca, even if I wasn't going to release my film then.

Bomb It cost us $300,000. I know we're better off now, though, than we would be had we just been sitting around waiting for a distributor and not done our theatrical, because our DVD sales were helped. We wouldn't be in the position we are now had we not done what we did. The film is coming out on VOD in November, three years after the release, on Time Warner, Comcast—traditional mainstream VOD. So we're still making money. I'm going to be penning my investor a check when I get home, not a huge check, but a decent check.

He just had a kid two years ago, so he's going to get all his money back by, I believe, the time the kid goes to college. It's a slow process and you need your investors to be patient, but had I known then what I know now, I probably would have spent half the amount money I did on the film. I would have way cut down on the budget, and it would have been easier to pay my investor back. I do recommend spending less money on your film now because it is difficult to recoup. It's not like people are walking up to you and handing you checks. This process is a lot of work. That's why I created that category of PMD, so that there is someone on board who's going do this work and who's responsible for this work.

LLOYD: Any last bit of advice you'd like to impart?

JON: The thing I'd like to say is that every film is different. The problem with the previous studio model is that they treated almost every film the same. Every film is different—it has a different audience and the filmmakers have different goals. So what you need to do is create a distribution strategy that is unique to your film and works for your film and to start that as soon as possible.

Chapter six

Film Festival Survival Guide, Part 6A, Section B17

You're a champ!

You've directed your own damn movie.™ You've produced your own damn movie.™ You've sound edited your own damn movie.™ You've even color corrected your own damn movie!™ You've shown your own damn movie to your mother and your frenemies so many times that they're stopped vomiting every time that one super gross thing happens. You know which part I'm talking about.[1]

So, we're done now, right?

---

[1] *Show Your Own Damn Movie to Your Mother and Frenemies So Many Times That They Stop Vomiting Every Time That One Super Gross Thing Happens!* will be published by Focal Press in March, 2017!*

   *NOTE FROM ELINOR: No, it will not.

Not![2]

But how do you go from showing your film to your friends and family to showing it to hundreds or thousands (or millions!) of people? Well, you could call up Steven Spielberg and ask him to take a look at your movie. I'm sure he loves getting those types of calls.[3] But if for some reason you can't get through to Spielberg or Tarantino, there is another way.

FILM FESTIVALS!

Festivals are a great way to get your movie out there in front of the public, also known as people who, unlike your mother and coworkers, have no reason to kiss your ass. And whether you end up getting a once-in-a-lifetime distribution deal or not, just seeing your film with an audience is one hell of an ego boost. Trust me, you'll love it!

FESTIVAL BREAKDOWN, WHICH IS EXACTLY WHAT I EXPERIENCE EVERY YEAR IN CANNES

When most of us think of film festivals, we picture Cannes and Sundance, with maybe a little splash of Tribeca or Venice. We envision them as these giant, magical events that are impossible for the little guy to get into, but if that little guy does somehow break the seal and get in, he's got it made. And that's not entirely wrong. But it's also not entirely right.

Over the past 300 years or so, festivals have become progressively more and more corporate. How else can you explain *Shrek IV*, a movie from a major studio with a $165 million dollar budget, which was both a critical and financial disaster, opening a festival that was supposed to be about undiscovered independent art? Even the Olsen twins, those pillars of free and independent media, had one of their films, *New York Minute*, premiere at Robert De Niro's[4]

---

[2] NOTE FROM LK: Elinor, please be sure this joke is effective by moving this paragraph to the next page. It will be hilarious!*

   *NOTE FROM LAYOUT DEPT: We discussed this "joke" and we think it's lame. We're not doing it.

[3] Actually, Oren Peli, director of *Paranormal Activity*, seems to have done this exact thing, so maybe it's not as farfetched as it sounds.

[4] Robert De Niro is best known for his role in Troma's *The Wedding Party*, available now at *http://buy.tromamovies.com*. BUY TROMA!

Tribeca Film Festival. Scroll through the Tribeca FF's online "vault" for more horrifying corporate offerings.

Don't get me wrong, I don't mean to call out Tribeca alone! After all, my lovely Pattie-Pie is the New York State film commissioner, and she might not like it too much if I focus on Tribeca's flaws.[5] The truth is, all the big, A-list festivals are slowly becoming these corporate mutual masturbation fests. Festivals need sponsors, and studios want their films to make money, so unholy deals are made and the Berlin Film Festival opens with *Sex and the City 2: The Sands of Time*.[6] Just look at Cannes! What, nobody knows who Woody Allen is? Allen is a genius, and I hope to someday become his next teenage Asian bride, but do his films really need a spot in a major festival? Shouldn't those precious spots go to films that truly need to be highlighted—films that would otherwise be overlooked?

FIGURE 6.1 *At Cannes Film Festival 2009, all 22 Troma volunteers had to sleep in a one-bedroom apartment. In Troma's defense, however, they really didn't get to do much sleeping. Here, a sleepy Toxie takes a moment to snooze on a nearby pillow.*

[5] Speaking of my lovely wife, in December, 2010 she was honored at the New York Women in Film & Television's Muse Awards. Move over Katharine Hepburn. There's a new Woman of the Year in town!

[6] This did not actually happen, but it could have.

But don't be discouraged. Or, at least, not too discouraged. There is a bright side! Even though you have an incredibly slim shot of getting a film into a festival like Sundance or Cannes, it *does* happen! These festivals do continue to discover good, deserving films and filmmakers. And even better, Sundance and Cannes aren't the only festivals out there! Put "film festivals" into Google and see what comes up.[7] There is absolutely no reason why you should not send your film out to as many film festivals as you can find! By the way, I have used Cannes not just for not selling our films, or for being ignored and insulted. It's also a great 10-day crash course in the current state of world entertainment.

ENTRY FEES

Okay, there actually is one reason why you may not be able to send your film out to every festival in the multiverse. Most festivals charge an entry fee, which can range anywhere from $10 to "money that would be better spent on paying off the credit card that you used to buy nachos for your film crew." Entry fees are a downer, for sure, but hopefully that money is going toward good promotion and not toward buying the festival staff nachos. There are plenty of ways to raise some cash for entry fees:

1. Ask your parents
2. Blackmail your parents
3. Ask your dentist or chiropractor
4. Sell cookies (this works especially well for Girl Scouts)
5. Sell real estate
6. Sell your body
7. Invest in a money market account
8. Get a job
9. Stop buying comic books
10. Go to Kickstarter.com and ask for donations[8]
11. Sell copies of your movie to the kids behind the school cafeteria dumpster. It's better than selling them drugs!

---

[7] No, seriously, do that. It might be more helpful to you than reading this chapter. I had a California roll for lunch, and it is also coming up.

[8] Kickstarter.com is a funding platform for creative projects. I recently posted a funding request for my long-awaited shot-by-shot remake of *All the President's Men*, starring my housekeeper, Julio. I have yet to receive any donations, but I have my fingers crossed.

I'm partial to numbers four and six, but you gotta do what you gotta do. Send your film out to as many festivals as you can afford. And remember, TromaDance doesn't charge any entry fees![9]

TROMADANCE

TromaDance is the first film festival wholeheartedly devoted to filmmakers and fans. Unlike every other film festival, TromaDance does not charge filmmakers to submit their films. Entrance to all screenings is free and open to the public. Also, there are no VIP reservations or preferential treatment regarding films, panels, or parties of any kind given. The organizers of TromaDance believe films are meant to be seen, especially when it comes to new filmmakers. Art—in all its forms—is for the people!

TromaDance features a range of films made independently, usually without big stars, big money, and far removed from the Hollywood studio system.

FIGURE 6.2 *Richard Taylor volunteers to help raise money at Tromapalooza for TromaDance and gets bands like Asbestos Tampons to play for free. Here he poses with Lloyd and Katy Perry (background), who follow the golden rule of Tromapalooza: amount of layers worn must be directly proportional to level of attractiveness.*

[9] For more information on TromaDance, read the rest of this book. Or go to *www.tromadance.com*. Or do both. And then, while you're on the Internet, review this book on Amazon!

The official selections of TromaDance have been made with nothing more than passion, courage, integrity, and raw talent.

Everyone at TromaDance is treated as an equal. The elite and the celebrated are treated no better or worse than the experimental filmmaker or the random moviegoer off the street. Admittance to all screenings, panels, parties, and events is strictly on a first come, first served basis. If there are any VIPs at TromaDance, they are the filmmakers whose blood, sweat, and hard work are on the screen.

TromaDance is an opportunity for everyone who's ever picked up a camera to have their work seen without the compromises required by elitist cartel interference. TromaDance is proud to be the first and only film festival of the people, for the people, and by the people.

FRIENDS FESTIVALS WITH BENEFITS (LIKE HAND JOBS DISTRIBUTION)

There are only a few film festivals that you, as a lowly independent filmmaker, have virtually no chance of getting into. There are hundreds of other festivals that you actually have a pretty good chance of getting into, if your movie is complete and has sound in all the places that you wanted there to be sound. On the flip side, there are only a few film festivals where, if your film is accepted, it has a good chance of getting distribution by a major studio. And then there are hundreds of festivals where, even if you get in, you have little to no chance of getting a distribution deal out of it. I'm going to give you a moment to guess the bad news here.

That's right! The small number of festivals where you'll probably get distribution is, unfortunately, also the same number of festivals that you have virtually no chance of getting into. So put aside your dreams of getting a pat on the back from Steven Spielberg as he watches your puppet musical comedy at Sundance, and let's focus on reality. I'm on my fourth vodka of the morning, and Long Island City is not a neighborhood that inspires dreams.

Distribution aside, getting into a smaller festival and getting the opportunity to see your film with an audience is a lot of fun! Maybe that joke that your sisters laughed at out of pity falls flat with an audience of strangers. Maybe your friend laughed when a character spit orange juice through his eye sockets because that exact same thing happened to you once and he remembers how funny it was!

But with an audience that doesn't get the inside joke, it doesn't mean anything. Seeing your movie with an audience can make your movie better, and it can even make you a better filmmaker! So when you make your next movie about a Holocaust survivor who gets eaten by a giant extraterrestrial shark, Steven Spielberg will be the first guy in line to buy a ticket.

OREN PELI'S *PARANORMAL* EXPERIENCES IN FILM DISTRIBUTION

Oren Peli's film Paranormal Activity, *made for $15,000 in 2007, became one of the most profitable movies of all time when it was released in 2009. For this, Lloyd Kaufman hates him. But that's really not Oren's fault.*

It is my belief, and it's naïve to some degree, that if you've got a good enough product, it will get recognized sooner or later. But I know in Hollywood, usually that's not the case. Usually the way to get a movie out there is to bombard the country with advertisements, and it's all about the first weekend box office. That was the exact opposite, though, with *Paranormal Activity.* In fact, we were deliberately holding back the number of screens and showings just to build some word of mouth. So in my particular experience, what worked was actually the antithesis of what usually happens when you're selling or marketing a movie.

FIGURE 6.3 *Oren Peli, director and producer of smash-hit, microbudget, kabillion-dollar-making* Paranormal Activity.

Festivals

When I was doing my initial research, I was really trying to figure out how to sell a movie. One of the first little bits and pieces that I learned was that you had to have a producer's rep. I tried to get a producer's rep, and nobody would talk to me. So then I said, "That's not going to work, let's try festivals." I got a book by Chris Gore called *The Festival Guide* and I read almost the entire book and then researched the festivals myself. While I was doing that I also created a website and trailer for my movie, hoping to get some notice. The website was very plain—it was just the trailer. There were no names of anyone involved or the actors—nothing. That was about April or May, so I knew that I could either wait for Sundance (and it may or may not get in there) or I could try somewhere else. So I decided to try and submit it to some of the larger festivals like Telluride and Toronto. I mean, I figure if I'm going to give up the premiere, I might as well go with someone big. I tried the San Diego Film Festival, which I thought I would have a pretty good chance of getting into, since I'm a local San Diego filmmaker and it was shot in San Diego, but they rejected me. Actually, all the big ones rejected me.

Then I tried Screamfest, here in Hollywood, and got accepted. It's fairly small, and it's just for horror films, but it has a good reputation. It's well-attended by the press and agents, so I figured we could get some good recognition. The problem was, the festival was in October, and I figured that by October, I still wouldn't know whether or not the movie had gotten into Sundance. So by playing Screamfest, I was basically removing any possibility of playing at Sundance. So should I go with the bird in my hand? It was a hard decision and I deliberated with my cast and my partners and we made our choice based on the philosophy of "if it's a good product, it will get recognized." We may not be able to do it the Sundance way like we had envisioned, with a midnight bidding war like *The Blair Witch Project*, but we'll find another route to getting there. Hopefully the movie will play well, and if it doesn't play well, then it wasn't meant to be. But if it does play well, if we get the recognition, if we get the good reviews and stuff like that, hopefully things will keep moving forward. So we decided to go with Screamfest.

Right off the bat, the festival director, Rachel, forced me to let people do reviews before the festival. I didn't want people to do reviews ahead of time because I was afraid the movie would get trashed. I just wanted it to play at the festival and let them review it there. She said, "Don't worry. Send it to the genre review websites like Dread Central and Bloody Disgusting. They're going to love it, don't worry about it." So I did. *LA Weekly* also gave us a good blurb, so we had really good reviews going into the screening. I was standing on street corners handing out postcards I designed. I was standing at Grauman's

Chinese Theatre with all the characters handing out these cards. I even cut a TV spot and aired it here in L.A. Before the screenings, I would go on 20 to 30 bulletin boards and spam. I was trying to get subscribers to my website with the trailer so I could send messages out to everyone at once. And with all that, the screening went great! It was well-attended, and the audience reaction was great. Immediately after the show, Rachel was dragging me into the lobby, showing me the guy that runs Dimension Home Video, and I was getting a bunch of business cards. A week later the movie got a couple of awards and we got a lot of interest—not from big studios but from medium-level distribution companies. I got a call from an agent at CAA, Creative Artists Agency, and he asked me a bunch of questions. Who are you? How did you make this movie? How much did the movie cost? And I was like, "Oh, 15." And he said, "Do you mean $15 million?" I said, "No, $15,000." He said, "Well, then I'd like to meet you and talk to you about CAA."

Somebody once said something along the lines of "When you're a nobody, nobody wants to talk to you." The only way to talk to them is if you have a personal referral, or if you're on the verge of becoming a somebody—then they'll

FIGURE 6.4 *At Cannes Film Festival, the only appropriate place to promote the Troma name is on your backside.*

find you. I had actually called CAA early on at one point when I was looking for a producer's rep and there was nobody to talk to. I said, "I would like to talk to a producer's rep," and they said, "Are you already represented?" I was like, "No." "Do you have a referral?" Another "No." So they said, "I'm afraid there's no one here to talk to."

Big Leagues

When I first met with the agent from CAA, he was talking about only representing me as a director, which I thought was awesome. A few days later I got a call from another agent who wanted to represent the movie and help sell it. So I thought, cool, everything is falling into place. At this time I made the mistake of sending the DVD to a lot of distributors. The problem was, I learned later on, is that you always want to bring the DVD to the person at the highest level because there have been cases where only a mid-level person saw it and rejected it without the top-level people even seeing it. You also want them to see it under optimal conditions, not on their laptop or at their office during the day when they're getting phone calls. Thanks to CAA, we got the movie to higher-level people. And then we got rejected again!

Next, my agent sent a DVD of *Paranormal Activity* to a few producers around town as a director sample, saying, "Here's a director for hire." One of the producers that got the DVD, David Schneider, sent out emails to his partners and other people saying, "This is the next *Blair Witch Project*, and we need to be in business with this guy." He brought it to the attention of his partner, Steven Blum. Steven used to work as the VP of acquisitions at Miramax, and he was one of the people who passed on *Blair Witch* back then. When he saw our movie he said, "I'm not making that mistake again." And this guy is well-connected; he can take the movie directly to heads of studios. So they got in touch with me through my agent, and I met them, I love them, I still work with them.

Even once we started talking to the big guys, what we heard most often was, "We love the movie, really scary, one of the scariest movies we've ever seen, but we don't know how to market it. It looks like home video, and there are no movie stars." Then someone named Ashley Brooks, who is an executive at DreamWorks, saw the movie. Now, DreamWorks isn't in the business of buying movies, they just make their own. So we weren't even thinking of trying to do anything with DreamWorks. But Ashley Brooks saw it and she had done a lot of movies like *Disturbia* and *The Ruins*, so she's the horror person there. She loved the movie and she brought it to the attention of the president at DreamWorks at the time, Adam Goodman. After nagging him for a while, she got him to see the movie. He said the same thing, "We love the movie, but we're not sure we know how to sell it." Then he said, "Maybe we can do a remake."

So now we had an offer for the remake, and I kept rejecting it. But after everyone in town had rejected us, three or four times, eventually everyone told me, "Oren, we know you're stubborn, but we tried really hard, and we couldn't get anything. Directing a movie for DreamWorks is not the worst thing on earth." And they were right. Even if you're directing a remake of your own movie, it's still a movie for Spielberg's studio. A lot of people would kill for an opportunity like that, so I reluctantly took the offer. But at the same time, I didn't want to give up on the original. So what we did was hold a test screening. Adam Goodman was there and Stacy Snider, the CEO of DreamWorks, was there, and when they saw how the movie played in a theater, that was the last time anyone said anything about a remake. After that, Stacy and Adam said, "We're just going to release this one."

However, that summer, DreamWorks and Paramount split. Suddenly, everything was on hold. Adam Goodman and Shelly Brooks, the original executives, moved to Paramount and took the project with them. That meant the movie had to be reintroduced to Paramount and things were in limbo for a long time because Paramount had some really big fish to deal with like *Transformers 2*, *Star Trek*, and *G.I. Joe*, and they were like, "What's this little home video thing from DreamWorks?" It wasn't exactly their top priority. Slowly things started moving, and they said, "Well okay, we'll give it a shot. We won't put too much money into it, and we'll just get it out there." Then about a year later, in June 2009, Adam Goodman was promoted from copresident of production to president of Paramount and that's when things really started moving.

Marketing by Demand

At this point, again, the problem was how do you market this film? And to their credit, Paramount Marketing, who just came from three summer tent poles, had to totally think out of the box. How do you market a $15,000 home video with no known stars? And that's when they came up with the idea of the demand system—that if enough people demand it, it will play in big cities like New York. There is a system that was already being used for bands, at Eventful.com, but this was the first time it was being used for a movie. The movie was getting a lot of buzz, and a lot of people were saying they wanted to see it. So we said, "If you want to see it, demand it!" We had midnight screenings in 13 cities and it was playing in college towns. The idea was to let it screen in these smaller places and college towns where people are very active on Facebook and Twitter and they'll spread the word if they like it. The screenings were packed, and we had really positive word of mouth. Pretty soon we were getting demands from New York, Chicago, L.A., etc., so we decided to show the movie in those markets. We did limited weekend and midnight showings as it started to expand.

And when it got to the point where we had a million people nationwide wanting to see it, Paramount said, "We'll release it wide." It only took three or four days and we got a million hits. So it was nationwide, but on only 150 screens. Then it went to 800, then over 2000 the next week. The peak was 2500.

Challenges

I think the greatest hurdle to a young filmmaker trying to sell their film is just the beginning. Trying to sell *Paranormal Activity*, I didn't know anyone in the industry. I had no contacts, and there was no friend that could give it to producers to get my foot in the door. People ask me if the success of *Paranormal Activity* will change the way people sell films in the future, but I have no idea. Ten years ago *Blair Witch* did the same thing, and nothing changed. Maybe next year, maybe five years from now, maybe sooner, there's going to be some movie that some kid makes in his basement for $5000 and it's going make $200 million. But studios are still going to make sequels and expensive sci-fi movies. Paramount has set up a division to work with microbudget movies. They'll make maybe 10 or 20 $100,000 movies with the hope that a few of them will turn out well.

As for the future, hopefully *Paranormal Activity* reminded studios and filmmakers about the power of the Internet. Big studios have always been advertising on the Internet, but here they took it to the next level in terms of getting the fans engaged. And I think we may see a little more of that. Paramount did it before with *Cloverfield*, and they were really good at getting good hype and releasing little bits of footage specifically for the Internet to keep the audience curious and engaged.

One thing that really, really helped us with the marketing, especially at the beginning, is that the film was supported a lot by fans from horror websites and word of mouth. When we started getting to the mainstream, the DreamWorks/ Steven Spielberg factor really helped us get mainstream notice. So if you're going to get Steven Spielberg to endorse your movie, that's always good.

As you can see from Oren Peli's experience, there are really no rules when it comes to festivals. Peli submitted his fantastic, no-budget movie to a festival that seemed so inconsequential that it wouldn't have even occurred to me to send my magnum ovum, *Poultrygeist: Night of the Chicken Dead* there. Yet he got an amazing distribution deal out of it! As of this writing, *Paranormal Activity 2* has opened in 3111 cinemas—more cinemas than *The Toxic Avenger, Parts I* to *IV* combined!

If you do get into a festival, *go*! Refer to the list of entry fee money-raising ideas if you are strapped for cash. If you do somehow manage to get into an A-list festival, they will probably pay your way. Midlevel festivals may pay the way for a few filmmakers, so it never hurts to ask. And if the festival that your film is accepted to can't afford to fly you out, get in your car and drive! Pick up a hitchhiker for some gas money along the way if you have to. Just having your film in a festival is okay, but you being there is what may make the difference between some mild applause and becoming the next Oren Peli, director of *Paranormal Activity*, or Lloyd Kaufman, director of *Para-abnormal Bodily Functions*!

FIGURE 6.5 *The TromaDance press conference held during AFM 2010. Lloyd was joined by Elton "Count Smokula" John and Neil Armstrong.*

And even if your movie isn't accepted into a film festival, *go anyway*! Going to Cannes or Venice is a crash course in the film industry.[10] Troma has never had a movie in Cannes, yet I attend

---

[10] Much like my books, *Direct Your Own Damn Movie!*, *Produce Your Own Damn Movie!*, and *Cater Your Own Damn Movie!*, coming in November, 2014 from Focal Press.*

*NOTE FROM ELINOR: No, it is not.

every year, usually with a small group of enthusiastic volunteers, and we have somehow developed quite a presence there. And over the years, we made lots of sales because of it. Of course, not all the attention was positive, and some people sort of hated us,[11] but did I mention that we made a lot of sales? Cannes is a small community, and if you go the first year, and you go the second year, and you're out there making a name for yourself, by year 15, everyone will know you! In the meantime, you'll be learning the business.

In 1980, I was at Cannes, obviously without a film in the festival, and after a night of heavy drinking, I stumbled down to the hotel lobby and met Robert Altman, who had also decided to have breakfast at 5 AM after a night of heavy drinking. If a drunken breakfast with the director of *MASH* and *Popeye* doesn't qualify as "learning the business," then I don't know what does.

When you do show up at a festival, do whatever you can to stand out. Now, you can go one of two ways with this. You can either make a spectacle of yourself, or you can wear a suit and look professional. Either way, you'll stand out from the crowd because everyone else is wearing a pretentious black turtleneck or an "I'm oh so cool" untucked open shirt and sunglasses-on-head uniform. At Troma, we try to play a little for both teams, if you know what I mean. We also try to balance making a spectacle of ourselves with looking professional. Michael Herz and I, over the past 38 years, have worked out the semiperfect system in which he wears an Armani suit and looks serious while I wear a powder-blue Men's Warehouse suit with a bowtie and walk the streets with a hideously deformed creature of superhuman size and strength and make a spectacle of myself. This system has worked pretty well for Troma; however, it has not worked very well for me. Maybe I've spent my career being too goofy. No one takes me seriously. People start laughing when I'm not trying to be funny. I knew this for a fact when I tried to inform friends about my mother passing away and they burst out in uncontrollable laughter.

Sigh. Bottom line, wear a suit. If nothing else, you'll be a hit with the gays.

---

[11] See *All the Love You Cannes* for an up-close and personal insight into just how much some people hate us. BUY TROMA!

BUDDY, CANNES YOU SPARE A DIME?[12]

Festivals are fucking intimidating. I've been going to Cannes for 40 years, and I still get a major anxiety attack every time I step off the plane in Nice. When you're in baggage claim, surrounded by all these "look at me, I'm so cool" shop girls from Miramax and DreamWorks, it's hard not to feel intimidated. They're getting picked up by chauffeurs, while I'm on the bus alone. They all seem to have such purpose, while I am just there to remind people that I'm alive. You'll press your face against the glass of the fancy restaurants where they are eating coq au vin and drinking wine on the company credit card, and you'll wander by the swank hotels where they are staying, and you'll feel like shit. But when I start to feel that familiar feeling, I am reminded of what Robert Altman said to me in the hotel lobby 30 years ago. In two years, they'll be gone, and you'll still be here. The fact is, 99% of those snotty bitches have never done a creative thing in their lives. And that's why Robert Altman was so nice to me when we had breakfast—I may not have had a film in the festival, but at least I was a fellow filmmaker. Also, the hand job I gave him under the table may have had something to do with it, too.

WHY WHORES LOVES CANNES

If I can impart anything to you in this slim book, let it be that there is nothing wrong with whoring for your art. So don't be afraid to go out there and whore it up! Oren Peli was out there in front of the L.A. Film Festival putting leaflets on cars. James Nguyen, the director of the absolutely horrendous, yet somehow mildly successful birdsploitation[13] flick, *Birdemic*, was whoring it around Sundance, even without the film being accepted into the festival. In fact, it was while Nguyen was driving a van around Sundance, on which the title of his movie was misspelled, that his spelling faux pas caught the attention of a Troma employee affectionately called

---

[12] NOTE FROM SARA: The original title for this paragraph heading was "I Cannes Has Breakdown?" Lloyd said he didn't get it, though, and made me take it out. I'm slipping it in here because if there is one thing I've learned from Lloyd, it's to never let a good (or very, very bad) pun go to waste.

[13] I started the birdsploitation genre with *Poultrygeist: Night of the Chicken Dead*, but am I the one being interviewed on CBS? No!

Manboy.[14] Manboy was fascinated by this odd piece of filmmaking and brought *Birdemic* to the attention of Michael Herz and me. However, I have a problem with promoting bad art under the guise of "it's so bad that it's funny,"[15] and both Michael and I were too pigheaded to see that we might make some money out of the deal, so we passed on *Birdemic*. Once Manboy had left Troma and moved onto another company, he convinced that company to acquire the film, and the rest is history. *Birdemic* is a minor hit on the midnight movie "let's make fun of this film" circuit, and Manboy gets his face on *The Early Show* for a few seconds. Everyone is happy. Except me, because I spat out my coffee and burned my fucking hand when I saw Manboy on *The Early Show*. But if James Nguyen

FIGURE 6.6 *James Nguyen, producer, director, and writer of the underground hit* Birdemic, *uses the Troma method of marketing at TromaDance Park City perfectly. The only small error he made was misspelling the title of his movie.*

---

[14] Actually, it used to be a term of affection. Then he punched another employee in the face during an argument about Radiohead, and we had to chase him out of Tromaville. Now I use the name very demeaningly.

[15] I feel this lessens the effect when something is actually both bad *and* truly funny, like *Citizen Toxie!* BUY TROMA!

hadn't been out there whoring for his art, then no one would have ever heard of *Birdemic*. The movie is being promoted as the worst film you'll ever see, but I can tell you with 100% certainty that there are worse movies out there. Several are sent to Troma each month. The only difference is that they weren't in the right place at the right time. It's funny, how Oren Peli sent his great movie to a shitty festival, while James Nguyen's shitty movie was discovered when he attended an A-list festival! Yin and yang![16]

While you're out there standing out from the crowd and whoring yourself for your art, don't forget to consider the media. Outfits from NBC, CNN, ABC, and every news network that you can imagine are sent to Cannes and Sundance and so forth every year, hoping for a story or at least a good shot of Angelina Jolie. Once they're on day 4, 5, and 6, and the stories are winding down, they are still under pressure to send home a story. So give them one! Troma got a segment on *20/20* one year in Cannes just because we were interesting. News reporters will love you if you make their lives a little easier! Judd Rose later moved from ABC to CNN and did another story on us. Unfortunately, he's dead now.

It's around noon, now, and I take another sip of vodka.[17] I've been at this writing thing for a few hours, and it's exhausting. And when I say "writing," what I mean of course is that I've been sitting in my office ranting, while my diligent co-writer takes notes. I glance over at Sara now, who appears not to be taking notes but instead scribbling sunflowers with sad faces in her notebook. A few seconds pass, and she must have noticed that I stopped talking, because she sits up a little straighter and clears her throat.

"Uh, what were you saying about Steven Spielberg?"

"I said no one is getting into Cannes."

"Right, right."

"Did you get what I said about the studios and festivals in a mutual masturbation fest?"

---

[16] Not because Nguyen is Chinese. I studied Chinese at Yale.*

  * NOTE FROM EDITOR: James Nguyen is not Chinese.**

  ** NOTE FROM LLOYD: Then take the yin/yang reference out. No one will get it if he's not fucking Chinese!

[17] Because I'm old and will die soon, I decided to step it up a bit and switch to Grey Goose. But Michael Herz hates the French, so I am not allowed to drink Grey Goose in the office. So I switched back to Smirnoff, which is actually just as good.

"Um, yep. Got it." She sighs and goes back to drawing bored flowers.

"This year during the Berlin Film Festival, this big German magazine, *Der Spiegel,* did a huge write-up on Troma."

"Oh really?"

"This is the *Time* magazine of Germany, and they're writing about Troma. And I don't know why! We don't have any distribution in Germany. But it was a great, big article. Five or six pages."

"Wow." She yawns. I don't think she believes me.

"Everyone else is spending money on billboards, and we get the lead article! Here, I'll send it to you."[18]

"Great."

(Twelve minutes pass as I search for the magazine on my BlackBerry. I also take a moment to send my assistant an email reminding him to call me in the morning, and I take a call from Count Smokula. This conversation, however, is not worth repeating here.[19] Finally, I find the article.)

"Ooh, there's a translation," I say. Sara chuckles slightly.

"That would be helpful. I don't speak German."

"I'll send you both."

Please note what I said about no one taking me seriously.

---

[18] Maybe it's because my name is Kaufman—a good German name. Now, where are those showers?

[19] NOTE FROM ELINOR: Neither is this one, really.

TROMADANCE

By Jonathan Lees, TromaDance Program Director

While there are an insufferable number of American festivals ratcheting up entry and attendance fees and fawning over corporate sponsors and celebrity involvement, there are a fistful that still retain the cineaste passion that kick-started the revolution. It wasn't until *South Park* creators, Trey Parker and Matt Stone, were rejected from Sundance for their film *Cannibal! The Musical* that TromaDance, one of the truly independent film festivals, was born. Created in response to that regretful rejection, Lloyd Kaufman started a little rebellion in elitist and unaware Park City, Utah. A festival, run completely by impassioned volunteers, that would represent the truly independent filmmaker—uncensored, provocative, and, above all, free. Free to submit, free to attend. This is TromaDance.

We fight for the right of largely unseen films to gain notice in an atmosphere sullied by publicists, gifting suites, and prepackaged events that are seemingly bent on distracting the audiences from the purpose of such a festival—the films and the filmmakers. Bullied by the Park City Commission, the local police, and security, TromaDance volunteers continued (loudly) to spread the word about our free film festival. Judging from some reactions, you'd think we were handing out HIV.

FIGURE 6.7 *Thousands of beer enthusiasts were enraged after showing up to "TromaDance Film Festival Headquarters Sept. 26-28" and finding out it was not actually the world's most refreshing beer.*

Armed with pasteboards, staple guns, lube, and smiles, we entered the noxious Park City atmosphere with an exuberance that frightened the masses who bore hours in the freezing cold to see Jennifer Lopez's ass walk up a flight of stairs. We screened movies off TV sets in a pizza shop, the dank cellar of a saloon, and even in our condo. To us, any screening, whether on a wall or the ass of a cow, was a success. We are promoting true independents—the kids who make films in their basements after school, grad students tweaking technique, masters experimenting with form. And really, what other festival has the director, programmer, and every volunteer pig piling in a small condo? You think Redford and Gilmore shared a room? Well, maybe when nobody was looking...

As we grew—bigger venues and standing-room-only audiences—and returned, determinedly, each year, our little "mixtapes of madness" had less to do with what was expected from Troma and more to do with carefully curating and presenting programs that defied typical festival models of whorish enslavement to the studios to attract attention. These included films from Giuseppe Andrews, who reinvented the modern comedy, utilizing lo-fi hardware and a trailer park cast of characters, with instant classics like *Dribble* and *Period Piece*, or *Rue Morgue* founder Rodrigo Gudiño, who stunned and

FIGURE 6.8 *Rodrigo Gudiño (front row, right) editor and chief of* Rue Morgue *magazine, and staff try to assassinate Lloyd by pretending to pose with him for a publicity "shot." See artfully disguised gun at top. Unfortunately, the gun misfired and ended up hitting Abe Lincoln.*

intrigued audiences with his first forays into subversive terror, *The Eyes of Edward James* and *The Facts in the Case of Mister Hollow*. These are just a few examples of how very different a festival could be when curated with passion, not profit, in mind. TromaDance's programs represent all the emotional makeup of our audience, an internationally seasoned array of imagery and sound that explores the horrific to the sublime, and all crafted with little to no money—just with the same drive, talent, and passion we all share.

BALANCING PASSION AND REALITY IN THE ECONOMICS OF FILM DISTRIBUTION, OR SELLING YOUR OWN DAMN VIDEO GAME

By Strauss Zelnick

Strauss Zelnick is the cofounder of ZelnickMedia. He also serves as chairman of the board of directors for Take-Two Interactive, the company that owns Rockstar Games, and has developed such family-friendly entertainment as the Grand Theft Auto *series and* BioShock. *He has also been a big shot at BMG Entertainment, 20th Century Fox, and Columbia Pictures. This introduction could go on even longer and list more accomplishments, but to quote Lloyd, "Don't overdo it, goddamn it."*

The motion picture business is a very tough business, as a business. And people are in it because they love it and they find it compelling. I always knew I wanted to be in the entertainment business. And I think if you look at the factors that are highly correlated with success, what really stands out is knowing what you want. I do think lots of other things matter, like working hard and persevering. I think a good education makes an enormous difference and I was fortunate that I had one. The common thread of highly successful people, though, is knowing what they want and staying focused on it. Education matters a lot. Knowing what you want probably matters even more.

As a pure economic model, entertainment is a very challenging business and has been since the 1950s. Executives can make money, and talent can make money, and certain producers and writers can make money, but as an investment proposition it's a tough business.

My advice for someone who has just made their first movie would be to go on the festival circuit. That will get you some publicity. Get into any festivals you can. If you have to fly around and deliver a print yourself, you have to do that. And go to as many markets and festivals, both domestically and internationally, as you can afford to. Go to the best ones you can, where stuff trades, like

Sundance or the American Film Market, or to some of the overseas markets. And if you show up at a market with a film and you have a screening, someone will show up, and if it's good you will get some word of mouth. Any opportunity to show the movie to people and get people to respond to it is a good thing.

There are plenty of people who do it themselves and sell their own movies—actually, hundreds of movies made every year in America and outside of America. Many of them never see the light of day. You still need to distribute that picture. You aren't going to get a lot of people to see it if you just post it on YouTube. An independent motion picture company can provide investment capital and can also provide marketing and distribution services. Can you do it entirely on your own? I can't think of too many examples of success where an independent filmmaker has both created and marketed and distributed a picture entirely by him or herself. I'm sure you could find one, but I can't think of too many. It's much more typical where someone does something like *The Blair Witch Project*, where it was self-financed, and then it was sold to another enterprise, and then that company put more money into it and actually marketed it and distributed it and created a success. That's more typical.

Just remember that selling a film and being rich and famous are not necessarily all the same thing. I think the advice I would give about success is to try to really focus on the kind of life you want and to understand that though it is tempting to think that you could have it all, you probably can't. You have to make choices. Make sure that the things you want are consistent with your skill set. At the end of the day, make sure that the things you are passionate about are the things that you are good at. And that the bull's-eye—what you're passionate about, what you are good at, and the business opportunity is there—that is the bull's-eye you want to hit.

Chapter seven

A Short Chapter about Short Films (and Short People)

I've always been a fan of *Match Game*.[1] If you were born too late to see *Match Game* during its initial run in the 1970s or too busy to catch the reruns on Game Show Network, let me catch you up. Genial host Gene Rayburn[2] would read a short parable of modern life, such as "Blind Betty couldn't see a thing. In fact, last week, she went to Coney Island to get a hot dog and ended up eating a BLANK." The point of the game would be for the young contestant to fill in the blank with the same answer as the celebrity panel, consisting of such notable names as Charles Nelson Reilly and Nipsey Russell. Now, at this point, the young contestant had

---

[1] When I graduated from Yale, I was destitute and I was a contestant on *Match Game* in an attempt to make some fast money. I was eliminated immediately, but Keir Dullea, star of Kubrick's *2001: A Space Odyssey*, was one of the celebrity panelists and he took me to lunch after the show.

[2] Actually, my mother dated Gene Rayburn. If things had gone right, I might have had quiz show host genes.

to make a choice. Would she go with the dirty answer and say "penis," thereby matching most of the dirty-minded celebrities but embarrassing her mother and husband, or would she go with the milquetoast answer, "snake," and lose the game. It was a moral dilemma that kept me watching week to week, I assure you. One Tuesday morning in 1977, Gene Rayburn read a little ditty that has stuck with me ever since. "The theater marquee," he read, "said 'Celebrity Shorts,' but all they had inside were pictures of BLANK."

Now, the first thing that popped into my mind was images of undies, but that's not unusual for me. Of course, the young, nubile contestant agreed with me and stated her answer with the slightly more refined "underwear." But leave it to the unsinkable Brett Somers, that raspy-voiced beauty, to give an answer that brought the house down. "Celebrity shorts?" she said. "All they had inside were pictures of Sammy Davis, Jr. and Mickey Rooney!" The crowd cheered! Rayburn was floored. And I, who was actually wearing nothing but boxer shorts, wept with delight. For the first time, I realized how funny short people were! And I've never forgotten it! If you're ever casting a film and you have a choice between a short person or an average-sized person, go with the short person! Not only is there something inherently funny about their entire presence, but likely their small stature has given them something of

FIGURE 7.1 Broken Poultrygeist Embraces, *a low-budget film coming to a theater near you!*

an inferiority complex over the years, and they will work like a dog for you to prove themselves worthy. I can say with certainty that my own inferiority complex has its roots, not in being an under-respected and underappreciated underground filmmaker, but in being shorter than my childhood friend Oliver Stone. If I'd been a few inches taller, maybe I'd be the one winning Oscars and he'd be the one sitting home at 2 AM watching reruns of *Match Game* and masturbating to Richard Dawson.

And speaking of shorts...

If you went to film school, you probably threw this book away halfway through Chapter 2. But if you did go to film school and you are still reading, you were probably encouraged to make at least one short film in-between learning about deconstruction theory and how to log and capture your professor's wedding video. If you didn't go to film school but you are interested in being a filmmaker, you

FIGURE 7.2 *Penelope Spheeris* (top row, far left) *and Fred "The Hammer" Williamson made inspiring speeches at the TromaDance Press Conference in 2008, to the delight of TromaDance "Spirit of Independence" Award winner Todd Dornfeld* (top left), *Elske McCain, director of* Jessicka Rabid, *Count Smokula, and Kurly Tlapoyawa* (front row, right), *who runs TromaDance New Mexico.*

probably got high with your friends one time and talked about how you were going to make a short film. And oh man, it was gonna be fucking awesome, right? Well, let me stop you there. Short form is both dead and more alive than it's ever been.

A SHORT SUMMARY OF SHORT FILMS

The film industry began with short films. When I began making films in the 1960s, shorts were still being made, and they would play before the feature when you went out to the movies. Hell, sometimes you even got a double feature! At Yale, in the 1960s, plenty of the kids I knew were getting into film school and making shorts. Then they would use these shorts to get grants so they could make features. By the 1980s, shorts were out of the theaters, and advertisements had taken their place. Double feature? Not likely. Incredibly overpriced ticket? Sure thing! However, short films were still being used as calling cards for rich kids from USC. They'd send the short around and get a directing job at Disney.

Fuck, I should have made short films.

I actually never did. I skipped straight to features, but oddly enough, shorts have come back! They're not being watched in a movie theater, but on computers and iPads galore!

Troma has a YouTube channel, where we have hundreds of short pieces that we've put up over the past few years. A short video that we filmed on net neutrality has more than 25,000 views! Of course, that's nothing compared to Lady Gaga's 1 billion views. But when you type "media consolidation" into YouTube, our video pops up before anything from James Carville or Bill Moyers!

Short films may seem to be dead, but how many sweaty fat kids watch YouTube for seven or eight hours at a time? It seems that all you need to do is film a cat doing something funny or a fat person falling off a trampoline and you'll be a star. Even *Two Girls, One Cup* is a short film, albeit not a discreet and tasteful one like the *Human Centipede* trailer.

In retrospect, I wish that we had used this medium more during the distribution of *Poultrygeist: Night of the Chicken Dead*. We could have filmed short webisode-type videos featuring side plots and side characters and then used those to draw attention to the actual movie. But don't let my stupidity stop you! By all means,

FIGURE 7.3 *Long-time Troma fan and volunteer Kyle Elderly shows his appreciation by creating this work of independent art. It is currently hanging in the New York Museum of Modern Art's newly built chicken wing.*

put your special features and (nonboring) deleted scenes up on the Internet when you are promoting your movie!

Until someone figures out a way to make money from short films, using them to bring in viewers is still great. We spent two days in Tromaville filming a short piece on the BP oil spill. We put it up on YouTube, and within a couple of weeks it had 5500 views. Again, that's nothing compared to the video of Justin Bieber imitating a cat,[3] but it's more than most of Sarah Palin's speech videos get. And while reminding 5500 Troma fans that we still exist is rewarding enough in its own right, there is also a possibility that many of those 5500 views come from people who don't have a clue what Troma is. Environmentalists, BP executives, and concerned animal lovers around the world may see our BP oil spill short and be inspired to order *Class of Nuke 'Em High!*[4]

---

[3] I am not making this up.

[4] Which is available now from *http://buy.tromamovies.com*. BUY TROMA!

THE BATTLE FOR THE MIND OF NORTH AMERICA WILL BE FOUGHT IN THE VIDEO ARENA

Lloyd's Interview with David Cronenberg in the Autograph Line at *Rue Morgue*'s Festival of Fear

David Cronenberg is the incredibly talented and successful director of such iconic films as Scanners, The Fly, Crash *(the very good 1996 film, not the shitty 2004 Paul Haggis film), and* A History of Violence. *Lloyd caught up with (accosted) Mr. Cronenberg at* Rue Morgue*'s 2010 Festival of Fear while David was trying to sign autographs for fans. Lloyd had less than four minutes before security arrived and forcibly removed him (Lloyd) from the convention, but he really thinks that he made every second count.*

FIGURE 7.4 *Acclaimed director David Cronenberg.*

LLOYD: David, can you tell the young directors out there what it is that you, as a director, do to sell your own damn movie?

DAVID: You start selling the movie before you make it, and that's something people don't understand. Often, even at the Cannes Film Festival, I'll go there and talk to French film distributors, Finnish distributors, Norwegian distributors, and try to convince them to come into the movie and finance it before we've made it, because that's all part of financing and independent film, and you are basically selling the movie. You're pitching it, selling it, and telling them how you think it could be marketed. If you have some stars in it, you're pitching them as well. So the selling of a movie starts before you get to make it, and if you don't sell it, well you might not get to make it. I just made a movie with Jeremy Thomas, who is a very well-known producer. He has made over 50 movies and won Oscars for *The Last Emperor*. And still, we had a hell of a time getting *A Dangerous Method* made, which is a movie about Freud and Jung starring Keira Knightley and Viggo Mortensen. It was an independent movie—intelligent, articulate, in other words, it's not an easy sell. And we had 11 entities financing that film, some of them government, some of them independent billionaires interested in investing in films. The sell for the film started then. Once you make the film, that doesn't mean anyone is going to see it, because you have to have the interface between you and, you hope, many countries. And that's where the presale counts. If you can get, let's say, a French distributor to put money into your feature, then they have vested interest in promoting it in France. So if it's an independent film, selling the movie begins with financing the movie. It's like a Frankenstein stitching together many financing entities. The old days of going to a U.S. distributor are over for independent filmmakers. It's really quite rough.

LLOYD: What about in your own career? Do you have a cautionary tale about something that was mismarketed?

DAVID: It's interesting, because sometimes it happens in a particular territory. My film *eXistenZ*[5] was distributed by Dimension and Bob Weinstein, and I was very unhappy with what happened to that film in the U.S. It was the #1 film in France, and in the U.S. it did nothing because it was only released in 35 theaters, even though we had a contract that guaranteed a minimum of 600 theaters. But various things happened, negotiations, and for various reasons Dimension was not happy with the film and they didn't want to release it. It was very disappointing, and not at all like their pitch to me where they said they were aggressive and inventive marketers. They had a test screening that they felt didn't go well, and instead of trying to figure out what they could do to sell the film, they were deflated. So you are in the hands of your distributors, and you can only do so much. If you're lucky enough to have any other countries in the world pick you up, you could have the same thing happen again in each country.

You could have one country where your film does great and you realize it was because your distributor understood your movie, understood the audience, and did the right advertising. I can't tell a Japanese distributor what's the best way to sell a movie in Japan. My movie *Spider* is an art film, not a horror film, though it has horrific elements involving schizophrenia. When I went to Japan to promote it, I saw that their poster had an image of the boy from the movie sitting in a chair, and behind him was this giant spider. Now, there are no giant spiders in the movie. "Spider" was the kid's nickname, and I said to them,

[5] Not to be confused with Ron Jeremy's miracle cure for flaccidness, ExtenZe!

"I know that you know your market, and that the Japanese culture and market are very different from North America, but it seems to me that this is going to mislead people into thinking there are giant spiders in this and that it's a horror movie." And they said, "No, don't worry, we know what we're doing." The film totally bombed. Now, I don't know if the film could ever find an audience in Japan or not—maybe it'd never find one—but I was right, and my instinct as an outsider was this is a bad sell for this movie, as it proved to be. So your struggle is not over when you've made the movie. It continues. It continues and continues, and it continues maybe even into the DVD sales.

LLOYD: What about the Internet?

DAVID: Now the Internet is a fascinating entity. At the moment, it's still very hard to make money from Internet distribution of movies, as everyone knows. Everyone is still trying to find the right model, whether it's iTunes and Apple or whatever. But still you must use the Internet to sell your film. I mean, it's been three years since I made my last movie, and everything has changed since then. There's Twitter, there's YouTube, there's viral stuff. If we're going to start a so-called viral campaign for this movie, *A Dangerous Method*, we have to use all those things. We have to use Twitter, we have to use Facebook, and YouTube and all those things. And this is all new to me, because the last time I did a movie, this stuff wasn't around. It's fascinating and it's great, but it is a struggle.

LLOYD: One quick thing, before I let you go. Is there one piece of advice that you, as an incredibly successful director, could tell young people today about the selling of a film?

DAVID: Other than that you have to do it? No. But that might actually come as a shock to them. You have to really understand that once you've finished a movie and you've said, "I did it, I've done it, at last," you're really not finished because you have to get people to see that movie. So the struggle continues. That's the message.

LLOYD: Thank you so much. Thank you. How much was the autograph?

DAVID: You know it's $40, Lloyd. Please keep the line moving.

DISTRIBUTE YOUR OWN DAMN INCEST

By Cory J. Udler

Cory is the writer/director/producer/sick mind that came up with Incest Death Squad. *Lloyd only wishes that he had thought of it first.*

FIGURE 7.5 *Cory Udler* (right) *with an exuberant Stuart Gordon in front of an* Incest Death Squad *poster.*

Self-distribution is only as successful as you are shameless in your promotion. It's one thing to tell your friends your movie is done and ready to buy on DVD. It's another thing for people in New Zealand, Australia, the United Kingdom, and Canada to know about it.

So how did I go about it? The old-fashioned way. I first bribed Lloyd with the promise of 72 hairless, castrated Asian twins in the afterlife, but Lloyd said he'd already had enough of that here on earth. My next step was to distribute my own damn movie!

My film, *Incest Death Squad*, is the story of Jeb and Amber Wayne, an incestuous brother and sister who kill tourists in the name of God. I've been crucified (kind of like that Jewish carpenter, Neil Diamond) for having such a controversial title and for casually pairing religious iconography with brother-and-sister sex, male-on-male necrophilia rape, and blood orgies. When the film was complete, I couldn't imagine a distribution company saying no to it! Not only was it exploitative (boobs, blood, bad words), but the acting was far superior to anything I had seen from a no-budget film. It's stylish, the music is great, the story is engrossing, and it did what I think all important genre films do—it tackled a controversial topic (organized religion) and made a social statement.

I contacted every single horror distribution company I could think of in the hopes that someone, *anyone,* would want in on the incestuous fun that is *Incest Death Squad.* Nothing. Not one bite. Not one call. Not one email.

The prospect of getting distribution at the onset, to me, was incredibly attractive, kind of like getting head in a wayside bathroom from a toothless grandmother. Sure, it's hot and moist, but once the horse tranquilizers wear off you realize that you have nothing to show for it.

Most distribution companies will not give you any money up front. You'll sit around and wait for reports to come in along with that 12¢ check every quarter. Distribution companies, more than likely, are just going to grab your film and bury it amid all of their other titles. They will not be spending any money on marketing the film, so therefore nobody's going to know it exists unless they shuffle through the company's website catalog to find it. Basically, you are giving away your heart, your soul, and your art to a company that isn't going to believe in it the way you do.

Twenty years ago, self-distribution was basically a way for a filmmaker to ensure that nobody would take his film seriously. In 2010, self-distribution is the *best* way for a filmmaker to go, and it is not an admittance of a poor-quality film. Many people seek out self-financed, self-distributed films because those are the films with balls—with passion. These are the films that don't treat their audiences like they're a bunch of shit-covered mongoloids. People want to see honesty from art. The best place to get that is from a filmmaker like you who has something to say and has invested everything they have into making their dream come true. With *Incest Death Squad*, I didn't spend much money to make it. In all honesty, the total budget for the film was under $10,000. But that figure also accounts for a brand new Canon XL2 camera and a big bitch Mac. So really, the film itself cost probably under $3000 to actually produce. So, in a short period of time through self-distribution, I was able to make back what I spent on the movie. You're not going to get that by giving your film to a distribution company that gives you no cash up front for the film.

I have been selling my film from our official website (incestdeathsquad. com) and also by buying artist's tables at horror conventions. An artist's table usually runs about $100 for a weekend. *Incest Death Squad* sells for $10. All I have to do is convince 10 loyal horror fans to give the film a shot and I've already broken even. I have had no problems doing very well at any convention or screening we've had.

A big part of that is the fact that Lloyd is in the film. I've had people come up and see Lloyd's name and plunk down $10 just for that fact. Another big factor is that horror fans are the most loyal film fans you could ever hope for. And they are more than willing to take a chance on a horror film they haven't heard of before. But a big part of my success at horror conventions is the fact that I am the one at the table the entire weekend selling the movie and talking to fans. Nobody can talk about your film like you can. People can sense your passion and that's what will ultimately sell your film—*you*! I have been to distribution companies' tables at horror conventions, and they're usually manned by some disenfranchised guy who knows nothing about the films he's selling and has nothing to gain from you buying the films or not buying the films. If you, the filmmaker, are there, essentially they're buying *you*. It means more to film fans to meet the guy responsible for a reprehensible smut fest like *Incest Death Squad* than to just buy a DVD from a guy who doesn't even want to be there.

I can only speak from personal experience when it comes to getting your film out locally, nationally, and internationally. If you're like me you blew your wad on meth—I mean, on a dead hooker's face—er, I mean, on making the film itself. That leaves you with no money to do any national advertising. Luckily enough, with a title that includes the word "incest," I've scored some great free publicity on incest prevention websites! Local press is an easy one. If you're not from L.A. or New York, or that other hub of independent film, International Falls, Minnesota, a film being made in your area is newsworthy. Your local papers, TV stations, and radio stations will jump all over the fact that a film is being made in your town. Trust me, just call them. So there's your local press. Nationally, hopefully you've scored a huge Oscar-ignored star like Lloyd Kaufman to be in your film. If that's the case, write up press releases and send them *everywhere*! Put that star's name on *everything* you do. Trust me, the genre magazines and websites will pick it up! Internationally, Twitter, Facebook, Myspace, and all other social networking options are *free* and they work! Abuse them like I abuse my wiener up to six times a day! Facebook has been invaluable in the success of *Incest Death Squad* getting interest from fans overseas.

One thing you have to remember is if you're going to distribute the film yourself, you have to have your legal ducks in a row. An LLC is cheap and prevents you from headaches that could possibly arise. If you do conventions, make sure you get a seller's license. Be smart. Don't use copyrighted songs in your film, either. I recently went to a screening of a Wisconsin-made film that was full of copyrighted music. When the filmmaker announced they were "going national" with it, I couldn't help but wonder how that $9000 budget was able to secure the rights to use Elvis Presley's music. If you are going to distribute your own damn movie, think *everything* through. Don't just assume that because you're an indie that you're safe—you're not. If you make your own damn movie, then distribute your own damn movie; just make sure you research everything you can. Don't give anyone, anywhere any reason at all to come after you. This is your film. Reap the rewards by being smart on the business end and completely shameless on the promotional end.

One last piece of advice. Every single day you should do at least one thing to promote your film. Whether that's contacting a website, sending a screener out for review, telling a homeless crack addict that the $10 they just stole from a blind kid would be better served going toward a copy of your film than it would going to more crack cocaine, whatever! That's actually advice from the guy who wrote the "Chicken shit for your soul" books, but it applies to what you're trying to accomplish!

Now, if you'll excuse me, I have to try and hunt down a hermaphrodite with a large supply of Vicodin or else I'm not going to be able to convince Lloyd to be in *Incest Death Squad 2* (coming in 2011).

DISTRIBUTING YOUR OWN DAMN DOCUMENTARY

By Jason Connell

Jason Connell is the president and founder of Connell Creations, Inc., a Los Angeles–based production and distribution company. In 2007, he produced and directed his first feature film, a documentary called Strictly Background, *which went on to win several festival awards. Connell also runs the United Film Festival in six cities around the world, including Los Angeles, New York, and London.*

FIGURE 7.6 *Jason Connell, director of* Strictly Background, *for some reason decides to promote* Beyond the Pole.

In 2007, I completed my first feature, *Strictly Background*, a charming and heartfelt documentary about background actors trying to make it in Hollywood. The film received high critical praise and won six Best Documentary Awards on the film festival circuit, so I assumed distribution would be a cinch. I quickly learned it was not that easy. I hired a producer's rep and a PR firm, but it took another year before we eventually accepted a deal from a third-tier distribution company. Although they got us some retail and online presence, no energy was put into marketing and we never saw a penny.

With our second film, the quirky fan favorite *The Rock-afire Explosion* (2009), we made the choice to self-distribute so that we could ensure control of the film and see a profit. While ultimately a successful choice, we had much to learn about navigating the distribution landscape.

1. *Have realistic expectations.* Be honest about what you hope to achieve, whether it's getting your money back, seeing a profit, or simply gaining exposure for your film. A documentary can achieve all three, but each priority comes with different strategies and timelines. Too often, filmmakers feel that once a movie is finished, their work is done. But marketing it is equally as difficult, and you truly get out what you put in.

2. *Know your audience.* Documentaries without big name stars or a hot-button issue to exploit can seem hard to market, but every strong documentary has a niche audience. As the filmmaker, you probably have a good handle on who that audience is. It's important to get creative when thinking about how to market specifically to that demographic, with special merchandise and events that will reach the people who will get the most excited and will keep spreading the word about your film.

3. *Know your strengths.* Rather than flounder in fields that you have no experience in, form partnerships with knowledgeable companies that can help you gain access to these areas. For example, companies that can help get your film on iTunes or Netflix will save you a lot of time and stress. If you've already created an impressive website, continuing to devote energy to your online presence through social networking can prove to be a beneficial use of your time.

4. *Don't be afraid to make money.* For your documentary to be successful, you have to maximize every opportunity to reach your audience. Film festivals are an amazing way to gain exposure, and many times festivals may sell your merchandise, pay screening fees, and ultimately continue to push viewers to your website where you can continue to reach people by having your film available on DVD or as a digital download. If a distributor becomes interested, the hard work and energy you put behind your film's packaging and network can only work in your favor.

5. *The most important piece of advice: make a good movie.* Putting energy into the initial product is invaluable. A good film will always find its audience.

Documentaries about niche subjects that don't have controversial subject matter to help garner attention can be tough for distributors to initially connect with, so self-distribution can be a particularly appealing option for this genre. It affords you, the filmmaker, a large amount of control. We have chosen to

FIGURE 7.7 Strictly Background *poster art.*

self-distribute our next two documentaries, *I Do, I Don't* and *GLOW,* and have since launched our distribution division, United Films, which is currently seeking further acquisitions, applying this grassroots mentality to more documentary and narrative films.

Chapter | eight

Mo' Distribution, Mo' Problems

A few months ago, while I was in Cannes, I sat on a bee and got stung.

----------------------Original Message----------------------

To: lloyd@troma.com
From: elinor@focalpress.com
Date: August 18, 2010 10:21 a.m.
Subject: RE: Explosive Distribution

Lloyd,

Let me stop you right here, before this chapter veers into uselessness like several of the others. I have tried, repeatedly, to explain to you that we would like this book to be full of practical information. Your sense of humor is wonderful, and we think it adds a great deal of value to hear relevant stories from your past that illustrate current trends. However, as I have told you, often your stories, funny as they may be, tend to ramble into incoherence.

Our focus panels have emphasized that they would like some practical advice in this book, much as we suspected, yet you refuse to believe. According to the book outline, *which you submitted* back in January, this chapter is about distribution with a major studio. It is not about bees. Please remove all references to bees and focus on distribution.

Regards,
Elinor
Focal Press

-----------------------End Message-----------------------

Let me start again.

A few months ago, while I was in Cannes, I sat on a bee and got stung.[1] Normally, this would be a bad thing, or at least pretty annoying. But after I was stung, I noticed that the arthritis that had been "bugging" me for a few years suddenly felt a little better. In retrospect, this may have been because my brain was so focused on the pain of the bee sting to worry about an achy joint, but at the time, I thought I had stumbled on something brilliant. When I got home, I instantly jumped on my CrackFairy and Googled "bee sting arthritis." After skimming through a few bee sting and arthritis fetish sites, I found the website of Dr. Jules Westen, a certified bee therapy practitioner in Connecticut. Turns out, someone else had discovered the healing power of bees many, many moons ago, and there is an entire secret industry of certified bee sting venom therapy practitioners throughout the tri-state area, and probably some more in California.

A week later, the bee doctor was in my house. He presented me with a plastic jar of female bees, and then spent three hours teaching me how to pick up a bee with one set of giant tweezers, then press the bee against my heaving loins with another set of giant tweezers, and then wait for it to get angry enough to sting me.[2] I don't really feel comfortable doing this to myself (read: I am a weenie) so my lovely Pattie-Pie volunteered to sting me the next time. I didn't expect her to be quite so eager to do this, and the devilish little twinkle in her eye sent a shiver down my shaft.[3]

---

[1] I don't think Elinor reads these chapters twice, trusting soul that she is. But if you know Elinor and you are reading this book, please do not mention that this chapter is 73% about bees.

[2] With human gynos, as opposed to gyno bees, this only takes about 2.5 seconds.

[3] Next week, when Pat goes to India, I may need my beautiful assistant Justin to sting me. I can't wait to be shirtless in front of him—exposed and vulnerable!*

*NOTE FROM LLOYD'S CURRENT ASSISTANT: Lloyd, Justin quit eight months ago. I told you, I'm Allison. And I'm not touching you, tweezers or not.

The idea of all this bee business is that after several stings, I will become immune to the sting, my legs and back will no longer puff up like pulsating red balloons, and my body will no longer itch. After this, good things will happen!

The saddest part about all of this, other than my own discomfort, which is pretty sad, is these poor bees. As someone who doesn't eat meat, I have a hard time killing 30 to 40 bees a week. And as if they know what's coming, these poor, sad bees spend their entire day trying to figure out how to get out of their plastic jar prison. Last week, two actually did manage to escape, but after a few hours, they came back. As Dr. Jules explained to me, once a bee has been touched by Lloyd Kaufman, no other hive will accept it.[4] Now I leave a dead bee in the bottom of the plastic jar, as a warning to the others, like Vlad the Impaler.[5]

FIGURE 8.1 *German filmmaker Marcus Jurchen, creator of Troma fan film* Attack of the Tromaggot *flew Lloyd and three Troma films to Germany. He hoped a Troma-tour in Berlin and other German cities would attract theaters to his movie. Lloyd and Marcus didn't attract any theaters, but they did attract quite a posse of handsome partygoers!*

[4] Funny enough, this applies to human gynos as well!

[5] And I'm paler than Vlad, believe it or not, even though he was Russian and I am a swarthy Jew.

After a few months of hideous welts and guilt about the dead female bees, I noticed that my arthritis actually seemed to be getting worse. So I let all the bees go free. I even played "Born Free" on the piano to encourage them to leave, but they all refused. Now we have a small beehive of all female bees in our backyard. Are they lesbians? How hot and Tromatic is that?![6]

Now, you were probably expecting some brilliant connection between this bee sting story and major distribution, and I swear I tried to come up with one. But really, I just wanted to tell the story. So let's just go with some metaphor about the bee that stung me being an independent filmmaker and I, as the giant studio, being sold on something by this little prick. Or maybe I am the independent filmmaker, and the major studio is the bee, trying to convince me that major distribution, or a bee sting, is actually good for me, when it's really just kind of pain in the ass. Hey, that's not bad! Let's go with that!

Now on to distribution!

MAJOR DYSENTERY, AND OTHER PROBLEMS THAT COME WITH MAJOR STUDIO DISTRIBUTION

For those filmmakers who are too lazy to attempt to sell their movie to the general public, or for those who, ridiculous as it sounds, want a little bit of respect, having a film bought and distributed by a major studio seems like an ideal situation. The studio does all the work and you get all the money and credit! Woo hoo!

And however fantastic major distribution sounds in theory, it can, in reality, be just the opposite—a depressing, soul-destroying practice that turns an enthusiastic and idealistic young director into a sad, bitter onion skin of a man or gyno.

But I don't want to get ahead of myself. Many young directors, like Quentin Tarantino and Robert Rodriguez have had their amazing films distributed by major studios, and as a result, everyone knows who they are and they make money and win Oscars. So, of course, there are good things that can come of it. And I, as a bitter, sad, onion skin of a man, would never want to discourage you from attempting to get your film distributed by a major studio. It could turn out great for you!

---

[6] They are so hot! I'm watching those hard-bodied lesbian bees right now as I type.

However, 99.9999% of the population is never going to have their film bought by a major studio, so if it doesn't happen for you, then hold your chin up high. It just means that you're normal! The other nine chapters in this book are for you, and you can still be a star!

FIGURE 8.2 *While Lloyd poses with Meatloaf front man Matt Shaw, Toxie's eagle-like eye catches a seemingly open button on Matt's jeans.*

And if you are in the (far less than) 1% that is allowed to enter the magical land that is the big studio system, be sure to keep your hands inside the vehicle at all times, wear your sunscreen and mosquito repellant, and remember what Unka Lloydie is about to tell you.

THE BENEFITS

Everyone has heard a story about a young director who made a movie, which got into Sundance, and was bought by a giant studio. The director got an $8 million advance, and his little movie was an overnight sensation. And maybe it's even happened once or twice in the entire history of the world. But true stories like this are few and far between. If a studio does want to buy your movie, it is very unlikely that they will swoop in and throw $8 million at your dirty Sketchers-covered feet.

The reason?

They don't have to!

Imagine that you made a film with a $5000 budget. Luckily, that year Sundance is just dying to open the festival with a musical set in outer space,[7] and since you just happen to submit a musical set in outer space, you are accepted! Your film is a hit with the festival crowd, and an executive from Disney tells you that they might be interested in buying your outer space musical and using it as a vehicle for Justin Bieber. You're over the moon with excitement at this point, with all your pathetically unrealistic dreams about to come true. Now, are the first words out of your mouth, "Show me $8 million, you studio pig!" or "Yes sir, Mr. Executive. Shall I sign the contract with my own blood?"

The people who run the big studios aren't stupid, although they very often seem to be.[8] They know that young, inexperienced directors are usually so eager to see their work on the big screen that

FIGURE 8.3 *As the Guinness World Record holder for most rejections of all time, Lloyd was a natural choice to be featured on the discussion panel for the film* Official Rejection *at the Dead Center Film Festival.*

[7]Speaking of musicals in outer space, please see Troma's *Vegas in Space*, a musical with transvestites in outer space by Philip Ford. It's a big hit at festivals!

[8]For instance, continuing to cast Renée Zellweger in anything.

they will give it away for next to nothing,[9] and they use this naïveté to exploit. The first thing that you need to accept before you enter the ring with a giant studio is that you will not get rich quick. In fact, let me take it a step further.

RULE 1 OF DEALING WITH MAJOR STUDIOS

When making a distribution deal with a major studio, *you will not win*. You may make some money, but the studio will always make much, much more. You may retain some semblance of control over your film, but the studio will always have more control. You may get something good out of the experience, but the studio will always get more. If there has to be a winner and a loser, you will always be the loser, and the studio will always be the winner.

RULE 2 OF DEALING WITH MAJOR STUDIOS

Always get a parking space next to the cafeteria.

"Gee, Lloyd," you are probably thinking to yourself right now, "Speaking of giant studios, you are a giant fuck! All I want to do is find out how to get my movie distributed by a studio, and here you are doing the fucking Macarena on all of my dreams. I knew you were bitter, Kaufman, but I always thought it was kind of funny before. Now I just think you're a fuck."

Listen friend, like I said, I'm not trying to discourage you from anything. Also, your repeated use of the word "fuck" is going to get this book banned in Alabama, and I don't appreciate that. I just want you going into this fucking shit with your fucking eyes open,[10] and without any illusions about what is going to fucking happen. Speaking of things that could happen...[11]

THINGS THAT CAN HAPPEN

When you hand your film over to a giant studio, you are basically giving them the right to do whatever they would like with it. Now, some people, like David Carradine, get off on loss of control, but you may not be one of them. In an abstract sense, loss of control

---

[9] So will co-writers, I've found.

[10] Also what I said to the bum behind the 7-Eleven before I gave him $8 to make sweet, sweet love to me. He's cute, but it's way hotter when he keeps his eyes open.

[11] If you would rather follow the train of thought, "Speaking of fucking..." then turn to page 183. I don't know what's there, but it's probably fucking hilarious!

may not sound so bad. But as David Carradine learned before you, in practical application, it can be really annoying.

CIRCUMCISION, AND WHY IT CHANGED MY WORLDVIEW

Like many other Jewish boys, I had part of my penis cut off at a very young age. This isn't nearly as pleasant as it sounds, and 65 years later, I still occasionally have nightmares about bearded men standing over me with dull knives. These dreams, also, are not as pleasant as they might sound.

Perhaps my distaste for cutting up films can be traced back to this singular event, or maybe I just don't like destroying movies. In either case, when you give your film to a giant studio, be aware that they have the right to recut it any way that they see fit.

In 1953, Judy Garland[12] produced and starred in the brilliant film *A Star Is Born*.[13] Critics were going gaga over the movie and calling it Oscar worthy. Then, Jack Warner, head of Warner Bros. and someone who would have worn a lot of Ed Hardy shirts if they had existed in 1953, got the idea in his head that this brilliant and perfect film was too long. A two-and-a-half hour movie could only have so many shows at the theater each day, but a two-hour or one-and-a-half hour movie could have, like, two extra shows each day! And that would be, like, an extra $5 in his pocket! So he took this amazing and perfect film, and he cut the hell out of it. The critics who had either seen it in its previous, complete form, as well as critics who had heard such great things about it, were shocked. Even Judy Garland was shocked. You see, little Jack Warner had, in his cutting spree, somehow destroyed the plot of the film. All of a sudden, it didn't make any sense anymore! People who saw it in the theater left scratching their heads. Then, to really piss everyone off, Warner destroyed all of the cut footage, so that even later, the movie could never be restored to its original glory.[14]

---

[12] A favorite of the gays, and coincidentally, one of my favs, too.

[13] *A Star Is Born* was directed by George Cukor, who also directed *The Philadelphia Story*, *The Marrying Kind*, and *My Fair Lady*, among others. You should see *all* of his movies!

[14] Back in the 1980s, film historians found the audio track of the film's original version, and used it, along with several promotional photos, to try and recreate the missing portions of the movie. However, the result is a somewhat boring middle section of the movie. Although it is worth checking out for an example of studio bullying.

Hopefully this won't happen to your movie, but anything is possible. Of course, not all studio cuts will be bad. A different perspective or fresh idea might be what takes your movie from pretty good to awesome. Staying open-minded to suggestions is great. However, if you made the movie that you wanted to make and you don't want it changed, be sure that final approval is written into your contract before you sign it!

50 WAYS TO DUMP YOUR MOVIE

Once the movie is in its final condition, chopped up or not, the studio also has ultimate control about how they decide to market it. And some great movies, like *Office Space* and *Observe and Report*, have been horrendously marketed, to the point of financial death. Worse yet and just as likely, the studio can also choose to *not* market your movie. In 1989, Warner Bros. was to distribute *The Toxic Avenger II* on home video.[15] Warner Bros. made a big deal to us about how *Toxic Avenger II* would be the lead Warner video release the month of the Video Software Dealers Association yearly convention,[16] and they suggested that Michael Herz fly out to Las Vegas[17] and see what a great job they were doing selling Toxie. However, when Michael got to the convention, the front of the hotel was covered with giant *Batman* cutouts and posters. He couldn't find a single leaflet about *Toxic Avenger II*! Toxie had been completely dumped, and Troma ended up with a $2000 gambling debt from Michael's depression-induced night at Caesar's Palace. A week later, I finally got Warren Lieberfarb, the president of Warner Home Video, on the phone. He was, I believe, in his limo at the time, and he accused me of harassing him. Then we got into a heated argument about the correct pronunciation of "harass" and he hung up on me. I've often thought that Anita Hill may have been in the limo with him, because this was before the big Anita Hill trial, and you rarely heard the word "harass" before that. So you see, Warren Leiberfarb, who built Warner Home Video for Warner Studios, which was built with money from parking lots and

---

[15] Our deal had actually been with Lorimar, but then Warner Bros. ate Lorimar.

[16] Now called the Entertainment Merchants Association, this convention is where all the distributors pitch their new videos/DVDs to the Wal-Marts and Best Buys. And they probably suck a lot of cock as well.

[17] Although, in their defense, getting Michael Herz to go to Las Vegas is pretty easy.

FIGURE 8.4 *This is an example of a Troma booth at a convention. As you can see, Troma puts much importance on its mission of understated elegance.*

funeral homes and other businesses that are often associated with the Mafia, was actually a genius! He almost prevented a right-wing black Newt Gingrich from becoming a Supreme Court justice!

Giving your movie to a giant studio can be great, but it can also be shit, just like a bee sting that pretends to cure arthritis. A great deal of the time, the studio will do whatever it can to screw you over. At Troma, we screw people over too, but it's okay because we don't make any money off of it, whereas a smarter studio will probably make some money off your film, no matter what.

THE ART OF ORDERING AN ICED TEA

It's a Thursday night, and Sara wants to meet and discuss the future of this book project. It's been 10 months, and I have yet to pay her, and apparently, this may be a problem. I have suggested that we meet in an Australian pub that serves a mean kangaroo.[18] She, instead, suggests a Barnes & Noble in Midtown. "Shit," I say aloud as I walk up to the bright, Disney-esque storefront window. This place probably doesn't even stock my books, and yet I am meeting here to discuss my next book. "Shit," I say again.

---

[18] The drink, not the animal, of course. This would have no appeal for me, as I am a vegetarian. The kangaroo is a deliciously fruity drink that makes me kanga-rude in no time.

I walk up to the second-floor café and scan the overhead menu. "I'll have a vodka tonic," I say jokingly to the black-clad gyno behind the sticky counter.

"Excuse me?" she says, without a hint of humor.

"Um, I'll have an iced tea, please. Two iced teas."

"Would you like black or passion?"

"Can I have both?" I wink at the girl, but I don't think she notices because her eyes are slightly glazed over.

"Would you like black tea or passion tea?"

I panic, and turn to Sara, who is holding our table before it is taken by one of the circling homeless.

"Black tea or passion tea?"

"Black," she says.

"Uh, one black and one passion."

"Would you like a tall, a grande, or a venti?"

I turn back to Sara. "A tall, grande, or the other one?"

"A tall," she says.

I turn back to the café gyno. "Uh, venti is the big one? Just make it two big ones I think."

"Sweetened or unsweetened?"

"Shit. Really?"

I turn to Sara. "Unsweet," she says before I say anything.

"Unsweet," I repeat.

"Okay, one venti unsweet black iced tea and one venti unsweet passion iced tea. Would you like a cookie or a scone to go with that?"

Now my eyes have glazed over as well. Drool has started to accumulate in the corner of my mouth. I reach into my pocket and take out a $10 bill. I hold it out to the girl in befuddlement.

"Do you have a membership card to save 10%?"[19]

The exchange has left me with zero appetite and no desire to ever purchase an iced tea again, exactly the opposite effect than I believe was intended.

That's what happens when corporations get involved in art. At one time, bookselling was the realm of people who liked books. Now, it is in the hands of Barnes & Noble and Amazon, who

---

[19] NOTE FROM ELINOR: Why is this conversation being included? Please cut this entire section and make a point about distribution. Please, Lloyd, I'm begging you!*

* NOTE FROM LLOYD: I'm getting there. This will be the best chapter so far! xoxo

apparently like selling shitty coffee and devices that allow you to read books without actually touching a book. By micromanaging and sanitizing the filmmaking process, studios have virtually eliminated the possibility of truly unique and innovative art, just as Barnes & Noble virtually eliminated any chance that tea gyno and I had of engaging in a real conversation. In many ways, the corrupt studio system that exists now is even worse than the system of the 1920s to 1950s. At least back then, studios made good movies once in a while, and the people making money were somewhat closer in proximity to the film industry, even if that meant just having an office on the lot where they could count their millions! Today, the people making money off *Eat Pray Love* are the CEOs of oil companies, Wall Street brokers, and Julia Roberts. These people don't care about art! They care about what makes more money. And if that means greenlighting *Shrek 17* instead of your character-driven ensemble piece, then so be it! But what these incredibly, incredibly rich people are forgetting is that corporations have no business in art. Barnes & Noble is dying, and no amount of upsizing iced teas is going to save it! Monopolies don't always work. Just ask Parker Brothers!

If a studio wants your film, let's be honest, you'll probably give it to them. If anyone had ever wanted anything that I did, I probably would have given it to them, too. Just be smart, and realize that you probably won't get from the experience what you think you'll get out of it. Instead, you'll get a little knowledge and street smarts.

Hopefully, you'll also get some prestige, and if you can spin that well, you can use it to get your next job!

Brad Kembel is the executive vice president of international distribution at Summit Films. He was directly involved in the marketing of Twilight, *the film series that turned millions of normal tweens into emo freaks and, hopefully, future-Troma fans! Brad graciously agreed to do this interview, unaware that Lloyd had an odd fascination with and slight sexual attraction to the star of* Twilight, *Robert Pattinson. Brad would like to state, for the record, that had he known, he would not have allowed Lloyd into his office.*

LLOYD: Brad, fledging filmmakers would be interested to know the realities of selling your own damn mainstream movie. When *Twilight* was developed, was that something that started in-house? And did that make it easier for you to market it?

BRAD: Well it was actually a major studio, who will remain unnamed, who optioned the first book in the series. They decided after a year that it would come to Summit. The thing that was really amazing—it was an unusual project where we were interactive with the audience and the author in everything we were doing to develop the series. It was in development for a year and a half during that publicity period, and it went on to the phenomenal success that it is.

LLOYD: Sounds like good timing.

BRAD: Absolutely, it was a fantastic, lucky fluke that we got our hands on it for Summit.

LLOYD: I imagine when you see a film through from conception to completion, you really have a huge motivation to get it out to as many people as possible. What about films that come in already produced for distribution? Is Summit open to working with independent filmmakers? Perhaps old, perverted ones, such as myself?

BRAD: Absolutely. That was the core beginning of Summit's business 20 years ago. That they were one of the key sales agents on the international side that was helping major production companies in Hollywood, but also helping the independents go to market with their films. It has always been a core part of our business and even though in the last 3 or 4 years we've received a lot of funding to grow into this new version of Summit that's this bigger mini-major company, we still handle a lot of sales agency stuff on the side. It's probably still a good third to 50% of our international sales activity.

LLOYD: What do you mean by sales agency?

BRAD: Sales agency is basically the business of going to market to represent for foreign sales for producers. Basically it's the process whereby you need to raise funding to make your movie. Banks need to lend you money and in order to do so, they want to see that you've made international sales so you can offer those contracts as collateral to be loaned money to make the film.

LLOYD: Can you talk a little bit about what Summit might be looking for? First, with a project they would produce in-house and, then more important, what you might want to look for in a film somebody else produced?

BRAD: Well it's a really interesting question because I don't think we are limited in any way anymore. There was a time when perhaps we might have been limited by budget or by other considerations, but now we're basically in a position to look at anything from a $1 million budget to a $150 million movie, and that's perhaps a bit of a unique circumstance in that we are one of the companies that might be interested in smaller films. We've probably moved a bit away from that in the last few years, but if the right sort of project comes along, like many years ago we were involved in *The Blair Witch Project* when we were helping to represent the company Artisan, which eventually got taken over by Lionsgate. You couldn't be more "indie" than that film.

LLOYD: Any interest in *Toxic Avenger V: Toxic Twins* or *Poultrygeist II: Day of the Egg*?

BRAD: Excuse me?

LLOYD: Can you tell us a bit about *Twilight,* and how did Summit decide to get involved and sell this movie?

BRAD: Well actually it was a nice bit of luck and happy circumstance. During the time that we were developing the project was actually when the book series started to explode with book sales and publicity. So a lot of this business is luck, and we were lucky in that regard.

LLOYD: What was it about *Step Up* that Summit saw and made you decide to pounce, because it looks like a high-budget movie that was done economically with unknowns?

BRAD: This series has always been done economically, and that was sort of the idea behind it. That's one that was really organic and homegrown inside of Summit here. Our head of production, Erik Feig, really felt it was a genre that could be revisited and reinvented for the next generation. The timing was perfect, and he was right in that regard. The idea was to make it a star-making vehicle for young talent like Channing Tatum from the first one, and to make them young and fresh and low budget and really to get to the core of what a series like that needs to be, which is really the dancing.

LLOYD: Getting back to *Twilight*, I would really love to meet Robert Pattinson. Is he that beautiful in real life?

BRAD: Um, is that a real question?

LLOYD: Yes.

BRAD: He's a very attractive young man, yes.

LLOYD: So we understand that budgets are usually big budgets.

BRAD: Um, yes. Right.

LLOYD: Let's say that an indie filmmaker has pretty much nailed what Summit is looking for—the genre is something that Summit might be interested in, the actors are not huge but are convincing, everything was done on a budget, and Summit is seriously looking at it. What sort of things should that filmmaker be looking to get out of Summit? What should they get out of a distribution deal? What is generally regarded as unacceptable? Can you speak to that?

BRAD: That's a very big question. I think honestly one of the preoccupations we have at this company is about the viability for the international marketplace. It's a very important consideration for us because most of the funding for our movies is going to be driven from international sales and those contacts that are put into place. Summit started out 20-odd years ago as an international agent and, over the course of many years, became known as one of the top companies at doing that type of business. That business is going to market with independent producers/films to sell them to the international marketplace and then you can, as a producer, take those international contracts to banks and lending facilities to raise the production budget or a portion of the production budget for your movies. And that's still a really core part of Summit's business. It's also how we finance our own productions. Other than that I would say the major things that we are looking for are unique stories and commercial viability—domestic and international.

LLOYD: Can you give hints to independent filmmakers who might have a film that meets your criteria? Does Robert Pattinson sparkle in real life?

BRAD: You're joking, right? Is this weird stuff for your DVD?

LLOYD: I'm very serious. I don't even think we're filming this. I just wonder how you could accomplish that special effect on a low budget, so I thought perhaps you cast a sparkly actor?

BRAD: No, he doesn't sparkle.

LLOYD: Oh, okay. Fair enough. Is there any advice you can give for an independent who might be making a deal with a major studio? Are there any points an independent should know when making a deal?

BRAD: Bring your agent or manager to the room. Actually, Lloyd, I'd like to bring someone else into the room now if that's okay.

LLOYD: Sure, sure. Are there any things, when you're dealing with a big company, that a filmmaker should look for?

BRAD: Well, it's difficult to even get your foot in the door when you're dealing with a major film company. It's difficult to get the meeting; it's difficult to be successful and unique in the context of the meeting anymore. There are hundreds of meetings that take place between development and creative teams at the major companies. What can I suggest, other than that you try and sparkle a bit like Robert Pattinson?

LLOYD: Brilliant! Regarding international sales, today we're getting a lot of competition from each country's local movies. Everyone's making movies. Regarding American movies, is there an American type of movie that is appealing to international sales?

BRAD: It's a tough question because the international marketplace is a very complex one and what might be the right answer regarding that question for France might be the wrong one for Germany, or all the major territories that really matter. Asia might have very different tastes in movies than Eastern Europe does, which is very different than Latin America. There's no one answer. There are certain genres that seem to work well—basically action, adventure—the more universal the better. Same thing with comedies, if their very slapstick and not dialog driven. But that's not to say that if you're *Juno* and a very smart comedy, that you can't do business around the world. So I can't say that there are any universal rules. The market is constantly changing and evolving internationally as well. What once worked and didn't work in one country is constantly changing for us.

LLOYD: Is there one that might be safer to go into, like star vehicles?

BRAD: Definitely star vehicles, definitely A-list stars that are propping up any of your material. And that as well is constantly changing. It might be Tom Cruise right now, but it might not be Tom Cruise five years from now, and it might not have been Tom Cruise five years ago.

LLOYD: In your mainstream area, can you determine what percentage of revenue comes from international sources?

BRAD: I think basically we just see it continually growing in the 20 years that I've been in the international side of the business. At this point, we fully expect for very commercial product to be probably be 60% to 70% of our worldwide grosses.

LLOYD: Do you prefer to partner with other distribution companies?

BRAD: We have five different output deals in major countries around the world and even some informal output arrangements.

LLOYD: Can you describe the output deals?

BRAD: An output deal is a fantastic thing that does not exist very much anymore. You have guaranteed to the independent distributors that you sell to, that you can come up with a viable amount of film product every year that they would want, and that they would need to prop up their slates. And so you enter into an agreement whereas basically, as long as a movie meets certain criteria, like budget or star level, they will automatically get that film for their country's proportion of what the budget of the film would be worth. For example, if France is worth 8% of the worldwide gross, then they will cough up 8% of the budget in order to have your steady stream of films for a period of time, like two years, five years, or whatever you have decided. In some cases this is often two or even three years in advance of when the actual product gets delivered to them, so they are of course obligated contractually and also out of pocket, as they have given you some down payment for the steady stream of films coming to them.

LLOYD: Is there some advice you can give the readers about mistakes that have been made with international markets?

BRAD: Well, I suppose there are always stories, like the film we delivered to the Philippines that caused a riot in the theater where the audience tore up the seats and set a fire in the corner.

LLOYD: Why did they do that? I don't think one of Troma's films has ever caused a riot!

BRAD: We basically delivered them a Macaulay Culkin picture not long after the *Home Alone* series. It turned out to be more of an opera piece, *The Nutcracker*, with a ballet mixed in, which they weren't expecting.

LLOYD: So the lesson there is tell the buyer what they're getting?

BRAD: Yeah.

LLOYD: There is the notion that even if the fledgling filmmaker makes *Rocky*, he cannot go out and do what you're doing. Why do you think that is?

BRAD: Well, I think you're really relying on the expertise of your sales agent to participate in the film markets each year—to go to them and to be responsible for selling the product. They are the ones who have access to the independent distributors in each country, that have the meetings and make the sales and the ongoing business. I think we're in a really unique position at Summit because we've had this long history of being at the top of the heap in the international sales market. We have the ongoing relationship with the key distributors in the market who often have similar market shares in their territory to the major studios, and that type of relationship is very important when trying to get your film sold and out to the marketplace in those places.

LLOYD: Do you think the market has become bifurcated between the low-budget Troma types and the Summits of the world? Do you think the traditional $4 million to $10 million movie is more of a tough sell now?

BRAD: Definitely, I think there's a bifurcation between companies that do the lowest budget films and the sort of companies that do the major independent sales agents and mini-majors like the Summits and Lionsgates. There used to be a real market for the American independent film from the mid-1990s up until a couple of years ago. That seems to have really dried up in the last couple of years because the product needs to be star driven, at least at some level or another, more often than not. And it's really rare for companies to stick around for 20 years or for 37 years like Troma has. And I think you might be lucky for a few more.

LLOYD: I think we'll be very lucky for a few more. My wife and business partner probably wish that we wouldn't be. So maybe the advice for someone who can't get the $40 million is to keep the budget really low, like micro budget?

BRAD: It's not a bad way to go because at this point those films are being very heavily marketed through the film festival system as well, and thank God that advantage is still there.

LLOYD: I thank God for Robert Pattinson and the *Twilight* films every day.

BRAD: Um, that's great.

LLOYD: Any final advice for the students?

BRAD: We actually struggle as much as lower-budget stuff in this business. These are difficult times. There are a lot of factors that come into play— there's piracy, sales are difficult, et cetera. Some reliable territories like Japan have fallen into the toilet the last few years. We've been able to compensate with a few territories coming up in the past few years, but not at the level that it used to be. There's always something going on in the marketplace to make our lives more challenging, and it makes life difficult for filmmakers too.

LLOYD: That's kind of a depressing note to end on.

BRAD: Maybe, but I think this interview is ready to be over.

MY OWN DAMN TESTIMONIAL

By Phil Nichols, Writer/Producer

When I attended AFM (American Film Market) in 2010 for my own damn movie, *Renfield: The Un-dead*, I used the self-promotion guerilla marketing technique of dressing in costume, which Lloyd Kaufman pioneered. Dressed in full regalia and makeup as Renfield the Undead (the character I played in the movie), I stalked AFM. Assistants followed me, passing out flyers and sell sheets on the movie and information on the suite where *Renfield: The Un-dead*'s rights were being sold. This technique created a wave of excitement and interest in the project. It also increased foot traffic to the sales suite!

I had always wanted to make my own damned Dracula movie. After researching the best guide books on making and marketing independent movies, I found *Direct Your Own Damn Movie!* and its companion, *Produce Your Own Damn Movie!* The wealth of information contained in these books, and the way that information is presented by the brilliant Lloyd Kaufman, is invaluable and should be required reading for every indie movie maker and every college film and video production class. *Renfield: The Un-dead* probably would never have gotten made and marketed if I hadn't found Lloyd's books. Lloyd Kaufman told me to direct, produce, and sell my own damn movie, and then he showed me how. *Renfield: The Un-dead* was the result![20]

FIGURE 8.5 *Troma's Head of Sales, Matt Manjourides (right), doing business at the American Film Market. Unfortunately, the "business" that was done was in his underwear.*

---

[20] EDITOR'S NOTE: In case you are tempted to think that Lloyd wrote this ridiculously flattering sidebar himself, as I originally thought, I insisted that Lloyd provide a picture of the real Phil Nichols. I'm still not sure I believe it, but it seems that at least one person, other than his adorable wife Pat, admires Lloyd. Go figure.

ADAM GREEN ON COFFEE, DONUTS, AND THE PITFALLS OF MAJOR DISTRIBUTION

FIGURE 8.6 *Adam Green (right), director of Sundance Selections* Frozen *and* Hatchet II, *which featured Lloyd as the "cookie platter passer."*

Adam Green is the writer, director, and producer of the 2006 horror hit Hatchet. *His latest film,* Frozen, *was selected for the Sundance Film Festival and features a woman wetting herself with fear. Watching this terrifying scene caused Lloyd Kaufman to wet himself. This, in turn, caused an entire audience of horror fans to wet themselves with laughter at Lloyd's expense. As a result of this incident, Lloyd will not be watching Adam Green's* Hatchet II, *which came out in 2010, even though he appears in it for a big three seconds.*

Coffee & Donuts, 2000

Coffee & Donuts was a movie that I made for $400. At the time, I had a job with a cable advertising company in Boston. You know, when you're watching ESPN late at night and that really fucking terrible commercial comes on, with the dude in front of his carpet place and his family is waving?—that's what I was doing. But I took the job because I was able to steal their equipment at night and make my own short films.

My partner Will Barrett (and when I say "partner," I don't mean that in a gay way; not that there would be anything wrong with it, but we're not gay) and I made *Coffee & Donuts* for $400, and we shot it on Beta SB. We edited it tape-to-tape, the old-school way, and we just put it into film festivals. Disney wound up buying the movie, but not so that they could distribute the actual movie; they bought the idea to turn into a sitcom, which I wrote for UPN. At the end of the day, it was not ethnic enough for UPN, and I'm somehow the only one who didn't see that coming.

We still haven't distributed *Coffee & Donuts*, because, frankly, I didn't know what I was doing then. I used copyrighted music, copyrighted logos on my T-shirts the whole time, et cetera. So we can't really do much with it now, unless we reshoot it. But this time it's gonna be fuckin' $800!

Distribution

Distribution, unfortunately, in my opinion, gets worse every single year. Ever since the foreign market just kind of gave up, it's been really, really hard. You used to have, like, a magic number—like the $2 million genre movie—where just between foreign sales and TV sales and other things, even if the movie wasn't very good, your investor was probably going get his money back. But that's not really the case anymore. You have distributors worldwide that'll sometimes not even offer you an acquisition fee. They'll just say, "Well, we'll put the movie out, but we're not giving you anything, so take it or leave it."

A great example would be *Hatchet*, which sold phenomenally worldwide. When it came time to make the sequel, we contacted some of these foreign distributors who were begging for the sequel, and we said, "You know, it would really help if you would just tell us how much money the first one made, and/or how many units you sold." And they would always say the same thing, "Well, it didn't do very well." Yet they're begging for the sequel! Basically, they don't have to tell you, and you're never going to see their books, and even if you do see their books, it's not going to be honest. You're kind of fooling yourself if you actually think you're going to get your fair cut from any of that. So the idea is to make sure you get a decent acquisition fee and you keep your budgets low enough. Sometimes, like *Frozen*, for example, which we made, we presold most of the foreign rights before we even made it. So our producers knew that they weren't going to lose any money when we started making the movie. The good thing about preselling *Frozen* was you had Peter Block as the producer, who people knew from *Saw* and *The Descent* and *Cabin Fever*, and by then I had a pretty good reputation because of *Hatchet*, so based on the strength of the script, the concept, and our track records, we were able to presell for decent amounts, and that way we were able to make the movie with no risk. But when you're a first-time filmmaker, you can't really count on that unless you have some huge star attached to your project.

On *Hatchet*, we were in discussions with the original distributor about the sequel. We sat down with them and said, "Well, how much did you actually spend on marketing *Hatchet*?" And anybody who was alive in 2007 knows they didn't spend anything on it—there were no TV commercials, there were no billboards, there was nothing. But they were trying to claim, like, $2 million or something like that, in marketing on the movie. And in the room, you could see that they *knew* it wasn't true, but that's what they've been told to say. One of the things that we really caught them on was they said they spent something like $800,000 on prints. Now, there were 80 prints of *Hatchet* made, and each print costs $2300. How the fuck does that come out to $800,000 in prints? And when you point that out, they're like,

"Ehhh, well, you know, I don't know. You'll have to talk to Bob in accounting."

"Well, can I talk to Bob?"

"No, he doesn't work here anymore."

It's very shaky. But when you're a first-time filmmaker, I don't really think you're in the position necessarily to get a great bargain or a good deal with what you're doing. You just have to be happy that somebody's going to actually support your movie and actually put it out. It's about the next one.

LLOYD'S PUBLIC RELATIONS HUMILIATION AND MY HAPPINESS

By Allison C. Jones, Assistant to Lloyd Kaufman[21]

Ever since I became one of many in Lloyd's ever-revolving door of assistants, it seems that every ounce of joy in my life has been wrung out of me like perspiration out of a 1980s tennis star's mulleted sweatband. At this point in my life, nothing amuses me more than seeing Lloyd-O squirm. For example, I made one minor mistake out of the entirety of a 10-page, single-spaced itinerary/schedule of meetings this past November for Lloyd's American Film Market trip. Lloyd then proceeded to berate me over the phone for 20 minutes, expressing the many ways in which I had failed him on a personal level. Only Billy Bob Thornton in *Bad Santa* could rival Lloyd's creative use of profanities. So what if my small slipup meant he had to drudge from the Delta airlines entrance to the American Airlines entrance a quarter mile away in a crowded LAX with 100 pounds worth of luggage? That image actually put a little extra kick in my step that evening. It's the moments where Lloyd really gets his nose rubbed in it that I have learned to rely on for the little light and happiness that is still able to seep through my now-hardened soul.

(Sara, Lloyd won't be reading this, right?)

Speaking of Lloyd getting his nose rubbed in it, about four years ago, Lloyd ran for the position of chairman of the IFTA[22] board and unexpectedly beat out one of the trade association's founders, the Academy Award–winning producer of *Monster*, Mark Damon. The election was controversial—as was Lloyd's platform. He was all about fighting the media conglomerates and preserving net neutrality on the Internet, not to mention the fact that he runs Troma, the force behind most of the world's poorest excuses for films. By all rights, Damon should have won, but he didn't. It was as newsworthy and contentious an election as this important association had ever seen in its 30-year history.

Now, for 30 years, the trade publication *Variety*—a publication owned by the megaconglomerates themselves—has been writing about these elections. Yet, as interesting, hard-fought, and unexpected as this win was, for some reason, not one word of *Variety* or any other publication was expelled on Lloyd.

---

[21] Current assistant, I should say. I have a job interview at Kmart next week, and my fingers are crossed!

[22] Independent Film & Television Alliance, the MPAA for the independent entertainment industry.

I can picture him now, waiting with bated breath to see his name in print, only to end up moping in disappointment in his frilly pink bathrobe for days on end, crying like a little baby girl.

Nevertheless, this pattern pretty much continued for the duration of his four years of chairmanship, most recently during AFM 2010, the same trip in which I inadvertently forced him to make that torturous journey in LAX from airline to airline.

On the opening day of AFM, *Variety* printed a major article about IFTA, an article that spent much time quoting a former IFTA chairman but, curiously, not the current chairman (if you haven't been paying attention up to this point, that means Lloyd!). In order to rectify the situation, the IFTA publicists arranged for *Variety* writer David McNary to interview Lloyd on what was to be an AFM wrap-up piece. To Lloyd's understanding, he would finally get some column inches in the rag. His interest in attracting young visionary artists and the businesspeople of tomorrow to IFTA was to be a theme of the article. The publicists and *Variety* made a deal stating that if IFTA gave the publication the article exclusively, said article would appear prominently.

And boy, was Lloyd excited! He was finally going to be taken seriously! Every other chairman, it seemed, had a turn at being profiled with ample space by the trade publication, and this was Lloyd's. The Troma office at AFM was shut down and closed off to all visitors and meetings as McNary interviewed Lloyd for one and a half hours for this profile piece.

When the article surfaced two days later, however, not only was it not a profile on Lloyd; his name wasn't actually mentioned at all! Even though, under his chairmanship, IFTA had become more famous as a trade association than ever before, and on his watch IFTA succeeded in throwing a monkey wrench to the Comcast/NBC merger, and for the first time government entities in Washington, D.C., and around the world were calling the IFTA offices for information and advice, Lloyd was still getting ignored.

(Regardless of how amusing and pleasing this is to me personally, it really isn't fair. Not to mention that Lloyd's place and profile in movie history are arguably more significant than any IFTA chairman whom he succeeded.)

Independent artists beware: prepare yourselves to be shunned and ignored by the film community, unless you sell your soul to the megaconglomerates. Even if you've created the longest-running independent film studio, are known around the world, or have people waiting in line to add you while your Facebook page is at full capacity. Even if you've influenced numbers of award-winning film directors all over the world. Even if you've won lifetime achievement awards and are getting more than 25,000 views on the bizarre, esoteric YouTube videos you post. Even if you give all of the young, closeted foot fetishists of the world hope.

If you are an independent artist, to *Variety*, you simply may not exist.

Now if you'll excuse me, I must get back to my assistant-ly duties and find Lloyd an all-weather security camera to purchase so he can spy on the dogs defecating on the sidewalk in front of his house. I've been informed that this is my #1 priority for the day.

Chapter | nine

Foreign Agents, and Other Things up My Ass

I'm always hearing about movies that bombed horribly in the United States but made $500 million worldwide. Unfortunately, Troma didn't produce any of these movies.[1] Foreign distribution is an extremely hard nut to crack, but it is too important to ignore.

While technology is making it easier and easier to virtually spread your movie around the world like swine flu, other forces are making it harder and harder. Did you know that several giant, devil-worshiping megaconglomerates, like Disney, are actually making movies and creating content specifically for certain countries, such as India? So your $10,000 movie is now competing with a $50 million to $100 million movie specifically geared to a country's tastes and culture. Did you know that redheads are considered bad luck in some parts of Malaysia? Neither did I! But you can bet your ass that Disney knew that.

When you are trying to distinguish your film in the foreign market, you are not only competing against Viacom, but you are

---

[1] Troma movies don't discriminate based on color or nationality. We've dropped more bombs around the world than the U.S. government in Iraq, Afghanistan, and Vietnam combined. And on civilians, too. In some cases, we'll just lay an egg—as we did with *Poultrygeist*!

competing against foreign filmmakers[2] as well. Governments love to subsidize their own local filmmakers, and many audiences prefer films by homegrown directors who actually know not to put red-heads on screen.[3]

Sound tough enough yet? No? Okay, keep in mind that you may also be butting heads with the local media. In the United States, five or six giant corporations control almost all media outlets. In other parts of the world, only one or two companies may control the newspapers and television stations. The government itself may even control them! And if you expect the Scandinavian press to champion your film over one that they have a financial stake in, think again.

FIGURE 9.1 *On set producing a pro bono PETA commercial with some lucky Troma interns. Publicity developed from working without pay can lead to publicity for other projects, as well as a unique children's zoo!*

In the end, though, selling your movie in a foreign market comes down to the same thing as it does when you're trying to sell it in

---

[2] Of course, this is a very U.S.-centric term. They aren't the foreign filmmakers in their own countries. You are!

[3] You should also know that Jews are hated in all counties, except, perhaps, Israel. I am hated all over the world, but that has nothing to do with my being Jewish.

your own country—if it's good and it's something that people want to see, people will find it. Troma hasn't had international distribution for years, but we have fans around the world. And on the bright side, foreign distribution can even be easier in some ways, because piracy can give you a head start on your fan base.

FOREIGN AID (LIKE WHEN YOU BOMB A COUNTRY AND THEN SEND IN BAND-AIDS AND NEOSPORIN)

Most of the people reading this book will probably never have their film distributed by a major studio.[4] And again, there's nothing

FIGURE 9.2 *A member of the Castrato chorus on opening night at* The Toxic Avenger Musical *in Pyongyang, North Korea.*

---

[4] A NOTE FROM YOUR UNDERUTILIZED FOOTNOTE GUY: Is anybody reading this book anymore? I quit around Chapter 5.

wrong with that. It just means that you are average, just like your mother always told you. But just because you don't have MGM[5] by your side doesn't mean that you can't have some sort of foreign distribution. The best way to do that is to start looking for a foreign agent. And the best place to start looking for a foreign agent is inside Glenn Beck's ass. If you want a human foreign agent, however, the place to look is IFTA!

WHAT IS IFTA?

IFTA is the Independent Film & Television Alliance, an internationally recognized trade organization for independent producers and distributors, of which yours truly has been chairman since 2006.[6] By perusing through the current IFTA membership catalog, you can find an extensive list of independent production and distribution companies around the world.

Each year in September, IFTA also runs the American Film Market in Los Angeles. If you are serious about foreign distribution, it is definitely worth a trip to AFM to meet these international ("foreign") agents and reps in person and pitch your film.[7] They may not let you into their offices, but you can at least kick the tires a bit and get a sense of which seem cool and are doing business. The Troma AFM office will let you in, but it has no sales and is useless.

---

[5] Ironically, MGM is now bankrupt and no one wants to buy it, even with a film library consisting of *Rocky I* to *V* and 300 James Bond movies. Karma is a bitch, isn't it, MGM.

[6] I intend to follow the lead of New York governor David Patterson and serve until mutiny occurs.

[7] In addition to promoting independence in art, IFTA is also on the front lines to preserve net neutrality and a free and open Internet. To learn more, search for "Lloyd Kaufman media consolidation" on YouTube and enjoy my relevant PSA!

HOW TO WORK THE AFM

By Jonathan Wolf, IFTA Executive Vice President and Managing Director of the American Film Market

The American Film Market is a great place to pitch your project or film—if you have a plan. Use these steps to increase your chances of success.

Prologue

If you have a project or script, the most effective use of your time and money is to purchase an AFM Half Market Industry Badge, which allows access to all offices and most screenings beginning Sunday, Day 5. It costs $295 which is a big savings compared to the $795 Full Market Industry Badge. Buy your badge before October 15. After that date, the fees go up.

Step 1: Homework—Create a List of Target Companies

More than 400 production/distribution companies have offices at the AFM, but not all are right for your film. You will need to focus your time and effort on companies best suited for your project.

Begin on opening day (Wednesday) by walking into the lobby of the Loews (no badge required) and collecting the bumper issues of the key trades: *Variety*, *The Hollywood Reporter*, *Screen International*, and *Business of Film*. (The trades are free at the AFM.) These publications have profiles of most companies at the Market. Take the trades home or sit at the pool and read, read, read. Find the companies that look best for your film.

FIGURE 9.3 *Miss Piggy's American Film Market badge.*

Do further research on the web. Most AFM companies list their projects and films in The Film Catalogue at *www.TheFilmCatalogue.com*. Many are members of the Independent Film & Television Alliance (IFTA), producer of the AFM, so you can read additional profiles on the IFTA website at *www.IFTA-online.org*.

Once you have created a target list, count the companies on it. If there are fewer than 10, you're being too picky. ("No distributor is right for *my* film!") If there are 100 or more, your homework grade is "incomplete." Keep working. The target list for most projects is 30 to 50 companies.

Step 2: More Homework—Create a List of Target Executives

For each of your target companies, create a list of key executives. Most important is the person or people who are in charge of acquisitions, development, and production. Look for their names in the trades and company websites. If you can't find the right names, call the company's main office (not its AFM office) and ask.

Finding out who's who is critical. You will never get anywhere by walking into an office and saying, "Hi, who is your head of acquisitions? I'd like to meet with him (or her)." This makes you look too lazy to do advance work and might cause the company to question your work ethic as a potential producing partner.

Step 3: Prioritize Your Target List

Separate your list into two groups: companies with an office in the city where you live and those from everywhere else. Focus first on the companies that aren't based where you live. If you are unable to meet with a company from your home city during the AFM, you can always follow up with them after the Market. Use other factors (e.g., the budgets and genres of the company's AFM lineup) to create an A and B list with 20 to 30 companies on each list. This will help prioritize your time near the end of the Market.

Step 4: Work on Your Pitch

A good pitch can get a bad film made and a bad pitch can leave a terrific project languishing on the shelf. Pitching is part art (it's a creative process), part science (pitches need to be organized and follow a tight script), and part salesmanship. There are many experts and resources on pitching, so here is our only advice:

- If you are madly, deeply in love with your project, if it's your only child and the AFM is its first day of school, get someone else to do the pitch. Pitching it yourself will definitely convince people that *you* love the project, but it probably won't do much more.
- In the pitch meeting, remember that you are being evaluated along with your project. When a company commits to your project, they are also committing to work with you.

FIGURE 9.4 *A Troma poster made for AFM 2010. Later it was more efficiently used as chimp cage liner at the Central Park Zoo.*

- Your mission during each pitch meeting isn't selling your project. You won't get a deal in one brief meeting. Your mission is simply: Get the second meeting!
- Consider attending the AFM's "Pitch Me!" seminar on Saturday morning.

Step 5: Make Appointments

On Thursday and Friday, call each target company's AFM office and request a 15-minute meeting with the key executive you identified in Step 2. AFM office phone numbers are listed in the AFM Show Directory—it's available at the Information desk in the Loews lobby. Don't use a cell phone. Use a land line in a quiet place. Ask for a meeting on Sunday, Monday, or Tuesday as most companies will be too busy during the first few days and your Half Market Badge begins on Sunday. For companies that won't set a meeting (prepare yourself—there will be many), see Step 8.

Step 6: Prepare Materials

Here are some thoughts on what to leave behind after every meeting:

- Your business card.
- A synopsis.
- A summary of the film's unique creative and financial attributes. This could include a list of all people attached or committed to the project, a budget abstract that's less than half a page, any rights that aren't available, investors that are committed, production incentives that you know the film can utilize, and so on.
- If the script is done, bring one or two copies with you but don't leave it behind without first consulting with your attorney.

These are just our suggestions—every film and situation is different. Be prepared, but don't bring copies of letters or documents that "prove" anything. It's too soon for that.

Step 7: Work the Show Before You Go

Done with your homework? Made your appointments? Confident with your pitch? Materials ready? Great. There's still plenty you can do at the AFM before you get your badge on Sunday:

- Go to AFM seminars.
- Attend the AFM finance conference.
- If this is your first AFM, attend the AFM orientation. You will receive an invitation after you register.
- Purchase your AFM Half Market Badge in advance so you will be ready to go on Sunday morning. Register online.
- Read the trades to stay on top of trends and deals.

Step 8: It's Showtime!

Here, in order, are your priorities for Sunday–Day 5, Monday–Day 6, and Tuesday–Day 7:

- Arrive at every scheduled meeting on time. Be prepared to be "bumped" or delayed. Don't take it personally—selling comes before buying.
- Visit the companies that wouldn't schedule a meeting with you on the phone. Remember, always ask for an appointment with a specific person.

- Visit companies on your B list and those you couldn't easily profile in Step 1. Get a feel for the product they handle and the culture of the company to see if they are right for your film. Consider being a "stealth participant" by picking up brochures and business cards without introducing yourself. Don't ask for a meeting while you are there. (If you've just walked in and asked a bunch of questions, stuffed your bag with their collateral, and grabbed every business card, it isn't likely you'll get a meeting.) Instead, wait half an hour and call the company to schedule a meeting . . . with a specific person.

Additional Steps: Producers with a Finished Film

The preceding steps were written for producers, filmmakers, and writers with projects and scripts. If you have a completed film and are looking for global distribution, congratulations! Everything above generally applies but you will need to move up the timetable:

- One month before the AFM, prepare a 5- to 7-minute reel of selected scenes. Do not create a consumer-type trailer. Acquisition executives will want to see complete scenes to get a feel for the film. Put the reel on a website so companies you contact can see it before committing to a meeting.
- Do your homework (Steps 2 and 3) and contact your target companies three to four weeks in advance of the AFM. Include the link to your reel.
- Set your initial meetings with each company in the first four days of the Market. Let them know you are arriving on Wednesday and will close a deal before the market is over.
- Purchase a Full Market Badge. (You've invested a lot of time and money—don't get cheap now!)
- Make sure your attorney will be available to you throughout the AFM.

  And good luck!

---

[8] EDITOR'S NOTE: Jesus, Lloyd, do you even have permission to include this here? Just because Nina Paley shares her art, that doesn't let you off the hook when something specifically says, "do not reproduce this." Please take this sidebar out or get written permission to include it. We do not want to get sued.*

  *LLOYD'S RESPONSE: Jonathan Wolf is great! I am sure he won't mind! xoxo

INTERNATIONAL PERSONS OF MYSTERY

Before signing with a foreign agent or distribution company, or even beginning talks with one, there are two things that you absolutely must do:

1. Find out what cross-collateralization is, and do not permit it.
2. Find out what a "most-favored nation" clause is, and make sure you get it.

Cross-collateralization means that the agent can deduct any expenses for any medium from your total revenue. So if they spend $100,000 on theatrical distribution and only make $10,000 back, they can then deduct the other $90,000 from the profits that you would have made on home video or TV sales, which is where you'll make the real money. If you have any leverage in negotiations, try to get the agent to keep all expenses in separate columns. Also be on the lookout for agents who take out an ad that promotes themselves as much as it does your film and then bill you for the total amount.

A most-favored nation clause basically says that if movies are sold together in a package, no movie will get a bigger percentage of the profits than yours. So if you make *Paranormal Activity*, and the distribution company sells it in a package deal with their very own film, *My Big Fat Shitty Movie*, for $300, they can't turn around and give you $100 and keep the other $200 for themselves, when it was your movie that the buyer wanted in the first place.

Like you, your agent is out to make money. And, unfortunately for both of you, neither of you can make *all* the money. It has to be split up somehow, ideally with you getting 70% to 85% and your agent getting 15% to 30%.[9] However, your agent has the advantage of receiving any money that comes in first, so it's ultimately up to him how much he gives you. And boy, are agents smart! They have spent years working out all sorts of creative ways to fuck you over! Sometimes one of Troma's sales agents will tell me some reason why he doesn't actually owe us money, and even though I know he's lying, I am so blown away by the creativity of the explanation that I let him get away with it out of respect for his superior intelligence.[10]

---

[9] I shouldn't have to say this, but whatever he gets and whatever you get should add up to 100%. I feel the need to say it, though, because many Troma fans who may be reading this book are legally retarded.

[10] Also, I'm a giant pussy.

For example, a foreign agent will take your movie to Cannes to try and sell it. He will also take the movies of nine other people and try to sell them as well. Now, most contracts are set up where an agent will take his 20% (or 15%, or 30%, or whatever deal you have worked out) of the profits and then, from your 80%, deduct any expenses that he incurs while selling your film. So the agent will get his money, and then also deduct the cost of his hotel and his French whore. Then you get what is left over. Now, logically, if an agent is selling 10 movies in Cannes, he should deduct 10% of his hotel from your profits, 10% from Filmmaker B's profits, 10% from Filmmaker G's profits, and so on. But the problem is, you don't *know* that he is selling nine other movies in Cannes, so little smartass agent has no trouble deducting 100% of his hotel from your profits, 100% of his hotel from Filmmaker B's profits, and so on. God, it's genius! And very, very upsetting.

Another creative way that agents can cheat you is slightly less immoral but still results in the agent making a lot of money and you making very little. Say the agent is selling 10 films in Japan. Now, a Japanese television executive offers the agent $1000 for all 10 films. For the agent, that sounds like a great deal, because he is going to make his 30% off all 10 filmmakers, resulting in $300. However, each filmmaker is only getting a tenth of that $1000, and that's before the agent's percentage is figured in. In the end, each filmmaker walks away with $70—absolute chickenfeed! At Troma, we serve as our own agent to avoid these very problems. But somehow, we end up with even less money. We were offered about 10¢ for *Poultrygeist* in Japan. The offers for international distribution were so insulting that we turned every one of them down. Maybe that was stupid, because now I can say that we literally haven't made a dime back, but as I said, I would rather give the movie away to people who love it[11] than make 10¢, minus an agent's sushi expenses.

When you're hammering out a deal with your foreign agent, there are a few things that you can ask for that may help you make a few bucks down the road. For instance, you can ask that any expenses be taken off the top, before the agent takes his 15%.

---

[11] And thanks to our good pirate friends in China, Thailand, and other countries, my fowl movement has indeed been given away—for free! Go to YouTube and type in some combination of "Lloyd Kaufman," "Chinese bootleg," and "Poultrygeist" for more.

You're still paying for his French whore, but he may be encouraged to choose a hand job over a blow job if he is paying for part of it, too. You can also ask for an advance on the profits. If an agent goes on and on about how great your movie is and how he can do such a fantastic job of selling it, then he shouldn't have any problem handing over a few thousand "good faith" bucks ahead of time. There is nothing wrong with using someone's cockiness to your advantage.[12]

It's hard to give too many details about contract negotiations, because so many permutations are possible. I could write a whole book on that subject alone![13] When you start making demands, though, just keep in mind that the harder you make it for the agent to make money off your film, the less motivation he has to sell it. And unless your name is James Cameron, Steven Spielberg, or George Lucas, you're probably not going to get everything that you want. And as a bonus, if your name is Lloyd Kaufman, you won't get anything that you want. Because even if you do get a great deal on paper, that still doesn't mean that you're going to get paid.

In 1980, Troma had a 2% gross deal on the film *The Final Countdown* starring Kirk Douglas and Martin Sheen. That meant we should have gotten 2% of any money that the film made, even before budgets were recouped, marketing costs covered, and so on. But even though the film did very well overseas, and I know for a fact that it recently sold about 500,000 copies on DVD in the United States alone, it's 30 years later and Troma has never gotten one single buffalo nickel. We could hire a lawyer, but who do we even sue at this point?[14] If Sylvester Stallone can't get paid for *Rocky VI*, as he said in a recent interview, what chance in hell do I have?

As much as I don't like lawyers, when you are dealing with agents, especially foreign sales agents who can used funny-sounding

---

[12] The beautiful young males who work for Troma use my cockiness to their advantage all the time.

[13] Well, I couldn't, but someone who actually has successful foreign distribution probably could. I could write a whole book on married gay men who love musical theater, but I don't know if the demand is there.*

*NOTE FROM CHINESE FOOTNOTE GUY: Now you're talking. Can you include a chapter on Asians?

[14] If you are reading this and you have made any money from the movie *The Final Countdown*, please email me at lloyd@troma.com so that I can sue you. And please review this book on Amazon!

terms like *proper apportionment* and *voulez-vous coucher avec moi* to confuse and intimidate you, it's worth it to have a good lawyer look over your contract before you sign it.[15] Involving a lawyer doesn't guarantee that you'll make money, but it can certainly help.

Some people will say that studios and agents are honest, while others will say that there is no way to get any money out of them. The truth is, I don't know. I've never had a studio deal. The closest that we ever came was *The Final Countdown*, and we had the best deal you could get. *The Final Countdown* was to be distributed by United Artists. Cool, huh? Then UA decided to go bankrupt just at the time that it released *The Final Countdown* in the United States. As I recall, Troma's raunchy comedy *Squeeze Play!*, with a $150,000 budget, came out at the same time and was getting better-quality screens than the $8 million *The Final Countdown*.

Then again, Chris Watson, who produced Troma's *Slaughter Party* has managed to make money off his film. I have no idea how, because I'm pretty sure Troma has sold about three DVDs of *Slaughter Party*, but somehow he has managed to make enough to finance his next project.

TO DUB OR NOT TO DUB

I enjoy Twitter. I really like getting twittered at. Or tweeted at. Or twatted at.[16] The tweets sent my way are generally pretty positive, with the occasional "I < 3 toxie," or "loyd rulez!" I am essentially "iltwitterate" and I can't do any sort of fancy posts, so I appreciate the simplicity of the above shout-outs.

So imagine my shock last week when I received a twat[17] from a very irate Brazilian Troma fan. She was extremely angry that none of our films had been dubbed into Portuguese. As if we, who have no distribution in either Brazil or Portugal, had the option of dubbing in Portuguese but just decided not to for the hell of it! As I

---

[15] Michael Herz graduated from law school at NYU and passed the New York bar exam. He was planning on becoming a lawyer before I convinced him to abandon all ambition and become cofounder and vice president of Troma. His wife, Maris, has never forgiven me.

[16] NOTE FROM PROOFREADER: That means something else. Please cut.

[17] ANOTHER NOTE FROM PROOFREADER: Seriously, that means something else. Really needs to be cut.

struggled to tweet out an explanation to her in 140 characters or fewer, I became more and more frustrated. How does one get a point across in 140 characters or fewer? It leaves absolutely no room for puns! But it also made me think a little about dubbing and what advice to pass on in this tome.[18]

I wish that we, at Troma, could dub our films into every language. We have fans in nearly every country around the world, except Greenland, so why not? Why not, you ask? Because it's fucking expensive! We don't even have foreign distribution, so we definitely don't have money to dub *Tromeo & Juliet* back into the original Italian, as much as I would love to. This also goes for closed captions for the American deaf fans of Troma, and we feel terrible about it. We are running on fumes, though. Strike that—we are running on the memory of fumes.

If you are strapped for cash, I recommend, at least at first, skipping the dubbing or subtitling. Your foreign distributor may even take care of it for you. And luckily, the young people of the world are very good at speaking English. And if you're lucky and people love your movie, maybe a fan will even make subtitles for you. Marc Gras, in Spain, has made Spanish subtitles for *Poultrygeist: Night of the Chicken Dead* because he is a fan.[19]

A Swedish fan sent me a link to a website that he created. He has every Troma movie's key art on one page, and then when you click on a film, it links to that movie's trailer. I emailed the page's link to Troma's webmaster with a subject of "why can't you do this?" or something similar. After all, our own site forces you to type a password in Swahili before you can figure out where the trailers are located.[20] A few minutes after I sent the email, it occurred to me that instead of trying to recreate this fan's genius and efficiency, why not just link to his page on the Troma site?

---

[18] NOTE FROM ELINOR: Lloyd, 37 pages does not qualify as a tome. Also, please respond to the proofreader's notes and remove the references to twats.

[19] He also produced a full-blown documentary about Troma in Spanish called *Troma Is Spanish for Troma*, featuring well-known Spanish directors. It will be shown at the Sitges Film Festival, and maybe it will help us get some distribution in Spain!

[20] Just kidding. I don't think we even have trailers on our site. BUY TROMA!!

DUBBING: DON'T SHIT A BRIC!

So if someone wants to do your work for you, for free, then great. But if you do decide to invest in some dubbing, resist the urge to dub your film in only French or Spanish, or other pretentious-sounding languages. Instead, use the language of the people. Billions and billions of people (read: potential fans) live in just a few countries and speak just a few languages. Brazil, Russia, India, and China (BRIC) are the most populous and fastest-growing countries in the world. And, shockingly, they don't speak French there. So if you're going to dub your movie, perhaps do it in Portuguese, Russian, Hindi, and Chinese.[21] Of course, the BRIC countries also happen to be the most expert at film piracy, so once again, dear readers, life is hopeless.

LLOYD KAUFMAN: EXPENDABLE

To dub or not to dub is an important question. But you know what is better advice than the advice above? Sell a movie that doesn't need dubbing in the first place!

If you are making *Pulp Fiction II* or some other quirky master-piece that depends on lengthy dialog and wordplay, you are going to have a much tougher time trying to sell it to an international audience. That's because humor doesn't always translate across languages and cultures. If I said to you, "What do you get when you cross a sheep with a kangaroo? A woolly jumper!" you'd probably punch me in the face and then spend the rest of the day wondering what the fuck a woolly jumper is. But British people apparently find this joke hilarious because a woolly jumper is what they call a sweater.[22]

Action, on the other hand, is internationally understood. No one needs to dub a gunshot to the face or a kick in the groin. That's why *The Expendables* will make a billion dollars worldwide. If you want to know what international markets are *not* looking for, just take a look at the films I've been making for the past 10 years.

---

[21] As a side note, we also occasionally get hostile emails and tweets from deaf people who are angry about our movies' lack of closed captioning. But I'm much less scared of deaf people than I am of angry Brazilians.

[22] I still don't think it's especially funny, but that's not the point.

PRESTIGE WORLDWIDE

However your movie does in the United States, international attention can be incredibly important. Troma was just paid hundreds and hundreds of dollars by a reputable, Oscar-winning producer for the rights to remake *The Toxic Avenger* as a big-budget studio flick, while *Citizen Toxie: The Toxic Avenger IV* has never even played on U.S. television. But I have a feeling that Akiva Goldsman typed "toxic avenger" into Google one day and immediately realized what a gigantic and passionate audience Troma has around the world. If there were a way to make money off of passion, we would be rich. It hasn't gotten to the point where you can really make money from an Internet presence alone, but that doesn't mean it will always be that way. Someday, someone will figure it out. It may even be you.

But that brings up another point as well. Right now, you, too, can type "toxic avenger" or "troma" or "garbagepail kids fetishism" into Google and see what comes up.[23] The sweaty, fat 14-year-old kid in his basement blogging about *Piranha 3D* has as much chance of his website being seen as Disney or Justin Bieber. There is a level playing field, and if someone puts up something good, it will be seen. That is called "net neutrality." The Internet is currently the only democratic and truly diverse medium. We need to preserve net neutrality on the Internet so that when the day comes and the Internet becomes a source of revenue, we indies have a seat at the table.

But if we do not fight to preserve net neutrality, all that you will see when you open up the World Wide Web is what the megaconglomerates want you to see. They'll be able to buy the bandwidth and turn the Internet into ABC-CBS-NBS spoon-fed baby food.

In closing, recently I attended the Berlin International Film Festival, hoping to sell some Troma movies and eat a lot of mashed potatoes. While I was there, I agreed to act in underground filmmaker Michael Huck's *Midnight Orchids*. A few weeks after I returned to Tromaville, I got an email from this young director telling me that he had seen *Poultrygeist* and *Citizen Toxie* on German television. Now, as I think I've said about 14 times, Troma has almost no international distribution, so there was no way that any of our movies should be on German television. We did a little

---

[23] I can tell you exactly what comes up when I type in "garbagepail kids fetishism."

detective work, and it turns out that two American guys had been going around saying that they represented Troma and selling our films. This, of course, was untrue. Michael sent them a very hostile email, and they apologized, but refused to give us any money. Now, Michael is going to sue the fuck out of them. So we didn't actually sell any movies in Berlin, but we picked up a great lawsuit! However, I am left wondering, why the fuck won't the German television buyers just buy our movies directly from us?

Eines tages wirst du glücklich sein, auch![24]

---

[24] I was a little wasted when I wrote this, so I don't remember exactly what I was trying to say here, as I don't speak German. I believe the intent was something to the effect of, "May you one day be as happy as I am." I think it was meant to be ironic, but again, I really don't remember.

Epilogue

I met a beautiful woman when I was 15. Her name was Epilogue.

The long history of Troma is filled with irony. Sticky, sweet, twizzler-infused irony. Between the upcoming mainstream big-budget *The Toxic Avenger* and *Mother's Day* remakes and the revenue from Hulu, YouTube, iTunes, Xbox, Sony, and the like, it seems that the only money Troma gets these days comes from giant media conglomerates. In the real world, this is great! I don't owe anyone money—not through Troma, my house, or student loans—and I was able to send my daughters to good schools so that they can grow up to become far more respectable than me. I'm just thankful that we're still in business! However, what do I make of the fact that, if Troma survives, it will be because of the very devil-worshiping media conglomerates that I have vilified?

Meanwhile, the scent of irony lingers on in the Troma building. Though we have made, and continue to make, arguably, some of the most offensive, tasteless films in the history of cinema, our branding model is based on Disney, the major studio with an image so family friendly it induces diabetic comas. The Toxic Avenger is our Mickey Mouse—he's on everything we do, from films to books to business cards to condoms. Over the past 40 years, I have become a brand as well. A loud, bowtie-wearing, underground P.T. Barnum, proclaiming loudly, for everyone to hear, that a Candide-like Troma fan is born every minute!

And as Barnum himself said, "Without promotion, something terrible happens ... Nothing!" My goofy, clownish behavior has helped to sell a few cinema tickets and DVDs over the years, and if I had retained my dignity, who knows where Troma would be today. At least I get recognized in airports!

It is often necessary to search the world over for Troma fans. Here, Lloyd meets Marek Dobes in the Czech Republic. He wants to be referred to as "Troma Ambassador," but Lloyd prefers to refer to him as his "Prague-tologist."

In fact, a few months ago I was in an airport, coming back from the Czech Republic, when a young woman recognized me and started telling me about how Troma had influenced her life. I apologized, and once she had forgiven me, we began discussing the decline of the bouquinistes along the banks of the Seine. I mentioned something about attending Yale, which I always try to work into every conversation. This led to a mention of George W. Bush having been in my graduating class. Just then, an old man sitting next to us, eavesdropping, perked up.

"You went to school with George Bush?" he asked.

"Yes, yes," I answered. "But he hasn't taken my calls since we spent the night together in Austin."

"George Bush is a real hero of mine," said the old man.

"Oh, good, good," I said, trying to extract myself from the conversation without injury.

"You know, he was in the Battle of the Philippine Sea with my uncle."

That was when I realized that he was talking about George Bush, Sr., the fucking 86-year-old father of the George Bush that I went to school with. Godammit, the old fucker thought I was 86 years old!

And that is the thought that I will leave you with. Being an independent filmmaker and selling your own damn movie is all about humiliation. It's about putting yourself out there, ego be damned. God wouldn't even allow me 10 minutes of ego-boosting celebrity status before some eavesdropping old shit thought that I was 86 years old.

Sadly, that wasn't the first time. And it probably won't be the last.

Lloyd's Best-of the-Best Guide to Film Festivals

If there are any festivals that afford you a good chance of getting a big distribution deal, these might be for you. However, as we saw with Oren Peli and *Paranormal Activity*, there are no rules to this game. *Paranormal Activity* was picked up at a festival that ordinarily wouldn't have made this list, even if the book had to be 500 pages long!

Hopefully, this short list can help you focus your search for the best festivals, but it is in no way complete. That would have taken away from my FarmVille time. For a great guide to international film festivals, check out Chris Gore's book *The Ultimate Film Festival Survival Guide*. But buy it only if you haven't already bought all my books!

CANNES FILM FESTIVAL

- Cannes, France
- *www.festival-cannes.fr*
- No entry fee for short films of 15 minutes or less
- Entry fee for feature-length films varies depending on the medium; 50 € for films submitted on DVD, VHS, or

Blu-ray; feature film on 35mm film print: 200 €; feature film on DCP (Digital Cinema Package): 300 €; 350 € for films on HDCAM/HDCAM-SR

In spite of the corporate-ness of Cannes and the fact that it pays far too much attention to big-budget, star-filled, utterly useless movies, it does occasionally unearth some treasures. If your film is selected at Cannes, be sure to remember your ol' buddy Lloyd, who showed you the way.

TORONTO INTERNATIONAL FILM FESTIVAL

- Toronto, Ontario, Canada
- *http://tiff.net*
- Entry fee is $50 for feature-length Canadian films, $25 for Canadian short films, $80 for international feature-length films

Playing your film at Toronto is prestigious, so go ahead and submit. Just keep in mind that the festival is run by a bunch of star-fuckers who tend to follow trends rather than lead them.

SUNDANCE FILM FESTIVAL

- Park City, Utah
- *www.sundance.org*
- Entry fee is $50 for short films and $75 for feature-length films

The callousness of Sundance and its disregard for independent art was what originally led us to create TromaDance. However, in the past few years, Sundance seems to be returning to its roots and treating independent filmmakers with more respect. Perhaps it was some sensitivity training? If you are accepted at Sundance, you're in for a treat. Just remember that, even as a Sundance-selected filmmaker, you will still be on the B, C, or F list. It'll provide your accommodations, but you'll be staying at the Super 8 while Lady Gaga is at the Ritz!

VENICE FILM FESTIVAL

- Venice, Italy
- *www.labiennale.org/en/cinema*

- Varies year to year, but the entry fee is usually 60 € for all films

This is a very prestigious festival, and a growing number of deals are being made there, thanks to the newly attached film market. And if you don't make a million dollars, there are plenty of canals to drown yourself in!

BERLIN INTERNATIONAL FILM FESTIVAL

- Berlin, Germany
- *www.berlinale.de/en*
- Entry fee is 50 € for short films and 125 € for feature length

This highly regarded festival is like a junior version of Cannes, but with subzero temperatures! But hey, at least no one is shoving you in an oven.

TELLURIDE FILM FESTIVAL

- Telluride, Colorado
- *www.telluridefilmfestival.org*
- Entry fee is $45 for short films, $95 for feature films, and $35 for students regardless of the length of the film

This festival is so exclusive/elitist that I've actually never been able to attend. I've called and called, but no response. It's so cliquey, in fact, that no one even knows what the selections are until they show up! It consistently shows good movies, though, and distribution deals do occur. The skiing is great, too, from what I've heard.

SAN SEBASTIÁN INTERNATIONAL FILM FESTIVAL

- San Sebastián, Basque Country, Spain
- *www.sansebastianfestival.com/in/index.php*

Very prestigious, and it seems to be pretty sincere about selecting visionary movies.

SOUTH BY SOUTHWEST

- Austin, Texas
- *http://sxsw.com*

- Not just a film festival, but also a major music, art, and cultural event
- Entry fee for shorts is $25, $40 for feature-length films

Unfortunately, this major arts festival seems to be moving in the direction of Toronto as far as being starfuckers.

HAMPTONS INTERNATIONAL FILM FESTIVAL

- East Hampton, Southampton, Montauk, and Sag Harbor New York
- *http://hamptonsfilmfest.org*
- Entry fee is $60 for short films, $35 for student films, $75 for narrative or documentary films
- Focus on new filmmakers from all over the world

It seems that a disproportionate number of Hamptons' selections go on to be nominated for major awards, so they must be doing something right!

TROMADANCE FILM FESTIVAL

- Asbury Park, New Jersey
- *www.tromadance.com*
- No entry fee, and all screenings are first come, first served!

The drunkest film festival around!

GENRE FESTS

Horror and fantasy film fests may not guarantee you a distribution deal, but at least they'll treat you right and you'll get some good local publicity. If you are invited to attend, you'll usually be on equal footing with everyone else, as there is no special treatment for A-list guests. More than that, though, going to festivals like these is a great ego boost. They're fun to go to because the other filmmakers are just like you, and the festivals themselves are fueled by real fans.

FANTASIA INTERNATIONAL FILM FESTIVAL

- Montreal, Quebec, Canada
- *www.fantasiafestival.com/pre2011/en*
- Accepts an eclectic mix of films—not an exclusively horror or sci-fi fest, but it is known for accepting a wide range of strange and genre-skewed films

- Claims to have a "low" entry fee; no entry fee for "Canadian productions of any length"

I believe this is the best-curated film festival in the world.

SITGES FILM FESTIVAL

- Sitges, Catalonia, Spain
- *http://sitgesfilmfestival.com/eng*

In my opinion, this is the most prestigious and serious festival of this type.

BRUSSELS INTERNATIONAL FANTASTIC FILM FESTIVAL

- Brussels, Belgium
- *http://bifff.net*
- No entry fee for feature-length films

Once, when I attended, I was seated next to Roman Polanski at dinner. I don't know if this was on purpose or not.

NEW YORK CITY HORROR FILM FESTIVAL

- New York, New York
- *www.nychorrorfest.com*
- Entry fee is $25 for shorts and $40 for feature-length films

H.P. LOVECRAFT FILM FESTIVAL

- Portland, Oregon.
- *www.hplfilmfestival.com*
- Slightly niche horror film festival emphasizing films based on the works of author H.P. Lovecraft
- No entry fee

PUCHON INTERNATIONAL FANTASTIC FILM FESTIVAL (PIFAN)

- Bucheon, South Korea
- *www.pifan.com*

When we showed *Poultrygeist: Night of the Chicken Dead* at PiFan, there were about 2000 people in the audience, about three quarters of whom were female. This was highly unusual, and the reverse of most other festivals. I love PiFan!

FESTIVAL FANTAZIE

- Prague, Czech Republic
- *http://festivalfantazie.cz/ff/en*
- Entry fee is 4 € and increases depending on how long you want your film to run

SAN SEBASTIÁN HORROR AND FANTASY FILM FESTIVAL

- San Sebastián, Basque Country, Spain
- *www.donostiakultura.com/terror/2010/en/index.php*

LONDON FRIGHTFEST FILM FESTIVAL

- London, England
- *www.frightfest.co.uk*
- No entry fee

Special (Non) Pullout Section of Five Decades of Troma Poster Art (in Glorious Black and White Because My Publisher Says Color Is Too Expensive for a Book That Is Only Going to Sell Four Copies)[1]

---

[1] Because Focal Press is too cheap to print in color, you will have to drop some acid to see these posters in true color, like I did when I was working on this section. Or, you can go to *www.troma.com* and see Troma's colorful history there.

FIGURE APPB.1 The Girl Who Returned *(1960s).*

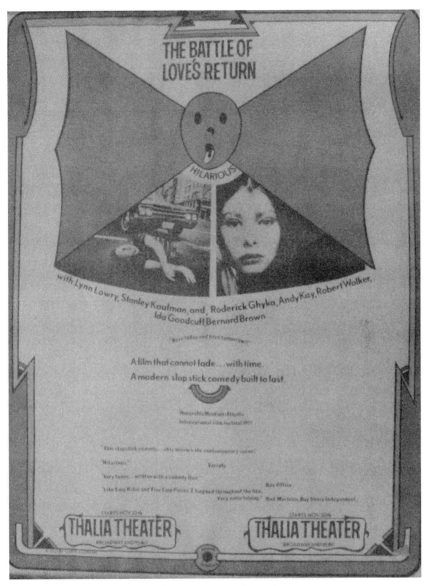

FIGURE APPB.2 The Battle of Love's Return *(1960s).*

FIGURE APPB.3 Squeeze Play! *(1970s).*

FIGURE APPB.4 The First Turn-On! *(1970s).*

FIGURE APPB.5 The Toxic Avenger *(1980s)*.

FIGURE APPB.6 Class of Nuke 'Em High *(1980s)*.

FIGURE APPB.7 Sgt. Kabukiman N.Y.P.D. *(1990s).*

FIGURE APPB.8 Tromeo & Juliet *(1990s).*

FIGURE APPB.9 Citizen Toxie: The Toxic Avenger IV *(2000s).*

FIGURE APPB.10 Poultrygeist: Night of the Chicken Dead *(2000s).*

FIGURE APPB.11 *Preliminary poster design for* Mr. Bricks *(2011).*

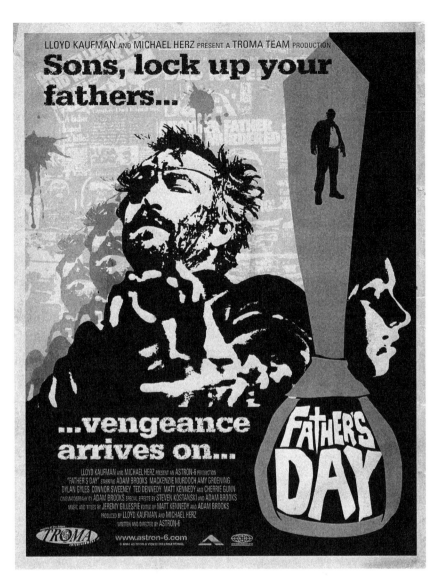

FIGURE APPB.12 Father's Day *(2011)*.

235 | Five Decades of Troma Poster Art

A Short Guide to Publicity and Sales at Conventions

By Ron Mackay

Conventions are good for more than binge drinking, hula-hooping, and leering at scantily clad women. If you play your cards right, you can get cost-effective publicity and you just might be able to sell a movie or two. To boost your sales at a convention, try to do as many of the following as (sub)humanly possible:

1. Have your film screened and/or do a Q&A. If people are able to see your film, you will sell more DVDs. If your film doesn't suck, you'll sell even more!

2. Have people associated with your film attend the convention. If you choose to have Lloyd Kaufman attend, make sure he doesn't whine about missing his "Pattie-Pie" all day, and try to take his BlackBerry away if possible. Otherwise he'll be on the phone with her all day and will not be selling DVDs! If Lloyd isn't in your film, having pretty actresses around is a

plus, but anybody fun and engaging will do the trick.[1] Keep in mind, though, that transportation and hotel expenses for all these additional people will eat up your profits quickly. For conventions that are close to New York, we will get Lloyd to come for just one day (preferably a Saturday) and then go home that night. That's usually enough to make a big improvement in sales without the costs being prohibitive.

3. Have fliers and other informational goodies handy to promote your film. Remember the saying, "Out of sight, out of mind," and then be sure that you're never out of sight!

4. Give time to your fans and convention goers in order to gain support for your projects. That can mean taking advantage of panels, if you get on one. It also means hanging around the booth instead of using your pass to check out the latest Wii game at the Nintendo area. And don't be afraid to talk to the fans that come by your booth. Most people will be content to browse (i.e., look quietly but not buy), so start up a conversation! Be creative and have fun with it!

5. Last but not least, make sure your audience knows you're serious about your cinema! No one can talk your film up like you, so give it a shot!

The following are some of the conventions where we have had the most success.

FAN EXPO/RUE MORGUE'S FESTIVAL OF FEAR

- *www.fanexpocanada.com*
- Toronto, Ontario, Canada
- Genres: Horror, sci-fi, comic book, gaming, anime
- 50,000 + attendees

This is one of the best conventions for sales, but, due to border patrol and customs, it can be very expensive to get your product

---

[1] At the Troma booth, we depend on our loyal Tromettes. Aside from being attractive/sexy/intriguing, the biggest requirement is that they must be willing to wear minimal clothing. On one occasion, when I didn't properly screen a Tromette, the result was a very cute girl who absolutely refused to wear anything less than three shirts and a sweater. This resulted in Lloyd referring to her all weekend as Super Tromette 7-Layeria. It also resulted in countless emails from Lloyd before almost every convention since, reminding me to not be an incompetent dolt, and to make sure that the Tromettes were willing to dress sexily.

there legally. One way around this is to explain to border guards that you are only going there to promote and that all of your product is only for displays and giveaways.

COMIC-CON

- *www.comic-con.org/cci*
- San Diego, California
- Genres: Comic book, sci-fi, horror, gaming
- 100,000 + attendees

Largest crowd and best media coverage of any convention, but the enormity of the con may adversely affect sales if people just can't find you.

DRAGON*CON

- *www.dragoncon.org*
- Atlanta, Georgia
- Genres: Fantasy, sci-fi, horror, gaming, comic book, anime
- 40,000 + attendees
- Lots of media coverage of parade and more

Very big convention that caters to one of the largest varieties of pop culture.

HORRORHOUND WEEKEND—INDIANAPOLIS

- *www.horrorhound.com*
- Indianapolis, Indiana
- Genres: All horror, all the time
- Flagship of *Horrorhound Magazine*'s conventions
- Very big draw for Chicago fans

This is one of the largest of the hotel-located conventions. It always has a diverse guest list, as well as fun after-hours activities. Past parties have included circus-style sideshows and horror-themed concerts. Horrorhound also puts on another smaller con in Cincinnati in November.

MONSTER MANIA—CHERRY HILL

- *www.monstermania.net*
- Cherry Hill, New Jersey, just outside Philadelphia
- Genre: Horror

- Two cons a year, March and August
- Consistently good draw of attendees

Good mix of popular and rare stars. Sales can vary dependent on attendees waiting in line for stars. Monster Mania also puts on a couple of smaller cons in Connecticut and Maryland.

CINEMA WASTELAND

- *www.cinemawasteland.com/show.html*
- Cleveland, Ohio
- Genres: Exploitation, horror, foreign
- Two cons a year, April and October
- Very open to screening independent films

Smaller convention, but sales often equal that of larger ones. Film screenings and parties every night. Very diverse guest list. The majority of the guests do not appear at other conventions, so this one is a destination for many fans.

CHILLER THEATRE

- *www.chillertheatre.com/main.htm*
- Parsippany, New Jersey
- Genres: Horror, television, rock & roll
- Two cons a year, April and October; October is the bigger one

Very busy convention. Big crowds can sometimes make it hard for people to get to your booth.

WONDERCON

- *www.comic-con.org/wc*
- San Francisco, California
- Genres: Comic book, anime, gaming
- 35,000 + attendees

Largest convention in Northern California.

SPOOKY EMPIRE

- *www.spookyempire.com*
- Orlando, Florida

- Genre: Horror
- Two cons a year, May and October

Parties, zombie walks, and good guests make this a popular convention.

TEXAS FRIGHTMARE WEEKEND

- *www.texasfrightmareweekend.com*
- Dallas, Texas
- Genre: Horror
- Zombie walk and car show

Good guest lists and fun extracurricular activities make this a popular convention.

FLASHBACK WEEKEND

- *www.flashbackweekend.com*
- Chicago, Illinois
- Genre: Horror
- Drive-in movies at night in the parking lot

This is the last, large genre convention in Chicago. The city has a good monetary base, and the convention always has a good location.

CREATION ENTERTAINMENT'S WEEKEND OF HORRORS

- *www.creationent.com/calendar.htm*
- Burbank, California
- Genre: Horror
- Costume contest

Celebrities are only accessible after their Q&As, leaving attendees more time to shop.

HORRORFIND WEEKEND

- *www.horrorfindweekend.com*
- Gettysburg, Pennsylvania
- Genre: Horror
- Celebrities include genre authors

Along with movie screenings, this convention also features readings by authors. Just over the Maryland border, this con pulls a large number of people from the Baltimore area.

ROCK & SHOCK

- *www.rockandshock.com*
- Worcester, Massachusetts
- Genre: Horror
- Concerts every night after the con
- Film festival
- Genre authors

Fun convention with a lot going on. And vendors get free passes to the concerts!

One final tip we've learned from years of conventions is to avoid any first-time convention like the plague. No matter what wonderful plans the organizer has, no matter what amount of advertising they do, no matter what grandiose guest list they have, you will tank at that convention. Run, screaming, from it, and stick to established conventions. If after a few years it still exists, then you might want to check it out.

Troma President Calls for the Survival of Net Neutrality at a Press Conference in the Troma Building, New York City

The following is an open letter from Lloyd Kaufman, president of Troma Entertainment and creator of The Toxic Avenger, *regarding the issue of net neutrality.*

August 23, 2010

Dear Fans of the First Amendment:

The Internet, the last free open and diverse democratic medium, is under attack. Net neutrality, which provides that no content is favored over any other and that content creators have an equal opportunity to freely disseminate their information, is being imminently threatened by greedy media megaconglomerates and their vassals.[1] It is urgent that we fight those who would sacrifice our freedom for a profit. Net neutrality will be the savior of independent art and commerce if we preserve it.

Three weeks ago, *The New York Times* reported on the recent Verizon-Google talks. What initially was clearly a conspiratorial plan to kill net neutrality and open the floodgates of a tiered, payment-based Internet is now being identified as a meeting of minds to discuss the possibility of a "parallel network." Verizon and Google are hiding behind vocabulary, convinced that by renaming an issue, they can fool the American public into acquiescence. Yet, whether it's directly setting up a payment-based Internet or conceiving and executing a parallel system, the issue is the same—by commodifying the dissemination of information, the media giants strike at the core values of freedom of speech and expression upon which this country was built. Verizon, Google, and their cohorts seek to begin construction of financial roadblocks in specific lanes of the current information superhighway, allowing only those of their choosing (those wealthy enough to pay their fines) to pass, leaving the rest of us on crappy, disconnected dirt roads where the public won't be able to find us at all. Instead, the megaconglomerates will allow access to only the most banal programming.[2] Thousands of independent suppliers of news, art, and entertainment will die. The Internet will be doomed like the mainstream media before it. It will be condemned to offer only spoon-fed baby-food news, art, and entertainment, while indies like us lose our fight for survival. Clearly, net neutrality is vital.

Right now, dear reader, your website, Troma's website, and Disney's website all have equal opportunities on the level playing field of the Internet. If your site or content is interesting, you can attract a larger public than Viacom, Rupert Murdoch, or Justin Bieber. And, should the Internet ever prove to be a source of great revenue, then you too will have your fair share of the profit. But the vertically integrated media conglomerates that control the

---

[1] The Motion Picture Association of America, the Screen Actors Guild, the Directors Guild, and the International Alliance of Theatrical Stage Employees, among others.

[2] Think 24 hours of *Full House* reruns.

traditional news and entertainment worlds are down in Washington, D.C., 24/7, spending kabillions of dollars lobbying to destroy this free, democratic, and diverse worldwide platform. They want their cartel to control the Internet. They want to control a kind of NBC/CBS/ABC world with no competition. Their many overpaid "suits" do not want to have to wake up in the morning and be required to actually *think*. Net neutrality on the Internet means that the media elites are forced to compete with you and me, which scares the shit out of them.

Historically, whenever new technology has become available, megaconglomerates sit back and allow the independents to take the risks and do the work to develop the technology into something with moneymaking potential. As soon as that technology starts to turn a profit for the independent visionaries, the megaconglomerates step in and begin to throw monkey wrenches into the works until they can co-opt the technology for themselves. For example, once videocassettes and home video became popular, the Motion Picture Association of America suddenly threatened that, because they could be shared, videocassettes heralded the end of copyright law and opened the doors to piracy and unmitigated pornography. They lobbied in Washington, D.C., spending millions and millions of dollars to get rules preventing the media monopoly repealed. The MPAA was simply using scare tactics and false logic to intimidate the masses; once the Mom and Pop video stores were destroyed by Viacom/Blockbuster et al., home video became the largest source of profit for the megaconglomerates.

Radio, television, film, and newspapers have already fallen prey to obscene media consolidation, having been converted into regurgitated, dumbed-down, controlled information at the hands of the vertically integrated media conglomerates. The Internet is our last space in which to defend our constitutional rights to free thoughts, speech, and art. Support the Internet Preservation Act of 2009. Representatives Edward Markey (D-MA) and Anna Eshoo (D-CA) propose to make net neutrality a U.S. law. Contact your elected officials and threaten to withhold your vote if they don't defend your interests. Let the Federal Communications Commission know how important this matter is to you. Post and pass along my relevant PSA and urge your friends and colleagues to do the same. Take part in the campaign to save the Internet. Now let's make some independent art!

Very truly,
Lloyd Kaufman, President
Troma Entertainment, Inc.

Anne Koester contributed to the writing of this letter.

Index